Financial Media Comment on *U.S. Savings Bonds: The Definitive Guide for Financial Professionals*

"Dan Pederson's knowledge of Savings bonds is amazing. No matter how picky the questions, he knows the answer and, better yet, can explain them clearly.
—Ronaleen R. Roha, *Kiplinger's Personal Finance Magazine*

"A good guide through the savings bond maze…."
—Janet Bodnar, Author of *Dr. Tightwad's Money Smart Kids*

"…a valuable tool for savings bond investors, who often find themselves at the mercy of uninformed bank employees. The book could pay for itself in extra interest earnings for investors who use it to determine the best time to redeem their bonds."
—Helen Huntley, *St. Petersburg Times*

"…[Pederson's book] addresses an investment issue that touches millions of people…. I will bet that your shelf of money books has nothing on this subject, even though you and your family own bonds. Buy one for your accountant, lawyer, and know-it-all uncle."
—Patricia J. Wagner, *The Bloomsbury Review*

"If balance sheets and maturity dates give you a headache. Dan Pederson is a numbers cruncher you should get to know. The southwest Detroiter's new consumer handbook…tells readers the pratfalls of bond ownership in sometimes blunt but always easy-to-understand language."
—Hawke Fracassa, *The Detroit News*

"…I recommend Pederson's book, well worth the…price…."
—Humberto Cruz, *Chicago Tribune*

"This book is THE authority on Savings Bonds and is easy to understand."
—Rick Doble, $AVVY DISCOUNT$ Newsletter, Smyrna, NC

"A plain-language guide…it offers tips on the best times to redeem your bonds, details on swapping EE bonds for HH bonds, tax aspects of bonds, and other goodies."
—Neil Downing, *The Providence Journal-Bulletin*

Financial Professionals Comment on *U.S. Savings Bonds: The Definitive Guide for Financial Professionals*

"The [304]-page paperback is well-written and, even more important, well organized. You'll find answers to your specific questions in the very complete table of contents. The guide has earned a permanent place on my reference shelf."

—J. Michael Martin, CFP, JD, NAPFA Advisor

"Written in a clear and direct manner, this well-organized guidebook provides all the information needed to understand, evaluate, and effectively manage a savings bond portfolio."

—Christina Bych, *The CPA Journal*

"This book and your firm are certainly the answer and what has to be considered the 'leading authority' on U.S. Savings Bonds. This combination certainly makes ME look good in the eyes and opinion of my clients. It also fills a large void in providing full investment service to my clients and their portfolios through a vital third party primary source of investment information and facts."

—Rhodes C. Palmer, VP Investments, Portfolio Manager

"Chapter 15, 'Summary Questions, Tips, and Opportunities,' and Chapter 16, 'U.S. Saving Bond Resources,' alone are worth the price of the book."

—Donald Ray Haas, CLU, *LAN Magazine*

"As a financial professional, I have always been surprised at the scarcity of reliable information about such a widely held investment as savings bonds. Determining bond values, understanding fixed and variable interest rates, and understanding tax consequences of transferring bonds are problems that I encounter frequently. Your book addresses these issues with clear, comprehensive answers."

—Barbara A. Warner, CFP

U.S. SAVINGS BONDS

The Definitive Guide for Financial Professionals

U.S. SAVINGS BONDS

BONDS

The Definitive Guide for Financial Professionals

Foreword by Robert K. Heady
founding publisher of *Bank Rate Monitor*

4th Edition
EXPANDED
UPDATED

Daniel J. Pederson

Sage Creek Press

Traverse City, Michigan

To My Loving Wife, Anna Marie

It is a great joy to partner with you on this road called life. What new terrain will the King reveal next?
Take my hand and we'll continue to follow.

For where your treasure is, there your heart will be also.
Matthew 6:21

Published by Sage Creek Press
121 E. Front Street, 4th Floor
Traverse City, MI 49684

Sage Creek Press

Publisher's Cataloging-in Publication
(*Provided by Quality Books Inc.*)

Pederson, Daniel J.
    U.S. savings bonds : the definitive guide for financial professionals / Daniel J. Pederson. —4th ed.
      p. cm.
      Includes bibliographical references and index.
      Previously published as part of U.S. savings bonds: a comprehensive guide for bond owners and finance professionals.
       ISBN 1-890394-28-9

      1.   Savings bonds—United States. 2. Government securities—United States. I. Title.

    HG4936.P43 1998   332.63'232
                               QBI98-1305

Editor: Christina Bych
Consultant: Ron Von Gunten

Printed in the United States of America
10 9 8 7 6 5 4 3 2

Disclaimer: While the author and publisher have made every effort to provide information which, at the time of publication, is as accurate and complete as possible in regard to the subject matter covered, it is acknowledged that mistakes, both in content and typography could exist. Current investment information should be obtained from the Department of Treasury, Bureau of the Public Debt, before making any decisions to buy, sell, reissue, or exchange any U.S. Savings Bonds. This publication is sold with the understanding that the publisher is not engaged in rendering legal, tax, accounting, and like services. If legal advice, tax advice, or other expert assistance is required, the services of a professional in that field should be sought.

For purchasing information, including quantity discounts, contact:
The Savings Bond Informer, Inc. at (800) 927-1901.

Contents

List of Tables and Figures

Tables

Figures

Foreword

As someone who writes a national newspaper column each week for millions of average investors, let me say that you've come to the right place with this book.

Why? Of all the investment vehicles that Americans park their money in, that financial professionals must give advice on, and that news media write about, U.S. Savings Bonds are easily the least understood. That's ironic, especially when you consider that savings bonds have been around longer than most of us have been alive. You'd expect that by now everyone would know everything about them.

Nothing could be further from the truth. Bond owners are desperate for answers to hundred of questions about these instruments. And more of your clients are bond owners than you think.

You'd think, wouldn't you, that with all the fast action on Wall Street in recent years—especially the great performances by stocks and mutual funds—that savings bonds would have become passe in investors' minds. Wrong! As the author Daniel J. Pederson points out, 55 million Americans own U.S. Savings Bonds, adding up to $180 billion. These are the conservative, security-conscious, safety-minded folks who make up one of the most solid investor blocs in the country.

Throughout the year, I get question after question from readers about U.S. Savings Bonds, ranging from how long earnings last, to how rates are calculated, and when bonds can be cashed. The main complaint is they're frustrated because they can't get straight answers from their bank or anyone else. This tells you something about the massive informational void that exists with U.S. Savings Bonds that does not exist with CDs and Treasuries.

For one thing, banks have little or no incentive to tell the bond story to their customers, and when they try the information is apt to be erroneous. In the same context, the consumer can't rely on stodgy government publications that need a United Nations translator to interpret what they're saying.

That leaves you, the financial professional, as the only trusted person to bridge the gap between bond owners and the information they need to know. Fortunately for you and your clients, Dan Pederson writes in an easy Main Street-style that anyone can understand. Plus, he has had hands-on experience as supervisor of the savings bond division at a Federal Reserve Bank.

Again, I have to keep coming back to the alarming lack of valuable information about savings bonds. Sooner or later, every financial advisor will be asked a savings bond question by a client. As an independent journalist, I have a file drawer of these questions from readers, and the place I've relied on for accurate answers has been Dan Pederson's company, The Savings Bond Informer, Inc.

You're in the same boat, because bonds are a critical part of many investment portfolios. Savings bonds can't be ignored or, even worse, mismanaged to the detriment of the bond owner.

When you consider that about $5.3 billion in savings bonds have stopped earning interest—money available for reinvestment—that fact alone should grab your attention. There's no reason why you can't be a savings bond expert now that you have this valuable reference at your side!

—ROBERT K. HEADY

Nationally syndicated newspaper columnist, "Robert K. Heady on Banking"
Co-author, *The Complete Idiot's Guide to Managing Your Money*
Founding publisher, *Bank Rate Monitor*

Acknowledgments

For the development of this book and The Savings Bond Informer, Inc., I am deeply grateful:

—To David Pederson, my brother, who urged me to write this book. Now it's your turn.

—To my associates at the FRB of Chicago-Detroit Branch. Especially my friends Robert Jones, Willie Mae Hall, and Larry Pasden: They provided invaluable counsel during my tenure at the FRB.

—To my outstanding associates at The Savings Bond Informer: Lydia, Maria, and Raquel Garcia, Paul and Sara Meriweather, Terreance Coleman, Marijane Grimaldo and Steve. Thank you for your dedication and commitment. The way you handle our clients with dignity and great service results in the numerous letters of "thanks."

—To my SEED Family, for investing, critiquing, and counseling that played an important role in shaping the direction of our company. You have always encouraged, believed and supported…thank you.

—To Soda, whether pedaling across America, trekking through India, or serving in an urban center, you have always sharpened and challenged me. I am forever grateful for your influence upon my life.

—To Brent Dawes. Thank you for insight into the foreign language of taxes. Whew!

—To Christina Bych, an exceptional editor and consultant. Your perseverance and insight again molded this text into a book that has received a tremendous amount of praise from financial professionals and the media. Your ideas and skills were critical to the success of this book. Thanks also for helping Anna Marie and me to lighten up and laugh. We really enjoy your company.

—Terreance, thank you for the long (late) hours and your keen eye for edits and layout. You helped us keep everything in perspective (not to mention making sure that I made those critical Tuesday meetings).

—Ron Von Gunten, you are gifted with words and wisdom and you also are skilled in your profession. This combination led to the essential revisions in this text. Of course, maybe what I am saying is simply an "Oracle of the Obvious."

—Sever Pederson, your eye for detail and your commitment to excellence made rough edges smooth.

—Last and most important, to my family, especially Anna Marie, my wife, best friend, business partner, and greatest supporter. My name may be on the cover, but you shaped this book. Your organizational skills forged the layout of the content. Your writing skills took concepts and numbers and translated them into user-friendly communication. From the initial concept, to completion, you kept this project on track. The book simply would not have become a reality without your skill, insight, and hard work.

Ron, Anne, David, and Debbie for listening and encouraging. Grandma & Grandpa Pederson for encouragement, and for blessing our children by watching them while we worked "overtime." Esther Marlow, for helping lay the foundation of our operation. Dan Marlow, for hours of consulting and marketing ideas. Anna Anderson: Nike must have studied her life before they coined the phrase, "Just do it." Whatever it took, she stood ready and "just did it."

Introduction

_____ **Introduction**

- ▶ *What to Expect from this Book*
- ▶ *What Not to Expect from this Book*
- ▶ *How to Use this Book*

During career day in my fourth grade classroom at Monroe Elementary School, I contemplated my obvious choices: professional baseball player, professional basketball player, professional football player, and firefighter. Never in my wildest dreams did writing a book about savings bonds enter my mind. In fact, had it entered my mind, there would have been very little excitement. Nevertheless, after four years as a supervisor of the savings bond division at the Federal Reserve Bank of Chicago-Detroit Branch, and after three years of directing The Savings Bond Informer, Inc., I felt compelled to share what I had learned in the first edition of this book. Ultimately, twelve years of serving thousands of bond owners and financial professionals across the nation led to the development of this fourth edition of *U.S. Savings Bonds: The Definitive Guide for Financial Professionals*.

Although the first three editions of this book were focused on reaching both the bond owner and the financial professional, this book is decidedly different. After watching the reactions of financial professionals at the seminars I conduct nationwide, I saw overwhelming evidence that, you, the financial professional, are involved in numerous savings bond "situations" each year. And because savings bonds are not part of your product line, you have received very little training on how to address these situations.

The purpose of this book is twofold: (1) to demonstrate the value of servicing savings bond owners, and (2) to provide the tools you need to successfully accomplish that. This guide has been completely revised and updated with tables, examples, and new strategies that will ultimately result in maximizing the value of your client's bond holdings.

What to Expect from this Book

The data presented is *not* an attempt to convince you that bonds are a "good" or "bad" investment; rather, the focus is on education: To accomplish this, the book has been broken down into four parts:

> Part I: Servicing Savings Bond Owners
> Part II: U.S. Savings Bonds 101: The Basics
> Part III: Beyond the Basics
> Part IV: Resources

Part I will give you a frame of reference from which to service bond owners. It begins with a basic, but critical, question: "*Why service savings bond owners?*" Information you need to know to reach this target market is presented, such as: where bond owners go for information (your competition); what is needed to evaluate their investment; and the dynamics of working with these investors.

Parts II and III help you sort truth from fiction when it comes to how savings bonds work. The material provided will also enable you to counsel investors on which transactions need to be performed and when. Step-by-step instructions explain how to get the job done. In addition, chapters include case studies and strategies for handling different financial situations: Part II, the simpler, and Part III, the more complex.

Several sections are particularly noteworthy:

- an introduction to the concept of selective redemption
- why searching for lost bonds almost always makes sense
- four ways savings bonds are double-taxed
- options for reporting savings bond interest upon the death of the owner
- issues to consider before retitling a bond into a trust
- how to help clients avoid "getting surprised" with a taxable event (due to savings bonds being retitled) in a divorce case

Part IV contains a wealth of information. It includes both government and non-government agencies that provide a variety of savings bond services. It also lists the various forms needed to complete savings bond transactions and where to obtain them. The directory of phone numbers and addresses will lead you to any additional help you may need.

What Not to Expect from this Book

This is not a book about municipal bonds, corporate bonds, bond mutual funds, Treasury bills, Treasury notes, or Treasury bonds. This book deals only with issues directly related to U.S. Savings Bonds: Series E, EE, I, H, HH, and Savings Notes/Freedom Shares.

This book is not a government publication, although several government publications have been used as reference. The tax chapter was researched by Brent Dawes, CPA, manager at American Express Tax and Business Services. The perspective of a CPA resulted in numerous "Tax Tips" and "Tax Traps." All documents used or referred to have been listed in the Bibliography.

Finally, you will not find advice on whether or not to encourage investment in savings bonds or what should be done with interest earnings upon redemption. You will be given the tools needed to evaluate and compare a bond investment with other options. And then it is up to you to best advise your clients, given their goals, objectives, and overall financial situation.

How to Use this Book

This book can be used as a guide or as a reference. As a guide, it explains the most technical information in an easy-to-understand manner. As a reference manual, it has been organized to provide quick and easy access to the data you seek. One approach would be to read Part I and then reference the remainder of the book on an as-needed basis.

The Contents provides not only chapter titles, but also the subheadings which describe the main points of each chapter. These subheadings are repeated at the beginning of each chapter; a quick browse will direct you to the proper section within a given chapter. The Glossary provides definitions of bond-related terms and phrases. Appendix A was designed to quickly put the characteristics of each series of bonds at your fingertips.

In an attempt to make the text easy to follow, you will find that some information is repeated. Often a piece of data applies to several issues; rather than refer you to other chapters, the needed information is summarized for immediate use, followed by directions to a more detailed section on the topic.

Millions of Americans have relied on U.S. Savings Bonds as a way to save and invest. The following pages will prepare you to competently advise and counsel bond owners while reinforcing your role as a multifaceted and informed financial professional.

Part I

Servicing Savings Bond Owners

_____Chapter 1

WHY SERVICE U.S. SAVINGS BOND OWNERS?

- ► *The Size of the Market*
- ► *The Worth of the Market*
- ► *The Need for an Expert*
- ► *Virgin Territory*
- ► *If You Don't, Someone Else Will*
- ► *Summary Points*

Because there are no commissions, fees, or revenue directly derived from handling savings bonds, working with them may mistakenly be viewed as unprofitable. This perspective is changing, however, due to the staggering amount of money invested in savings bonds, the number of investors involved, bond owners' need for efficient savings bond management, and the unique opportunity that this presents for the financial professional.

The Size of the Market

More than 55 million Americans own U.S. Savings Bonds: This makes bonds the most widely held government security in the world. (That is four times more clients than the largest U.S. mutual fund company currently boasts.) Every year 15 million people purchase bonds through a combination of independent purchases and payroll deductions. It is also anticipated that the introduction of the new Inflation Protection Bond (I bond) will further increase this number in the next few years.

According to government statistics, more than 40,000 organizations, companies, and government agencies participate in a Payroll Savings Plan. It is not unusual for investors who are in this program to have accumulated bonds monthly throughout their careers. Military personnel and government employees are highly encouraged (read "expected") to invest in bonds. This constituency alone accounts for over $3 billion in annual sales.

Whether you like savings bonds as an investment tool or not, the numbers cannot be ignored. Savings bonds have become an integral part of many Americans' fixed investment portfolios.

The Worth of the Market

Investors collectively hold more than $180 billion in savings bonds. Over $5.3 billion of this has stopped earning interest and needs to be repositioned. On average, almost 3% of the bonds owned by your clients fall into this category.

If you are like most financial professionals, you will be amazed at the amount of money some individuals have invested in savings bonds. It is not uncommon for the author to serve clients who hold more than $1 million. Anne called with this story.

I recently inherited bonds, along with four other people, from a relative whose entire estate consisted of savings bonds (over $2 million). The deceased was generous in leaving over a quarter of a million dollars to each beneficiary. However, the estate, tax, and retitling problems that we have encountered demonstrate that neither he nor the financial professionals in charge of the estate understood the intricacies of savings bonds, nor how to advise us.

An even greater number of investors hold $100,000 to $500,000. Depending on their financial aptitude and comfort level with other investment options, this may represent a significant portion of a person's net worth. In fact, it may be the only investment they have. But whether a client or potential client has a substantial amount in bonds or not, at the least your newfound savings bond knowledge will enable you to provide a "value-added" service that builds relationships and wins referrals.

The Need for an Expert

Most bond owners know very little about their investment. U.S. Savings Bonds are a do-it-yourself proposition. No one receives a statement from the government containing the precise details for each bond owned, such as those routinely sent for savings, checking, and mutual fund accounts. Material written for the layperson is scarce. Furthermore, rule changes have made savings bonds a deceptively complex investment. But interest rates and timing issues aside, investors may have little idea of the value of their holdings. Savings bonds have become increasingly difficult for the average person to track and manage.

As with any other investment vehicle you handle on a day-to-day basis, *your* level of savings bond expertise can either cost or save your clients thousands of dollars. Armed with the proper information, you can further demonstrate to your clients the value of their trust in your advice.

Virgin Territory

It is not often in the financial service industry that you encounter an opportunity that is truly virgin ground. In spite of millions of investors and a fifty-seven year history, very little has been done over the years to service savings bond investors. The government has focused most of its time, money, and efforts on marketing. Commercial banks handle bonds as a courtesy and often confidently supply inaccurate information to owners. (See Chapter 3, page 22, for the results of a recent bank survey.) This is where you come in. The void of reliable information about bonds creates an opportunity for a financial professional to address this need and stand out from the crowd.

If You Don't, Someone Else Will

In an increasingly competitive financial service marketplace, professionals see the need to provide solutions to their clients. Solve the client's "problem" and they are more likely to remain loyal. Address an unmet need and they will be grateful. Send them away empty-handed and someone else will meet their needs and capture their business.

A family was seeking financial advice. Dad had died and Mom was elderly. Mom had over $200,000 in savings bonds. The family interviewed several "financial experts/advisors" in search of someone who could help with her affairs, since all the children lived out of state. One advisor said, "Don't worry about the savings

bond interest, it will receive a stepped-up-basis upon your Mother's death."
Because the family had a previous edition of this book, they knew that bonds do
not automatically receive a stepped-up basis.

Needless to say, the advisor who offered this family incorrect savings bond information did not get their business.

Effectively managing savings bond investments can mean thousands of saved
dollars for your clients and many new working relationships for you.

Summary Points

- Millions of people own savings bonds and millions more purchase them each
  year. Investors collectively hold over $180 billion in bonds; of this amount
  over $5.3 billion has stopped earning interest—and is available for other
  investment opportunities.
- Investors have difficulty finding answers to their questions. There is a great
  need for accurate savings bond information.
- Very little has been done to meet this need, which opens a new market to you.
- Your knowledgeable advice regarding a client's savings bond holdings could
  save them thousands of dollars.
- If you don't have the answers bond owners need and want, they may entrust
  their business to someone who does.

Chapter 2

WHAT IS NEEDED TO ANALYZE A SAVINGS BOND INVESTMENT?

▶ *All Savings Bonds Were Created Equal*
and Other Popular Myths
▶ *Costly Mistakes*
▶ *The Need for a Savings Bond Statement*
▶ *The Composition of a Savings Bond Statement*
▶ *It Doesn't Need to Be Time-Consuming*
▶ *Summary Points*

Earning a reputation as a trusted advisor requires skill, hard work, and consistent attention to your clients' needs. In your initial consultations with a client, you gather a substantial amount of financial information. The next step includes obtaining data on each asset so that you can determine whether your client's current holdings are consistent with his or her needs, plans, and goals. This careful scrutiny of each asset is followed by an examination of how each fits into the overall plan. The savings bond portion of a client's portfolio should be no different. Any advice offered must be based on an evaluation of the client's savings bond holdings and then included as part of the whole. Unfortunately, the myths that are typically held about savings bonds often stand in the way of this process.

All Savings Bonds Were Created Equal and Other Popular Myths

Widely held and widely misunderstood, the size and scope of savings bond ownership does not rival the store of misconceptions held concerning them.

Many people treat savings bonds as though all bonds are the same. However, savings bonds operate according to different rules depending on their type (series) and when they were purchased. These rules, in turn, determine the unique set of information specific to each bond. This includes interest rates (two for most bonds), timing issues, maturity dates, accrued interest, projected future performance, and value. For example, two Series E bonds with the same face value, but purchased at different times, can come under different rules (which leads to different rates of interest and strategic timing considerations).

Just as there is unique data that apply to each bond, there are also unique rules that govern the various transactions, such as retitling, tax and estate planning, exchanging for HH Bonds, and using bonds (Series EE or I) "tax-free" for education. For instance, unlike many other investments, bonds do not receive a stepped-up basis upon the death of an owner. To assume that savings bonds behave as other investments risks your hard-earned reputation and your client's money.

Contrary to popular belief, knowing the redemption value of a savings bond is not enough to help a client make informed decisions. Knowing the detailed information that applies to each bond in a portfolio can make a significant difference on the return. Not knowing can mean forfeiting hundreds or, in some cases, thousands of dollars.

A couple had purchased $60,000 of savings bonds ($30,000 purchase price) in August of 1993. When inquiring about their bonds, they were told that the bonds were earning only 4%. They were not informed that when the bonds reached five years old they would receive a retroactive "catch-up." They cashed their bonds only sixty days before the five-year anniversary. The result is they forfeited over $1,800 that would have been theirs had they waited until the bonds were five years old.

In addition, issues such as a client's asset allocation and income needs, both pre-retirement and retirement, must also be examined to successfully integrate his or her holdings into a financial plan or strategy.

Unlike your typical fixed investment, there are several pieces of the savings bond puzzle that must come together so the picture can become complete, understandable, and usable. If the pieces don't fit together, or if one is missing, costly mistakes result.

Costly Mistakes

After every seminar, a line quickly forms with people eager to share "their savings bond story" with the author. Often the tale involves a financial mistake brought on by the advice of a misinformed person:

- A man redeemed all of his bonds right before retirement, during the year when he was in the highest income bracket of his lifetime. He had not been informed that all the interest income from the redeemed bonds had to be reported in that calendar year.

- A woman read a publication that advocated cashing bonds that had reached face value to purchase new bonds under the new rules. At the time, many of her bonds were earning rates of 7.5% under the old rules; the new rules' rate would have netted her substantially less.

- A woman recently widowed was advised to cash all of her bonds; she later learned that her bonds would have continued to earn interest for an additional eight years.

- A couple needed money for a down payment on a new home and so randomly cashed 50 of their 100 bonds. If they had applied the principles of selective redemption (Chapter 8), they would have realized an additional $1,000 to $2,000 to use toward the purchase.

- A financial planner learned that over $50,000 of his client's $240,000 bond portfolio had stopped earning interest over five years ago.

These mistakes could have been avoided. It all starts, however, with an analysis of *each* bond your client owns.

The Need for a Savings Bond Statement

The following letter changed the way the author thought about servicing bond owners and led to the formation of The Savings Bond Informer, Inc.

To whom it may concern:
We have over two hundred savings bonds (see attached list). We would like to know the value of each bond, how much interest has accrued, what interest rates they are paying, and when they stop earning interest. In addition, we may want to cash some of these bonds in and would like to know which bonds should be cashed first, which last, and why. Thank you kindly for your help.
—Retirees from Dearborn, MI

As the supervisor of the savings bond division of the Federal Reserve Bank of Detroit, I had learned that the answers to these questions were essential to proper management of this investment. In fact, on occasion I randomly recalculated savings bond transactions after redemption and discovered a disturbing pattern. Because they did not understand how to handle their investment, owners consistently and unknowingly forfeited interest that should have been theirs. I was convinced that if an investor was supplied information that was easy to understand and easy to use, this type of mistake could be avoided, but all that was available at that time were redemption tables. And this couple did not want general information about U.S. Savings Bonds, nor did they want charts and tables from which to attempt to pull data that applied to their holdings. They wanted the detailed facts that applied to each of *their* bonds. What they needed was a customized savings bond statement that would reflect their holdings.

The Composition of a Savings Bond Statement

A savings bond statement should contain information about each bond and reflect a summary of the client's entire holdings. Following is a list of questions that such a report answers, accompanied by a brief explanation of why each answer is important.

Questions to be Answered for Each Bond

1. **What is the bond worth now?** *Any given bond may be worth as little as half or as much as eight times its face value.* Knowing the exact value of each bond will provide you with an accurate assessment of this vehicle within an investment portfolio.

2. **How much interest has accrued to date?** For most bond owners, interest becomes a tax liability in the year the bond is cashed or reaches final maturity (exceptions may include bond owners who report interest annually, bonds that are eligible for the tax-free feature, and bonds exchanged for the HH bond upon final maturity). For tax-planning purposes, this information is essential. (See Chapter 14 for more on tax issues.)

3. **When will it reach final maturity?** *Remember: Americans are holding over $5.3 billion of bonds that have stopped earning interest.* Knowing the final maturity date of each bond can help both you and your client to plan ahead. Chapters 6 and 8 will help you do this.

4. **When does it increase in value?** Each bond issued before May 1997, that is over five years old, will increase in value twice a year. *Cash a*

bond one day before the increase date and six months of interest will be forfeited. **Note:** The increase date for bonds purchased prior to December 1973 does not always fall on the issue date and six-month anniversary.

5. **What is the guaranteed interest rate of each bond?** Each bond purchased prior to May 1, 1995, has a unique guaranteed and average market-based rate. Knowing this rate will help determine whether to sell or hold given current fixed investment yields. (Chapter 5 provides an in-depth explanation of interest rates.)

6. **What is the current earning rate?** This is the rate the bond is earning during the current six-month period. This is an exact indicator of the current performance. It is not a good indicator of performance beyond the bond's next increase date.

7. **What is the projected future performance of this bond?** Each bond needs to be rated for short-term and long-term performance. The Savings Bond Informer Rating System℠ offers an estimate of expected future returns. Each bond receives a rating based on the two-year and five-year projected performance. Since the bond program often produces spikes or dips in a yield that can skew perception of future performance, this rating system enables bond owners to make an "apples to apples" comparison of their holdings.

8. **When will the bond enter an extended maturity period?** Bonds purchased prior to May 1, 1995, assume a new guaranteed interest rate when they enter an extended maturity period. Many bonds that had been earning 7.5% dropped to a new guaranteed rate of 4% when they entered their extended maturity periods. You need to know which bonds are affected and when. The details on maturity and extended maturity periods are presented in Chapter 6.

9. **How did the bond perform in the last twelve months?** Many investors like to evaluate their investments at least once a year. Determining how a particular bond or the entire bond portfolio performed over the previous twelve-month period informs an owner of the "actual" recent performance.

10. **When will a bond reach face value?** Five years? Seven? Ten? Twelve? Eighteen? Any of the answers could be correct, depending on when a bond was purchased. The length of time depends on the purchase price and the interest rates assigned to the particular bond. The most important issue related to this question is the date upon which it reaches the end of the original maturity period (at which point the bond will be worth at least face value). At that point, the bond enters its extended maturity period.

Entering an extended maturity period results in a new guaranteed rate for bonds purchased prior to May 1, 1995.

Summary Questions

11. **What is the total value of the bond investment?** This is a key component to gaining an accurate picture of the client's net worth and distribution of assets across the risk spectrum.

12. **How much was paid for the bonds?** This is the original cost, that is, the cost basis even if the bonds were received as a gift. Some exceptions may apply.

13. **What is the total interest earned on the bonds?** This is the amount that would have to be reported as interest income if all the bonds were cashed at one time.

Once these answers are obtained, you can move toward integrating a savings bond investment into any plan or strategy.

It Doesn't Need to Be Time-Consuming

Providing an evaluation of your client's savings bond holdings does not need to be overwhelming or time-consuming. There are two primary options for quickly and effectively analyzing this savings bond investment. While they are just listed here, the strengths and weaknesses of each are further discussed in Chapter 18.

Options for Delivering the Answers

1. Let an expert do it for you (See page 18 for an example.)
2. Do-it-yourself: (See Chapter 18 for options.)
   a. manually
   b. via software and tables

Before choosing your data source or a combination of data sources, review the above options in light of your particular needs.

Summary Points

- Savings bond holdings must be treated with the same scrutiny as other investments.
- Savings bond myths often hinder this process and lead to costly mistakes.

- Efficient management starts with an evaluation of each bond and includes a summary of the entire savings bond portfolio.
- Providing accurate, detailed savings bond information in the form of a savings bond statement does not need to be time-consuming.

Figure 2.1 Sample: The Savings Bond Informer, Inc. Summary and Detail Listing

The Savings Bond Informer, Inc.
Account #:CS00040089

Savings Bond Statement For:
NAME OF YOUR CLIENT GOES HERE
October 1998

P.O. Box 9249
Detroit, MI 48209
Phone: (313) 843-1910
Fax: (313) 843-1912

Statement Summary:

Number of Bonds on this Statement:...........	4
Total Purchase Price:...........	$3,725.00
Total Interest Accumulated on Bonds:...........	$8,094.76
Total Redemption Value of Bonds:...........	$11,819.76
Interest Earned Year-to-Date:...........	$526.08

Consumer Notice: This statement reflects the rates, values, and rating system in effect as of the date of this statement. The government can change the bond program at any time and TSBI, Inc. makes no guarantee of any future returns. The "Statement Explanation" sheet (enclosed with your order) provides a description of each column including the exclusive Savings Bond Informer Rating System sm (Columns G and H). Thank you for using our service.

Detail Listing of Savings Bonds:

A Line Number & Series	B Issue Date	C Face Value	D Guaranteed Rate	E Guaranteed Rate Until	F Current Earnings Rate	G 2-Year Rating	H 5-Year Rating	I Increase Dates	J Last 12-Month Yield	K Current Value	L Interest Accumulated to Date	M Bond Stops Earning Interest	N Notes
1 E	MAY 1958	$500	0.00 %	N/A	0.00 %	F	F	No More	2.96 %	$3,662.40	$3,287.40	MAY 1998	
2 E	MAY 1972	$1,000	4.00 %	MAY 2002	4.00 %	D	NR	MAR & SEP	5.06 %	$4,365.20	$3,615.20	MAY 2002	
3 EE	MAY 1986	$200	4.00 %	MAY 2006	3.96 %	D	D	MAY & NOV	4.05 %	$226.16	$126.16	MAY 2016	
4 EE	SEP 1992	$5,000	6.00 %	SEP 2004	5.95 %	A	A	SEP & MAR	6.13 %	$3,566.00	$1,066.00	SEP 2022	
Page Totals:										$11,819.76	$8,094.76		

Page: 1

To order a savings bond statement,
see the last page of this book.

Chapter 3

WHERE DO BOND OWNERS GO FOR INFORMATION?
Your Competition

- ▶ *U.S. Savings Bonds Are Not a Bank Product*
- ▶ *Bank Service: The Good, The Bad, and The Ugly*
- ▶ *Government Service: The Good, The Bad, and The Scary*
- ▶ *Financial Professional Services: You Decide*
- ▶ *A Chance to Repent*
- ▶ *Summary Points*

Doesn't anybody know anything about U.S. Savings Bonds? It seems like I have called all over and every person gives me a different answer!

—A frustrated bond owner

Where bond owners choose to obtain information will largely be determined by whether they receive the help they seek. The two sources most frequently contacted for savings bond information are commercial banks and the government. A third source—financial professionals—is quickly gaining ground as a player in the savings bond information arena. This chapter will provide evidence that some of the most popular sources for savings bond information are not the most reliable. Understanding how to advise your client when it comes to discrepancies in the data is important to the integrity of your advice. Understanding the competition's ability—or inability—to meet your client's savings bond needs can help you determine how to gain a competitive edge and how to supply the kind of service that keeps clients from going elsewhere.

U.S. Savings Bonds Are Not a Bank Product

> Few other industries have been asked by the government to take actions adverse to their own interests in the way the banks have been exhorted to sell U.S. Savings Bonds through the years.
> —Paul S. Nadler, "Uncle Sam Out of Line,"
> *Banker's Monthly* (November 1992), p. 8

U.S. Savings Bonds are a product of the federal government. They are not, nor have they ever been, a product created and fully supported by commercial banks.

Most banks would not describe bonds as a moneymaker. They receive small fees for handling the bond purchase application and for redeeming bonds. They do not receive money for advising individuals on their bond holdings. As a result, most banks do not put a high priority on training their personnel in savings bond timing and interest rate issues. The training dollars are spent on bank products more likely to generate substantial revenue. Furthermore, banks have often been strongly encouraged to sell bonds at times when bonds competed with—and outperformed—their own product line. That was the unenviable position banks found themselves in during 1992: Bonds had a guaranteed rate of 6%, while savings accounts and some certificates of deposit (CDs) were struggling to reach 3%. Needless to say, the profit-minded bankers were not excited to see an all-time high of $17.6 billion in savings bond sales. Customers were taking their money out of bank products and investing in a government product—and the banks had to provide the necessary assistance.

Currently, banks handle bonds as a courtesy and provide various services, that is, if they handle them at all. It is not surprising that some banks are decreasing their level of service related to bonds.

Bank Service: The Good, The Bad, and The Ugly

The Good

Many banks act as a point of sale for bond purchase and a point of redemption for bond cashing. For the most part, banks do a good job determining what a bond is worth. They use standardized tables that provide redemption values. However, as with any money matter, it makes good sense to double-check the calculations.

Note: The government does check bond payment amounts through a system called E-Z Clear. However, it can take up to eight weeks for an adjustment on a pricing error to be made, and only differences over $25 are automatically adjusted (lesser amounts can be adjusted upon request from the financial institution). An adjustment on a price difference is not made directly with the bond owner. The government adjusts the difference with the financial institution; it is the responsibility of the financial institution to refund or seek payment from a bond owner in the event of an over- or underpayment. It is very important for bond owners to independently verify the correct amount they should receive upon redemption.

Suggestion: For alternatives to confirming a bond's worth, see Part IV, "Resources."

A financial planner recently called with the following story.

I was working on an estate settlement. The law firm needed bonds evaluated, so I used your service to provide a report for them. Today they called to tell me they had cashed some of the bonds. There was one problem, though: They received $1,000 less than they thought they should have. After checking your report, the law firm called the bank and asked them to recheck their figures. Sure enough, the bank amount was wrong. The bottom line is that had we not had the report, we would not have known we were being shorted.

Because the financial professional was informed, his client got the money due the same day. (In over a dozen cases that came to The Savings Bond Informer, Inc., last year, bond owners were able to identify valuation errors because they had procured an independent verification of the amount to be received; the adjustments were made either on the spot or very soon thereafter. For options on confirming a bond's worth, see Part IV, "Resources.")

Watch out, though. It works in reverse, too. If a bank overpays, the excess must be returned. Another financial planner reported that a client had been contacted by his bank several months after he had redeemed some bonds. The bank claimed that they had overpaid the client and requested that the money be returned.

The Bad

Bank tellers, who have not been trained in savings bond technicalities, are often forced into duty as bond consultants. Inaccurate information is the usual result.

In 1991, a man went into a bank in Michigan with E bonds he had purchased in the 1970s. He asked the teller what he should do. After consulting her charts, she informed him that the bonds were no longer earning interest and that he should redeem them. He followed her advice and liquidated all of his bonds from the 70s that he had purchased through payroll deduction.

This proved a disaster. First, his bonds had **not** stopped earning interest; they would have continued earning interest until after the year 2000. Second, when he redeemed the bonds, he had to declare **all** the interest income that year. The tragedy was that this man was two years from retirement and so was in **the highest income bracket of his lifetime**. Third, many of his bonds had been earning attractive rates of 7.5%. Understandably enraged by this experience, the man had no recourse. He, unfortunately, did not get the teller's information in writing.

Urge your clients *never* to trust verbal information about interest rates and timing issues for their bonds. If they choose to work with a bank, tell them to insist that all the information they are given be put into writing, including the name of the person giving the information, the date, and the location.

The Ugly

A 1998 phone survey of 100 banks nationwide revealed that less than 8% of the banks could accurately answer a question about interest rates and the dates a specific bond accrues interest. Of those questioned, 22% referred the caller to the "government"; 15% offered a wrong answer; and 22% simply responded "I don't know." Of those responding, 33% said to call 1-800-USBONDS for help. Of those who suggested the 800 number, all were asked, "Does that number have a person who will assist me?" Over 75% said, "yes." That number is a recorded line, which among other things, has referred bond owners back to their banks (until August 1998) for information about interest rates. It is no surprise that bond owners are often frustrated and angry at the lack of help they have received. They have become the proverbial dog chasing the tail. A few additional responses were especially noteworthy.

"Let me check this newspaper article I saved, because a lot of people come in here with bonds."

"The interest rate on your bonds varies, it doesn't stay the same and no one can tell you."

"Sometimes they change monthly, sometimes they don't, there doesn't seem to be any method to the madness that I can see."

This latest survey supports the findings of a 400-bank survey conducted in 1994. In that survey (documented in the third edition of *U.S. Savings Bonds: A Comprehensive Guide for Bond Owners and Financial Professionals*), 8% of the banks' answers about interest rates or timing issues were accurate. Of the 400 banks surveyed, only four banks answered all five questions accurately (a 1% chance of having all bond questions accurately addressed).

The problem is not bond valuation, although independent verification is always advisable; rather, it is untrained bank personnel trying to answer questions concerning interest rates and increase dates. By now you see the pattern.

Government Service:
The Good, The Bad, and The Scary

The Good

In the first edition of this book, I pointed out that the bond consultants at the Bureau of the Public Debt (BPD) were both helpful and knowledgeable. Although I was asked not to list them in the acknowledgments (for fear of an implied endorsement), I do want to point out that the BPD has worked hard, and with success, in recent years to make the bond program more user-friendly to bond owners. The most notable improvements in this area include quicker responses to information requests, the creation of a web site, and the bond valuation program titled "The Savings Bond Wizard." The bond consultants at the BPD are the experts and, in the author's opinion, the most reliable source of information.

The five Federal Reserve Banks (FRB) that handle savings bonds appear to be stepping up their efforts in the area of customer service as well. Calls are more closely monitored and the way in which inquiries are handled is a higher priority than in the past (in the late 1980s there was no measurement or ranking of call volume or the quality of the response to the caller).

The Bad

While positive steps are being taken, the specific help that each bond owner will receive remains at the mercy of the individual who happens to answer the phone. In addition, because of the sheer size of the market (55 million bond owners, plus the banks and financial professionals who serve them), the government has sought to "push" questions down the line (to banks or the FRB). Thus, we are back where we started. Although this reduces the number of calls handled by the BPD, it does not help the bond owner for the reasons already discussed. Finally, while the Internet site will be a great benefit in answering many questions, the unique nature of each person's financial circumstances will often call for a human response. And, as popular as the web is, many bond owners have yet to go online. Calling a FRB for answers does not assure accuracy, either.

A client of The Savings Bond Informer (TSBI) recently called stating that a FRB had informed him and his wife that their bonds (issued June 1993 to December 1994) would receive 4% a year until the bonds were 18 years old. Based on that data he was ready to cash them all in. But after an evaluation from TSBI, they discovered that the bonds would receive a "catch-up" upon turning five years old: In their case this would happen in the next twelve months and would result in a double-digit yield of over 10% for that twelve-month period. In addition, the bonds would then earn 4% to 5.5% under current market conditions. Needless to say, here the FRB information could have led the bond owners to a decision where they would have forfeited a substantial return.

Several times over the years the author has been at odds with a FRB about the finer points of a particular bond's performance (based on conflicting information offered to a bond owner). Once brought to their attention, FRB management has enlightened their phone representatives with the accurate information. Although the bond representatives at the FRB know a great deal, they are not always versed in the intricacies of each bond.

The Scary

As a financial professional, you know the mountains of NASD and SEC rules designed to keep you in line, but who monitors the government's performance? Who can bond owners appeal to?

The author has been chided by a savings bond official "to stop beating the drum" regarding the bonds that have stopped earning interest. But under what circumstances could you, as an investment advisor, sell a product and then, if the investor does not come to collect after a certain period of time, keep the money with no obligation to contact that investor? Why hasn't there been more effort and attention paid to locate and pay back investors whose bonds have stopped earning interest? Instead, rules have been passed that state if the bond owner doesn't come forward with exact documentation—each bond's serial number—by a certain time, they forfeit the opportunity to claim their money. Meanwhile, their money—about $5.3 billion—is being used interest-free.

Financial Professional Services: You Decide

Many financial professionals initially attend the author's seminars on savings bonds for two reasons: CE units and free breakfast. Many equate the excitement of this subject with that of wallpaper removal or trying to restore your computer system after a crash. After an hour of education and marketing techniques, however, attendees focus an incredible amount of energy on how servicing savings bond owners can be a part of the planning practice. When asked, prior to the seminar, about their level of service to U.S. Savings Bond investors, financial professionals give similar responses. Following are the top four views, accompanied by an analysis of their potential results.

View #1: "Huh, savings bonds? What a waste! I just tell my clients to cash them in."

Comments: While the last thing you want is to be slowed down, advising clients to "cash them all," could, in some instances, open oneself up to a lawsuit. As described in Chapter 2, savings bonds are not all the same and should not be treated as such. They operate according to different rules depending on their series and issue date. "Cashing them all" could create a host of financial problems for the client, including interest loss and tax liability.

People are becoming savvy about their investments and savings bonds are no exception. At the very least, financial counselors will be expected to document why they advised their client to "cash them all in."

View #2: "You know, I've had several clients who own savings bonds. Usually I just send them to the bank. I'm uncomfortable with the topic and don't see it as a way to enhance my business."

Comments: Although this provides a temporary solution, it does not weigh the cost of lost opportunity. Consider these three points:

1. Did the client get the help he or she needed? Most likely, no. Bank information on interest rates and timing issues is often inaccurate or incomplete. (Refer to the previous section, "Bank Service.")

2. You have just aided a competitor! The clever banks direct all clients with savings bonds to their in-house financial advisors. They know that the investor is moving toward a financial decision and they want to offer their input (read "products"). The savings bond advice can still be inaccurate or insufficient, but now your client has received a sales pitch from your competitor along with it.

3. You missed an opportunity to impress and provide a value-added service to this client. That translates to lost business and lost dollars.

View #3: "None of my clients own bonds, I don't need to spend any time on this."

Comments: Are you sure? Have you asked your clients if they own bonds? It's possible they haven't volunteered the information. Clients sometimes fail to tell their planner that they have bonds because:

- they forgot about this portion of their assets
- they are too embarrassed to mention they have bonds
- they do not think it is necessary
- they do not trust the advice they might receive
- they assume that only a bank or government resource could provide guidance regarding savings bonds

Many advisors have gone back to long-term clients to ask about ownership and have been surprised at their findings. **Note:** this is a good reason to contact inactive clients.

View #4: "I specifically inquire about bonds, help my clients evaluate their holdings, and often end up with increased business as a result of being knowledgeable and having the right resources to address the subject."

Comments: Because you have taken the opportunity to serve bond owners, you have brought them added value. Consequently, clients feel satisfied with your counsel, are sending referrals your way, and your business is growing. A letter I recently received from Steve, an advisor from Sun City, Arizona, illustrates this:

A client recently referred me to an elderly gentleman who came into my office with a summary of assets. I noticed a rather long list of savings bonds and immediately discussed with him what information your company could provide to us. He agreed to obtain a report and what he learned was very informative and very surprising. I asked him to guess what his US Savings Bond portfolio was worth. He guessed about $200,000. I showed him his report and he learned that his savings bond portfolio was actually worth $370,000. Additionally, we learned that twelve of his bonds were no longer paying him any interest. He was very thankful for the information and said that the fee was money well spent.

This savings bond owner will likely be telling his friends and family about how his advisor helped him.

A Chance to Repent

The temptation to harshly judge saving bonds as an investment is understandable, given the vigor of the stock market in recent years. Go head, admit it. You would no sooner recommend savings bonds to a client than you would refer them to their local bank for mutual funds. But financial planners are faced with a dilemma: Consumers continue to purchase and hold savings bonds at a rate that rivals some well-known mutual funds. But whether the motivation is patriotic, nostalgic, or simply family tradition, it appears certain that bonds will continue to garner an impressive number of investors who have precious little information available to them regarding their investment.

If you have not yet encountered a client with a sizable bond portfolio, you eventually will. Your ability to intelligently discuss the intricacies of U.S. Savings Bonds and, more important, to competently manage that which the client already has could mean the difference between the client looking elsewhere for advice and your securing an account for life.

Summary Points

- The two most commonly used sources of savings bond information are banks and the government.

- Because banks receive no payment for handling bonds, training dollars are spent elsewhere. As a result, banks provide inaccurate or insufficient information on savings bond interest rates and timing issues much of the time.

- While the government is the best source of free information for savings bonds, getting an answer specific to your situation is sometimes difficult and can also, on rare occasions, result in misinformation. An independent verification is advisable for any financial transaction.

- While a growing number of financial professionals are making an effort to service savings bond investors, the majority have not yet chosen to include service to owners as a part of their practice, thus providing you with a competitive edge.

_____ Chapter 4

HOW TO EFFECTIVELY WORK WITH SAVINGS BOND OWNERS

> ▶ *Asking the Question*
> ▶ *Understanding the Bond Owner Mindset*
> ▶ *Dealing With Bond Owners' Objections*
> ▶ *Starting the Evaluation Process*
> ▶ *Advice on Advice*

So, where do you start? Some bond owners may not feel comfortable giving you their bond information. Others may not even want help with their bonds. This chapter will help you get over some of the hurdles you may encounter when approaching clients about the savings bond evaluation process.

Asking the Question

An Oracle of the Obvious

Do not assume that clients will tell you that they own savings bonds—even if they have divulged complete information on all of their other assets. Many a financial professional has been working with someone for years only to learn after a direct question that the client holds bonds. An investor may not think it necessary to communicate this information to you since they are not planning to do anything with the bonds at this point anyway.

Once you know that your client has savings bonds, the following questions should help him or her understand the need for a savings bond statement.

1. Do you know how much interest has accrued on your bonds?

2. Do you have a plan for the bonds' use? Do you have a plan for passing them on to your heirs?

3. Have you considered the tax consequences?

4. If you need the money, do you know how much you have?

5. If you were to cash a few bonds, do you know which ones to cash and which ones to set aside for optimum return?

To make sound decisions regarding any investment, the investor needs to know all the facts. Encourage your clients to obtain a written report detailing each bond. Show them an example of a savings bond statement and explain how this tool can help them to understand and better manage their bonds.

Note: If an investor doesn't know whether he has bonds or not—that is, "I had several through payroll deduction when I was in the army, but I don't know what happened to them"—instruct him to file a lost bond claim form. See Chapter 10 for instructions. He may discover that he owns bonds that will be replaced free-of-charge with no interruptions on his interest accrual.

Understanding the Bond Owner Mindset

Because of the complex, yet somehow familiar, nature of bonds and the lack of helpful information regarding their working, three types of bond owners prevail. The following profiles will help you understand their perspective which will, in turn, better equip you to provide appropriate counsel.

Profile #1: *The "Haven't Given It Much Thought" Bond Owner*

Most bond owners fit this category. They do not know how savings bonds work and are unaware of the need to have their investment evaluated. Their bonds could be tucked in a safe deposit box, dresser drawer, or under the mattress. Management of their holdings follows a simple formula: Collect bonds over the years and redeem them when it is time to make a big purchase.

Profile #2: *The Frustrated Bond Owner*

It is common for savings bond investors to become frustrated in their search for answers to their questions. They often get no answers, inaccurate answers, and conflicting answers: The result, confusion.

A caller recounted her recent experience with this common loop of wasted time.

I began by calling the "1-800-USBONDS" number (a government line). A recording instructed me to contact a local financial institution for interest rates on older bonds, which I did. However, this line is also a recording. So I decided to call my bank. The bank instructed me to call 1-800-USBONDS.

By the time a bond owner talks with you, he or she may be rightfully angry. "Why can't I find anyone who can answer my questions?" This represents the perfect opportunity for you to build credibility by delivering the information your client seeks.

Profile #3: *The Over-Confident Bond Owner*

This will be the hardest sell. In fact, they may not see a need for any of your other financial advice either. They have all the answers and know all the rules—or at least they think they do. Once again, presenting the questions on page 30 will alert these investors to the fact that they do need savings bond information.

Common Misconceptions

Keep in mind that whatever their different point-of-view, most investors have misconceptions about bonds. These misconceptions will quickly surface as you begin to dialogue. You will probably hear comments such as:

- "I know my bonds will reach face value in seven years."

- "I bought these bonds when they were over 11%, but I think that's only good for twenty or thirty years."

- "I'm sure that all these bonds (from the 1980s and 1990s) are tax-free for education."

- "I'm going to hold my bonds because they earn interest forever."

- "The bonds I have from the 1990s will double in five or seven years."

All of these statements are inaccurate. However, your response to such statements and the proof that you can provide to the contrary may determine whether you build a bridge with that client or alienate him from your services.

Dealing With Bond Owners' Objections

Do not be surprised if your questions are met with skepticism, indifference, or anger. These responses are not a threat when you understand why they exist and how to respond to them. Following are common objections.

Objection: *"My bank has the information I need."*

Response: Banks generally are good at valuing bonds, that is, determining how much bonds are worth if sold. However, banks do a poor job of handling the crucial questions on interest rates and timing issues. An owner needs to know not only a bond's value, but also its current interest rate, maturity date, and the dates when interest rates change. (TSBI receives several cases a year where a bond owner received inaccurate redemption information from the bank. Investors who have an independent verification source are usually able to identify an error and, therefore, have it rectified the same day.) And, the bank may put more energy into selling you another product rather than helping you understand the product you have.

Objection: *"All I need are the government tables."*

Response: You would need several different tables and an abundance of free time to piece together the information the government provides. In addition, some of the data is not clearly presented. The tables are general, not specific to your clients' bonds.

Objection: *"I'm not planning to cash or exchange, therefore, I do not need an evaluation."*

Response: Your client could be one of the many investors who collectively hold over $5.3 billion in bonds that have stopped earning interest or the investment may be worth far more than suspected. Some bonds are worth up to eight times their face value.

A financial professional sent a list of a client's bonds to TSBI for evaluation. The client thought they had about $60,000 in bonds. TSBI's savings bond statement revealed that the client actually had $240,000. That changed the client's investment decisions. Furthermore, over $50,000 of the $240,000 had stopped earning interest five years earlier.

It can't be stressed enough: For any financial plan or strategy to be complete, your client must have a precise accounting of all investment portfolio holdings.

Objection: *"I'm just going to exchange for HH bonds."*

Response: Again a few questions may help.

- Have you considered the pros and cons of exchanging for HH bonds?
- Do you know the timing issues associated with an exchange?
- Do you know how to instruct the bank teller regarding deferral of interest?

- Do you know the interest rate HH bonds currently pay?

- Did you know that the interest rate you get when you exchange is locked in for ten years?

- Do you know the rate that your bonds are currently earning?

Exchanging for HH bonds is often an unattractive option. For answers to the above questions, see Chapter 9, page 103.

A Sentimental Objection

Objection: *"I know my bonds have stopped earning interest, but I do not want to cash them because of sentimental reasons."*

Response: These bond owners may have inherited bonds from Grandpa or Aunt Betty and it is their link to the past—to a person who meant a lot to them.

One solution may meet the needs of all involved. The Bureau of the Public Debt (BPD) says that photocopies of savings bonds can be made for record keeping purposes. So, the bond owner can make a color photocopy and then write a note on back stating that "this is a copy for record keeping only, the original bond was cashed on xx/xx/xx." Some bond owners may want to frame the bond(s) or create a special remembrance. The original bond can then be cashed. This solution will hopefully provide "the best of both worlds."

Starting the Evaluation Process

To start the evaluation process, a bond owner must create a list which states three pieces of information about each bond: issue date, face value, and series. If a client is unable, for whatever reason, to record this information, he or she can make photocopies of the front of each bond. According to the bond consultants at the BPD, photocopying and faxing copies of bonds is legal because photocopies can in no way be negotiated nor do they have any monetary value.

Note: While not needed for an analysis, for record keeping purposes it is important that the bond owner also have the following: the full serial number and registration (that is, the Social Security number, names, and address for each). The ability to provide detailed information to the BPD—should the bonds ever become lost, stolen, or ruined—will aid in the search. A record keeping form, which you can photocopy and give to your client, can be found at the end of this chapter. Providing this form will assist you in gathering the necessary data.

Creating a Savings Bond Evaluation List

The following instructions apply only to Series E, EE, and SN (Savings Notes or Freedom Shares), not to H and HH bonds. (See Chapter 9, page 103, for information on H and HH bonds.)

Figure 4.1

Series EE Savings Bond

Series. The series identification is listed on the front of the bond, usually in one of the four corners. For Series E and EE, it will also be at the end of the serial number.

Issue Date. The issue date can be found in the top right-hand corner of a bond. (Ignore the issue stamp which includes a specific day of the month and appears below the issue date.)

Face Value. The face value of the bond is the amount printed in the upper corner. The face value is *not* the purchase price. (The bond pictured above is a Series EE with an issue date of September 1986 and a face value of $75.)

In addition to the record keeping form on page 36, your clients will greatly appreciate the following list that will help them organize their holdings.

The Bond Owner's "To Do" List

✓ Organize bonds by series, then by issue date, face value, or registration.

✓ Use the bond record keeping form to note Social Security number, serial number, series, registration, issue date, and face value for each bond.

✓ Make a photocopy of the completed bond record.

✓ Put one copy of the bond record with the bonds; file the other somewhere else.

✓ Store the bonds in a safe place.

✓ Keep bond information with your will, stating the location of the bonds and the bond records.

✓ Do periodic checks of your holdings.

Advice on Advice

- A large portion of your client's savings may be tied up in this investment. Negative comments about savings bonds are the equivalent of attacking his or her judgment and, as a result, may alienate the person before you have a chance to help them.

- If a person holds misconceptions about bonds because he or she was given bad information, keep in mind that the source of this information could be a relative, close friend, or financial professional with whom the person has had a lifelong relationship.

- The discipline an investor has demonstrated through bond purchases over the years can mean you have a long-term investor/saver on your hands. Build on your client's strengths.

- The purpose of a savings bond statement is to have a factual vehicle from which to base decisions. Provide proof for the truth.

Figure 4.2

U.S. Savings Bond Record Keeping Sheet

Name(s) of Savings Bond Owner(s)

Issue Date (top right-hand corner)	Face Value (front of bond)	Series (E,EE,H, HH, I, SN,FS)	Serial Number	Social Security Number

Part II

U.S. Savings Bonds 101:
The Basics

_____Chapter 5

UNDERSTANDING INTEREST RATES

▶ *Why Interest Rates Are Important*
▶ *What Rates Are Your Clients' Bonds Earning?*
▶ *The Confusion Over Interest Rates*
▶ *Common Misconceptions*
▶ *Interest Rate Rules and How They Work*
▶ *October 1986: An Illustration of How
    the Interest Rates Work*
▶ *When Do Interest Rates Change?*
▶ *Quick Tips on Interest Rates*

No doubt Galileo and Einstein would have been intrigued with the savings bond program if they were alive today. Piecing together the data that has affected savings bonds is a challenge. And while knowing how to piece together the data may not lead to a scientific breakthrough, it will result in more money for your clients and a greater comfort level for you when fielding interest rate questions.

This chapter begins by illustrating why interest rates are such an important piece in the savings bond puzzle. Next, it looks at the interest rates that apply to your clients' bonds (at the time of writing) and when those bonds will stop earning interest. The chapter concludes with a brief discussion of the confusion that surrounds interest rates, the misconceptions this confusion has led to, and how the interest rates work. A special section details the October 1986 bond because you will likely receive more questions about this bond than any other.

Why Interest Rates Are Important

The current interest rate that a bond is earning and the length of time that this rate will be in effect provides a measurement for the bond's future value. It is essential to understand this when comparing bonds. As with a marketable Treasury security (a Treasury note or bond), a high interest rate (or coupon rate) gives one savings bond a greater future value than another bond with a lower interest rate (assuming both bonds have equal redemption value at present). On a practical level, if a couple wants to cash half of their bonds, a financial professional who can differentiate between the worst performing and the best performing bonds will better serve them. Consider the following example:

Robert and Rita own 150 savings bonds. The total value of their portfolio is $100,000—$30,000 of which is deferred interest. They want $50,000, but don't know which bonds to cash. One financial professional suggests cashing the oldest bonds first, while others insist that they should take the newest bonds. You, on the other hand, ask these investors for the issue dates, series, and face values of all their bonds. From that information, you obtain a detailed report, customized to their holdings. The statement reveals that half of their bonds are earning 4% and the other half are earning 6%. You identify the 4% bonds and the client cashes them first. The remaining bonds continue to grow at 6%. You just helped your clients realize an additional $1,000 a year in interest by identifying their best and worst performing bonds. Over the next five years, they will have earned over $5,000 that, had they haphazardly cashed some bonds, might have gone un-realized.

Age should not be the sole determining factor when deciding which bonds to cash; yield plays a significant role and needs to be considered. Current yields (for a six-month period) can be found in the government publication "United States Savings Bonds/Notes Earnings Report." (See page 240 to order.) This government yield along with a short-term (two-year) and long-term (five-year) rating of future performance is offered in The Savings Bond Informer Bond Statement. (See page 236 for more information.)

What Rates Are Your Clients' Bonds Earning?

Bonds do not all receive the same rate of interest. Current interest rates range from 4% to 6.1%, depending on series and date of issue (with one exception noted below).

Series H and HH bonds: Interest rates vary from 4% to 6%, depending on the issue date of the bond. Any Series H bond over 30 years old is paying 0%. Any

Series HH bond over 20 years old is paying 0%. (The first HH bonds issued in 1980 will stop earning interest in less than two years, the year 2000.)

Savings Notes/Freedom Shares: Those that still earn interest receive between 4% and 5%. All savings notes over 30 years old receive 0%. All savings notes will have stopped earning interest by October 2000.

Series E bonds and Series EE bonds over five years old: Interest rates range from 4% to 6.1%, depending on the issue date. No bond earns over 6.1%. Any E bond issued November 1965 or before and that is over 40 years old is earning 0%. Any E bond issued December 1965 and after, and that is over 30 years old, is earning 0%.

Series EE bonds less than five years old: Generally, these bonds range from 4% to 5.5%. However, bonds issued from March 1993 to April 1995 have a retroactive "catch-up" which is added to the value of the bond on the five-year anniversary. Thus, these bonds can yield over 10% in that fifth year. Bonds issued from March 1993 to April 1995 and that are not yet five years old will be the best performers in the bond program over the next one to two years. After they turn five years old, they will yield between 4% and 5.5%, if interest rates remain relatively flat.

Series I Bonds: The first I bond was issued September 1, 1998. The initial interest rate for I bonds issued in September and October 1998 was 4.66%. This is a combination of a fixed rate of 3.4% and a CPI-U (Consumer Price Index-Urban Consumers) based rate of 1.26% (when annualized). The rates on outstanding I bonds will fluctuate every six months dependent on changes in the CPI-U. The rates on new-purchase I bonds are reset every six months, in May and November. See Chapter 17 for more information on the I bond.

The Confusion Over Interest Rates

Savings bonds operate according to their type (series) and the rules in effect at the time of purchase. For example, two Series E bonds with the same face value purchased at different times may come under different rules. Or, two bonds purchased at the same time, but of different series (such as the Series E and EE bonds), may operate according to different rules. Over the last sixteen years, the bond program has undergone four major rule changes. This has meant six changes in the guaranteed rates and more than forty-four changes in the market rates. These changes have lead to confusion in three areas: the way in which the rates are defined; the way in which the rates are calculated; and which rates apply at which time.

Three Different Types of Interest Rates

Until 1982 there was only one type of interest rate—the guaranteed rate. The guaranteed rate assigned to a bond depended on the date of purchase and the specific maturity period a bond was in. In 1982 the government introduced the market rate. Designed to make bonds more attractive, this rate provided an upside potential: A bond can earn an interest rate above the guaranteed interest rate if it is held for five years or longer. Thus, the government began calculating two values for each Series E, EE, or Savings Note/Freedom Share (SN/FS).

Changes made in May 1995 and May 1997 both simplified and complicated the interest rate structures. The government's "new rules" simplified the issue by allowing only one interest rate to apply at any given point in time to Series EE bonds issued on or after May 1, 1995. The complication is that most bond owners hold bonds governed by the "old rules." The result is that there are three unique types of interest rates that apply to U.S. Savings Bonds: the guaranteed/fixed rate, the market rate (with four subcategories), and most recently, the CPI-U indexed rate. Every bond has either one or two of these rates that affect its performance.

Table 5.1 indicates which rate applies to each series of bond. While H and HH bonds have been included in this table, and are briefly mentioned at the end of the chapter, an in-depth discussion of these bonds appears in Chapter 9. The I bond is covered in detail in Chapter 17.

Table 5.1

Types of Interest Rates that Apply to Each Series

Series	Type of Rate
I-September 1998 and after	CPI-U Indexed Rate and Fixed Rate
HH	Guaranteed Rate
H	Guaranteed Rate
EE-May 1997 and after	Market Rate
EE–May 1995 to April 1997	Market Rate
EE–Pre May 1995	Average Market Rate and Guaranteed Rate
SN/FS	Average Market Rate and Guaranteed Rate
E	Average Market Rate and Guaranteed Rate

That the combined changes resulted in three different types of interest rates would be confusing enough. To add insult to injury, however, the way in which these rates have been defined and applied also has become complicated.

The Guaranteed Rate: Defined and Applied

The guaranteed interest rate is the minimum rate that a bond will yield until the end of the original maturity period (in some cases the bond may have to be held at least five years to receive this guarantee). For an expanded explanation of how this rate works, see page 49.

The guaranteed rate is sometimes referred to as a "fixed" rate. However, while the guaranteed rate is just that—guaranteed—the fixed rate, as in the case of the new I bond, may not be guaranteed. (That is, in the way we think of guaranteed; I perceive guaranteed to mean, "I will get this." However, a holder may get less than the declared fixed rate on the I bond in periods of deflation.) The following is a synopsis of how the guaranteed rate is applied to bonds purchased at various times throughout the history of the program.

I Bonds purchased September 1998 and after: A fixed rate is assigned to the bond at the time of purchase. An inflation-adjusted rate is added to the fixed rate (or subtracted from, if there is deflation) every six months to determine the actual earnings rate for each six-month period.

EE Bonds purchased May 1995 and after: There is no guaranteed rate.

E and EE bonds and SN/FS purchased prior to May 1995: A guaranteed rate is assigned to a bond at the time of issue. *This rate is only good for the original maturity period and can change each time a bond enters an extended maturity period.* (See Chapter 6 for an explanation of maturity periods.)

The Market Rate: Defined and Applied

The term "market rate" can mean many things: an average of many market rates, 85% of a six-month T-bill average; 85% of the five-year Treasury yield average; or 90% of the five-year Treasury yield average. It may help to understand that there are two benchmarks against which the market rate is determined: the six-month Treasury bill (T-bill) yields and the five-year Treasury yields. (See page 49 for an in-depth explanation of how the market rate works.) The following is a summary of how the market rate is applied, starting with the most recent changes.

EE Bonds purchased May 1997 and after: The market rate is 90% of the average of five-year Treasury yields. This rate is published every May and November. See Table 5.2.

EE Bonds purchased May 1995 to April 1997: The market rate is 85% of the six-month T-bill yield for the first five years and then 85% of the average of five-year Treasury yields after the bond is five years old. This rate is published every May and November. See Table 5.3.

E bonds, Savings Notes, and EE bonds purchased prior to May 1995: The market rate is 85% of the five-year Treasury yields. However, this individual rate is combined with other individual market rates to form the average market rate for bonds. And, the average market rate may or may not be what a particular bond is earning.

Note: Throughout the remainder of this chapter you will see reference to the following four rule changes:

- *September 1998 I Bond Rules* These rules apply only to Series I Bonds purchased September 1, 1998, and after.

- *May 1997 EE Bond Rules* These rules apply only to Series EE bonds purchased May 1, 1997, and after.

- *May 1995 to April 1997 Gatt-cha Rules* These rules apply only to Series EE bonds purchased between May 1, 1995, and April 30, 1997, and are a result of the GATT agreement. (See page 47 for more information.)

- *Pre-May 1995 Rules* These rules apply to Series E, EE, or SNs purchased prior to May 1, 1995.

Common Misconceptions

To help you answer your clients' most basic questions about interest rates, you must be familiar with the four most common rate misconceptions.

Misconception #1: *All bonds earn the same rate of interest.*

Pre-May 1995 Rules for E, EE, and SN/FS
No. Each bond can have a unique guaranteed and average market-based interest rate. Its issue date and series determine the rate for any given bond.

May 1995 to April 1997 Gatt-cha Rules for EE
No. Each bond receives a market rate (based on 85% of six-month T-bill yield) every six months for the first five years. After five years, the bond receives a new market rate every six months based on 85% of the five-year Treasury yield.

May 1997 Rules for EE

No. Each bond receives a new market rate every six months. This market rate is based on 90% of the five-year Treasury yields.

Misconception #2: *The interest rate that is quoted when you buy a bond is good for the life of the bond.*

Pre-May 1995 Rules for E, EE, and SN/FS

No. The guaranteed rate that was in effect when the bond was purchased is the minimum rate the bond will accrue during the original maturity period, that is, the time it will take the bond to reach face value at that rate. A bond will continue to earn interest well after the original maturity period, but the guaranteed rate can change each time the bond enters an extended maturity period.

May 1995 to April 1997 Gatt-cha Rules for EE

No. The rate published at the time of purchase has no bearing on future rates for these bonds. The market rate that is initially assigned to a bond applies for the first six months only (based on 85% of six-month T-bill yields). A new market rate is published every six months. This pattern continues until the bond is five years old, at which time the market rate is based on 85% of the five-year Treasury yields.

May 1997 Rules for EE

No. Each bond receives a new market rate every six months. This market rate is based on 90% of the five-year Treasury yields.

Misconception #3: *Older bonds have lower interest rates than newer bonds or newer bonds have lower interest rates than older bonds.*

Pre-May 1995 Rules for E, EE, and SN/FS

No and **no**. Older bonds can carry guaranteed rates as high as 6%. Many newer bonds earn only 4% to 5.5%. The interest rate varies from bond to bond. In some cases, older bonds may be earning only 4%, while a newer bond could be 100 to 200 basis points higher.

May 1995 to April 1997 Gatt-cha Rules for EE

Each bond in this time period receives a new interest rate every six months. The rates will generally not vary by more than 50 basis points from bond to bond. Often the spread is less than 25 basis points.

May 1997 Rules for EE

Each bond receives a new interest rate every six months. Historically, the rates have not varied by more than 60 basis points from bond to bond.

Note: The spread between these bonds and the Gatt-cha bonds has been 59 to 105 basis points, always in favor of the bonds governed by the May 1997 rules.

Misconception #4: *The market rate that is published every May and November is the interest rate for all bonds.*

Pre-May 1995 Rules for E, EE, and SN/FS

No. The individual market rate published each May and November has no significance by itself. This is not the rate these bonds are earning.

May 1995 to April 1997 Gatt-cha Rules for EE

The market rate in effect at the time of purchase will influence the bond for the first six months only. A new market rate will be published every following six months. This pattern continues until the bond is five years old, at which time a long-term market rate will effect the bond every six months. The first rate published under these rules has no effect on the bond's future rates.

May 1997 Rules for EE

If purchased May 1, 1997, or after, a Series EE bond receives a new market rate every six months. This market rate is based on 90% of the five-year Treasury yields.

Interest Rate Rules and How They Work

The most recent rule changes are the easiest to understand. This section starts with these recent changes and works back to the rules for older bonds.

May 1997 EE Bond Rules

Under these rules, bonds increase in value monthly and the interest is compounded semi-annually. They have no guaranteed rate, but are governed by a new market rate that is assigned every six months—May 1 and November 1. This rate is based on 90% of the average of the five-year Treasury yields for the preceding six-month period. Thus, the rate published in the government's most recent announcement (May 1998) will govern a bond for the first six months. For instance, if a bond was purchased June 10, 1998, the rate published May 1, 1998—the first rate assigned to all bonds purchased from May 1, 1998 to October 30, 1998—is applied to this bond for the first six months. On December 1, 1998, this bond will be six months old and the rate published November 1, 1998 will be in effect for the next six months. (For a history of recent rates, see Table 5.2.)

Note: Investors who cash these bonds before they are five years old suffer a penalty: They forfeit three months of interest. These are the first bonds in the history of the program to operate under this condition. For more complete information on the pros and cons of purchasing Series EE bonds, refer to Chapter 7, "Purchasing U.S. Savings Bonds."

Table 5.2

Interest Rates for EE Bonds Purchased May 1997 and After

Rate was Published	Interest Rate
May 1, 1997	5.68%
November 1, 1997	5.59%
May 1, 1998	5.06%
November 1, 1998	4.60%
May 1, 1999	
November 1, 1999	
May 1, 2000	

May 1995 to April 1997 Gatt-cha Rules

These rules were enacted as a result of GATT (the General Agreement on Trades and Tariffs). Although touted as better for investors, the rules have proven much worse for the owner who holds his or her bonds for at least five years. (Thus the term "Gatt-cha.") Because the public did not respond favorably, the Treasury changed the program May 1, 1997.

Under these rules, bonds increase in value semi-annually. They have no guaranteed rate, but earn interest at a market rate that is adjusted every six months. For the first five years, the market rate is based on 85% of the six-month T-bill yields. This rate is determined by measuring the three-month period prior to May and November. After the bond is held five years, a market rate based on 85% of the five-year Treasury yields for the six-month period prior to each May and November is assigned. Thus far, only rates based on T-bill yields have applied. The following table displays the rates published so far.

Table 5.3

Rates Published for EE Bonds
Issued May 1995 to April 1997

Rate was Published	Interest Rate
May 1, 1995	5.25%
November 1, 1995	4.75%
May 1, 1996	4.36%
November 1,1996	4.56%
May 1, 1997	4.63%
November 1, 1997	4.53%
May 1, 1998	4.47%
November 1, 1998	4.01%

Here's how it works: A bond purchased in December 1995 would have been assigned the rate of 4.75% for the first six months. On June 1, 1996 (six months later), that bond was assigned a new rate of 4.36%. This rate was in effect until December 1, 1996, when a new rate of 4.56% was assigned. Every six months the bond is assigned a new interest rate that is tied to the performance of the six-month T-bills in the first five years of the bond's life.

Pre-May 1995 Rules

This group probably represents the majority of bonds your clients hold. Before examining the complex nature of these rules, we must focus on EE bonds issued between March 1993 and April 1995. Although governed by the pre-May 1995 rules, they are given special attention here because of a unique occurrence.

EE bonds issued between March 1993 and April 1995: These bonds will be the best performing bonds in the program over the next one to two years. Why? Because they receive a fixed rate of 4% until they turn five years old. At the five-year mark, they receive the average of the market rates retroactive to the date-of-purchase. This can be a double-digit yield for the year in which that retroactive increase is added. After five years, these bonds will earn close to the individual market rate (based on 85% of five-year Treasury yields) that is published every six months (currently between 4% and 5%). One more important note: These bonds increase in value monthly until they turn five years old. After that, they increase in value semi-annually.

Now let's examine the rest of the bonds governed by the pre-May 1995 rules. A primary source of confusion is that few people understand that the government has established two independent methods for calculating the value of each bond. One is based on the guaranteed interest rates published during the life of the bond. The second method, totally independent from the first, is based on the average of the market-based rates published for a bond.

The Guaranteed Rate

As stated earlier, the guaranteed interest rate, which was assigned at purchase, is the minimum rate the bond will yield until the end of its *original maturity period.* (**Note**: In some cases a bond must be held for at least five years to receive this guarantee.) The guaranteed rate is not in effect for the life of the bond. This is a particular surprise and disappointment to bond holders who bought in the mid-1980s at 7.5%. They thought that rate would be good for as long as the bond was held. In reality, those investors were guaranteed 7.5% for the original maturity period only (ten years, in this case).

For Series E and EE bonds, original maturity periods vary from five to eighteen years, depending on the issue date. After that time, the bond enters an *extension* of ten years and is assigned a new guaranteed rate, the rate that will be in effect for that ten-year period. The original maturity period for SN/FS is four years, six months. A table of the original maturity period for each bond can be found on page 58.

For example, assume in the following illustration that the bond will be held to *final maturity* (when it will stop earning interest); in this case, that will be thirty years from the date-of-purchase. A Series EE bond purchased in July 1984 had a guaranteed rate of 7.5% and an original maturity period of ten years. In July 1994, the bond entered its first ten-year extended maturity period. The guaranteed rate for that bond during this first *extended maturity period* dropped to 4%. Why? Bonds are assigned the guaranteed rate that is in effect on the date they enter a new extension period. As of July 1994, the guaranteed rate was 4%, so this bond will have a guaranteed rate of 4% until July 2004. In July 2004, the bond will enter its last extension of ten years. The guaranteed rate for the last ten years will be whatever the guaranteed rate is as of July 2004. That final guaranteed rate is assigned to the bond until its final maturity in July 2014.

The Average of the Market-Based Rates

> The market-based interest rate is set at 85 percent of the average yield, during the time the bonds are held, of marketable Treasury securities with five years remaining to maturity.
>
> —"U.S. Department of the Treasury, Bureau of the Public Debt, U.S. Savings Bond Division, Savings Bond Buyer's Guide: 1993-1994," Pubn. SBD-2085

As stated, the market rates published every May and November are calculated on the previous six months' data for marketable Treasury securities with five years remaining to maturity. For instance, the rate published on May 1, 1994, was 4.7%. This was the first semi-annual rate for bonds purchased from May 1, 1994, to October 31, 1994. However, this is not the rate these bonds *currently* earn.

The key here is the difference between the *individual* market-based rate and the *average* of the market-based rates. A recent caller named Joan asked, "I bought bonds in the 1980s at 11+%. I know they are still earning that interest, but for how long?" How did Joan arrive at the inaccurate conclusion that her bonds were earning over 11%? Because the first *individual* rate published for her bonds was 11.09%. However, she never earned 11.09% because that number became part of an average once her bonds were held five years. Examine Table 5.4, page 57, for a comparison of individual market-based rates and the average of the market-based rates for a given time period.

The market-based variable rate generated enthusiasm when the 11.09% rate was announced with the program's introduction in November 1982. Joan thought she was buying bonds that paid 11.09%. But she was not. First, Joan would have to hold her bond for at least five years from the date of purchase to be eligible for the market-based rate program. If she held the bond for fewer than five years, the market rate has absolutely no effect. Second, all the rates published during the holding period of a bond (five years or longer) are averaged. This average is then rounded to the nearest quarter or hundredth (depending on issue date and/or the date the bond may have entered an extension). This rounded average is used to calculate a value for the bond based on the average of the market rates.

As you can see, Joan never received over 11% on her bond. In fact, the current value of her bond is about equal under both interest rate structures and her guaranteed rates actually produce a greater redemption value. Why? In this case, the value based on the guaranteed rate of 7.5% over the first ten years and 6% in the bond's current extension (average of 6.97%) is greater than the value using the average of the market rates of 6.87% (as of May 1998) over the life of the bond.

What is the bottom line? The significant number in the market-based rate program is the *average of the market rates for the specific bonds a person holds*. One thing you can determine from the *individual* market rate published every May and November is this: If the individual rate published is higher than the average, it will push the average up; if the individual rate published is lower than the average, it will pull the average down.

During a 1994 TV interview, the author mentioned that the guaranteed rate for bonds purchased that day was 4%, even if they were held for only one, two, or three years. Following the broadcast, an angry bond owner called in: "Bonds are paying 4.7% right now, the new rate was just announced this week!" This person did not understand that he was not getting "4.7% right now."

To qualify for the average of the market rates, bonds must be held for at least five years. All of the individual market rates published during this time will be averaged. If this average of the market rates produces a bond value greater than the value produced from the guaranteed rate (4%), then the investor would receive the average of the market rates.

Bonds purchased with a guaranteed rate of 4% (March 1, 1993 to April 30, 1995) will see a significant jump in value once they have been held five years. Why? Up to the four-year, eleven-month mark, the bond value is based on a guaranteed rate of 4%. Once held five years, the average of the market rates published over the life of the bond will be taken back to the date of purchase and compounded forward (if the average is greater than 4%). A bond purchased on March 1, 1993, had ten published rates over the first five years; the average of those rates is 5.19%. When the bond turned five years old (March 1998), this average rate of 5.19% was credited retroactive to the date of purchase. The result was a one-time double-digit yield for the fifth year.

As you can see from Table 5.4 (page 57), only four times out of twenty-two (twenty-two because only bonds at least five years old were counted) was the average market rate higher than the first published market rate. This is a historic view, and one that has been affected by falling interest rates in the 1990s.

An economy that produces rising interest rates over a long period of time could easily create an average market rate that is higher than the first published market rate. For example, a bond purchased November 1993 was assigned a first market rate of 4.25%. The second market rate assigned to this bond was 4.7%. The third rate was 5.92%. The fourth rate was 6.31%. The fifth rate was 5.16%. The sixth rate was 4.85%. The seventh was 5.53%. The eighth was 5.36%. The ninth was 5.28% and the tenth, 4.77%. This bond must be held five years to be eligible for the average of the market rates. These ten rates average 5.21%. As of November 1, 1998, that rate will be credited retroactive to the date of purchase. As you can see, the average rate of 5.21% is almost 100 basis points higher than the initial rate of 4.25%.

So, next May or November, when all the newspapers publish the government's press releases promoting the market rates, you will be able to anticipate the forecast. When some writers inaccurately say, "This is the new rate for all bonds held today," you will know better. Only the market rate based on 85% of five-year Treasury yields will apply to bonds purchased prior to May 1, 1995, and that rate will become part of an average that may or may not affect your clients' bonds.

October 1986: An Illustration of How the Interest Rates Work

During the last several years, one interest rate question has been posed to the author more than any other: "I bought bonds in October 1986 with a guaranteed rate of 7.5%. What interest rate are those bonds earning now?" Before we explore the answer to this question, let's examine why the question is critical and how the responses received from various sources illustrate the gross amount of misinformation that is disseminated about savings bonds.

October 1986 was the last month that bond owners could purchase bonds and lock in the guaranteed rate of 7.5%. And buy they did. Three days before the end of the month, the government announced that it would lower the guaranteed rate from 7.5% to 6% on November 1, 1986. That gave people three days to buy 7.5% bonds.

At the time of the rate change, the author was supervising the savings bond division of the Federal Reserve Bank of Chicago-Detroit Branch. This area typically averaged 50 applications a day for the purchase of savings bonds. During the last three days of October 1986, his area received over 10,000 applications. Other Federal Reserve Banks also recorded record volume. This represented the largest three-day purchase period in the bond program since World War II.

More recently, The Savings Bond Informer, Inc. has received calls from hundreds of bond owners who have been given incorrect or misleading information about the interest rates these bonds now earn. The source of much of this misinformation is the bank teller, as demonstrated in Chapter 3. In personal inquiries to over a dozen banks, the author was told that these bonds now pay more than 7%. This error is the result of bank personnel not understanding the data they have.

The author also received calls from people who reported that Federal Reserve Banks had told them that they were earning a market-based rate (4.85% for the period in question). In fact, even those who are part of the savings bond program sometimes have a tough time explaining how the interest rates on these older bonds work. In an article that appeared in *The Providence-Journal Bulletin* (October 8, 1996), a savings bond representative said this about the October 1986 bonds, "Technically your bonds are eligible to earn interest at a rate of about 4.85% over the next six months." We are all "eligible" for a lot of wonderful things, but experience shows us that we often don't get all that we are "eligible" for.

First, the market rate of 4.85% is irrelevant by itself. At the time of writing, not one bond out there is earning 4.85%. That rate, as described earlier in this chapter, is averaged together with other market rates published during the life of a bond. Thus, it is important only in relationship to the other market rates in effect for that bond.

Few understand the relationship between the guaranteed and the average market-based interest rates, and fewer still can explain it. Based on these two sets of rates, the government is calculating two unique redemption values. The bond owner receives whichever value is higher, based on whichever set of rates produces the greatest redemption value. The highest individual rate at any given point in time is *not* automatically received. This is important to understand as we look at the effect of the guaranteed rate and then at the effect of the average market-based rate.

The guaranteed rate was higher the first ten years (7.5%); after year ten, the individual market rate is higher than the new guaranteed rate (4%). Therefore, many people assume that they are automatically receiving the higher market rate. A bond owner does not receive the guaranteed rate for the first ten years and then convert to the market rate added onto the guaranteed rate from year eleven on.

A Value Based on the Guaranteed Rate

The October 1986 bonds had a guaranteed rate of 7.5% for the first ten years, its original maturity period. At the end of the original maturity period, the bonds entered an "extended maturity period." This first extension is ten years; a second ten-year extension will begin when the bond is twenty years old. When a bond enters an extension, it picks up the guaranteed rate that is in effect on that date. Subsequently, these bonds picked up a new guaranteed rate of 4% because that was the guaranteed rate on October 1996. This 4% becomes the floor for the next ten-year period. And, as the author tells clients of The Savings Bond Informer, Inc., 4% is the best representation of what one will actually earn for at least the first seven to nine years of this ten-year extension. Table 5.6 (page 59) demonstrates this by showing the value of a $1,000 bond based on the guaranteed rate (redemption value may vary from the government redemption tables by a few pennies due to rounding).

Take note that the average market-based rate has no place in column "C" where the value based on the guaranteed rate is calculated. You do not get the guaranteed rate for the first ten years and then automatically start earning the market-based rate. The guaranteed rate for the first ten years is followed by the guaranteed rate for the second ten-year period (4%). Nowhere does the average market-based rate affect values created by using the guaranteed rates.

The reason for emphatically stating that the market-based rates do not affect the values created by the guaranteed rates is because that is the biggest misconception being perpetuated. People think, "I got the 7.5% for ten years and now I automatically get the market rate which I know is 85% of five-year Treasury yields and certainly more than 4%." Sorry to be the bearer of bad news, but that view is wrong.

A Value Based on the Average of the Market-Based Rates

As you learned earlier in this chapter, what is now called the market rate (known as the "variable market rate" before the May 1995 rule changes) is published every six months. However, this rate has no significance by itself. Do not look at the rate by itself and assume, "Oh, this bond must be earning xyz% because that is what the government published as a market rate."

Once the October 1986 bond had been held for five years from the date of purchase, it became eligible for the average of the market rates, retroactive to the date of purchase. Over the five years, ten rates had been published—one every six months. At the five-year mark, the average of those ten rates was 6.93% (see Table 5.4, page 57, column 4). A redemption value based on that average would obviously create a lower value than that created by the guaranteed rate of 7.5%. So even though this type of bond was eligible for market-based rates, they had no effect at the five-year mark.

At the ten-year mark, a similar situation exists. Twenty market rates have been published for the October 1986 bond. The average of those rates is down to 6.2%, as seen in Table 5.4, page 57, column 5 (the low rates in years six through ten pulled the average down). Now it is even more obvious that 6.2% retroactive to the date of purchase will produce a lower redemption value than the guaranteed rate of 7.5% since date of purchase. The side-by-side charts in Table 5.6 (page 59) demonstrate this fact.

Significant Head Scratching Begins Here

Most bond owners assume now that the 7.5% rate has expired they will receive the 6.11% average market rate (the average of the twenty-two rates) or, at the very worst, the individual market rate of 5.53%. Um, sorry. Let's examine Table 5.6 (page 59) to see what actually happens.

The October 1986 bond is now over ten years old. What happened in year eleven and what will happen in the years beyond? In year eleven, as always, two values were created for this bond. One value was based on the guaranteed rates; the second, on the average of the market-based rates. For the guaranteed rate table, an interest rate of 4% (the current guaranteed rate in the extended maturity period) is used for year eleven. You now have ten years at 7.5% and one year at 4%. This produces the redemption value of $1,086.26 (see Table 5.6, the row labeled "23-eleven years?").

For a value based on the market rate at the end of eleven years, there are twenty-two market rates to consider. The average of those twenty-two rates is 6.11%. That average is taken retroactively to the date of purchase and then compounded forward to arrive at the redemption value of $969.37. This is much lower than the redemption value using the guaranteed rates ($1,086.26). At the end of eleven years, then, the market rate was still having no impact on the bond.

What is the best representation of what the bond actually earned in the eleventh year? The 4% guaranteed rate. (Note: the actual yield may be slightly lower or higher—3.97% to 4.07%—due to rounding.)

So, anyone who says that the bond earned the market-based rate in year eleven is among the uninformed. The proof, by the way, is in the pudding, and in this case the pudding is the redemption table (Figure 5.1). As of October 1996, the redemption value for a $50 October 1986 bond, was $52.22. The redemption value as of April 1997 was $53.28. The amount of increase is 2.03% or an annual rate of 4.06%. The author rests his case.

Figure 5.1

Redemption Values for an October 1986 Bond

"As Of" Date	Value of $50 Bond
October 1996	$52.22
April 1997	$53.28

Adapted from Form PD 3600, Tables of Redemption Values,
Dept. of the Treasury, BPD.

From the date the October 1986 bond entered the extension, how long will it be before the owner receives more than 4%? The answer is seven years, *if* the long-term rate averages 6.11% over the next six years—a generous assumption. If the market rate averages 5.2% over the first extended maturity period (October 1996 to October 2006), this bond will earn 4% during the entire ten-year extension. The actual annual yield will be between 3.97% and 4.07% due to rounding. Examine Table 5.6 (page 59) to see where the values based on the market rate begin to exceed the values based on the guaranteed rates on row numbers 35 and 38.

Many investors are very frustrated with a 4% return on a long-term investment product. This rate is lower than the three-month T-bill rate at the time of writing.

In the early 1990s, as interest rates fell dramatically, the Treasury was stuck paying what they had promised in 1986: 7.5%. That is, they were locked into paying a premium—more than market conditions would have paid—on the October 1986 bond. The investor had made a good choice and was actually beating the system. Now, however, the tables have turned. According to the rules governing savings bonds, bond owners are asked to swallow a guaranteed rate of 4% for as long as ten years if they want to hold onto their October 1986 bonds. The patriotic investor may feel that it all evens out in the end. However, if one looks at bonds as an investment, without the patriotic obligation, these bonds should be recognized as the worst performers of any savings bonds held.

When Do Interest Rates Change?

Series H and HH bonds: The interest rate assigned to the bond at issue is good for the first ten years. Every ten years the bond will receive a new rate. The rate for any bond entering an extension since March 1993 has been 4%. This 4% rate is set at the discretion of the Treasury and there is no schedule for rate adjustment.

Savings Notes/Freedom Shares: These bonds will earn between 4% and 5% through final maturity (thirty years). All savings notes will have stopped earning interest by October 2000.

Series E bonds and Series EE bonds over five years old: These bonds can be affected by either the guaranteed rate or the market-based rate. A new market rate is published each May and November. The guaranteed rate, which was 4% at the time of writing (October 1998), last changed March 1, 1993. There is no scheduled change for the guaranteed rate.

Series EE bonds purchased May 1995 and after: New market rates are published every May and November.

Series I bonds: The fixed rate for these bonds will be announced each November and May, but do not expect frequent changes. Since it is not tied to any index or security, the rate will probably remain relatively constant from one announcement to the next. The CPI-U (consumers price index-urban consumers) will change every six months. This will be announced each May and November. For a complete explanation of the I bond, see Chapter 17.

Quick Tips on Interest Rates

- An important measurement for the future value of a savings bond is the current interest rate a bond is earning and the length of time that rate will continue.
- The age of a bond should not be the only data used in determining which bonds to cash, the interest rate must be considered.
- Your clients' bonds are currently earning between 4% and 6.1% if they are over five years old and have not reached final maturity.
- Savings bonds are governed by the rules in effect at the time of purchase and by their type (series). All accrual bonds fall under one of the following sets of rules: September 1998 I Bond Rules; May 1997 EE Bond Rules; May 1995 to April 1997 Gatt-cha Rules; or the Pre-May 1995 Rules.
- There are three types of interest rates: the guaranteed or fixed rate, the market rate (with four subcategories), and the new CPI-U indexed rate.
- Being aware of the common interest rate misconceptions will enable you to answer your clients' questions.
- Interest rates can change when bonds enter extensions.
- EE bonds purchased between March 1993 and April 1995 will earn a double-digit yield for the year in which their retroactive increase is added.
- Many people have questions about October 1986 bonds. These bonds are no longer earning 7.5%.

Table 5.4

Historic View of the Market-Based Interest Rate on Savings Bonds Purchased Prior to May 1995

Issue Date	Average Market Rate Over the Life of the Bond	First Market Rate Published for Bond	Average Market Rates for an October 1986 Series EE Bond	
Through 4/30/83	6.80	11.09		
5/83 to 10/83	6.66	8.64		
11/83 to 4/84	6.60	9.38		
5/84 to 10/84	6.50	9.95		
11/84 to 4/85	6.38	10.94		
5/85 to 10/85	6.21	9.49		
11/85 to 4/86	6.08	8.36		
5/86 to 10/86	5.99	7.02	For an October 1986 bond, the average of the first ten rates was 6.93%.	
11/86 to 4/87	5.95	6.06		
5/87 to 10/87	5.94	5.84		
11/87 to 4/88	5.95	7.17		
5/88 to 10/88	5.89	6.90		
11/88 to 4/89	5.84	7.35		
5/89 to 10/89	5.76	7.81		For an October 1986 bond, the average of the first twenty rates was 6.2%.
11/89 to 4/90	5.65	6.98		
5/90 to 10/90	5.57	7.01		
11/90 to 4/91	5.48	7.19		
5/91 to 10/91	5.37	6.57		
11/91 to 4/92	5.28	6.38		
5/92 to 10/92	5.19	5.58		
11/92 to 4/93	5.16	5.04		
5/93 to 10/93	5.17	4.78		
11/93 to 4/94	5.21	4.25		
5/94 to 10/94	5.32	4.70		
11/94 to 4/95	5.40	5.92		
5/95 to 10/95	N/A	6.31*		
11/95 to 4/96	N/A	5.16*		
5/96 to 10/96	N/A	4.85*		
11/96 to 4/97	N/A	5.53*		
5/97 to 10/97	N/A	5.36*		
11/97 to 4/98	N/A	5.28*		
5/98 to 10/98	N/A	4.77*		

*This rate does not impact any bond purchased after 4/30/95.

Table 5.5

Guaranteed Minimum Rates
and Original Maturity Periods
For Series EE, E, and Savings Notes
(This table is for the month of September 1998.)

Issue Date	Original Maturity Period	Guaranteed Through Current Maturity Period	Life of Bond (years)
SERIES EE			
May 1995 to present	17 yrs.	no guaranteed rate	30
March 1993 to April 1995	18 yrs.	4.0	30
November 1986 to February 1993	12 yrs.	6.0	30
March 1983 to October 1986	10 yrs.	4.0	30
November 1982 to February 1983	10 yrs.	6.0	30
May 1981 to October 1982	8 yrs.	6.0	30
November 1980 to April 1981	9 yrs.	6.0	30
January 1980 to October 1980	11 yrs.	6.0	30
SERIES E			
March 1978 to June 1980	5 yrs.	4.0	30
December 1973 to February 1978	5 yrs.	6.0	30
December 1972 to November 1973	5 yrs. 10 mos.	6.0	30
June 1969 to November 1972	5 yrs. 10 mos.	4.0	30
October 1968 to May 1969	7 yrs.	4.0	30
December 1965 to September 1968		no longer earn interest	30
June 1965 to November 1965	7 yrs. 9 mos.	4.0	40
January 1961 to May 1965	7 yrs. 9 mos	6.0	40
June 1959 to December 1960	7 yrs. 9 mos.	4.0	40
October 1958 to May 1959	8 yrs. 11 mos.	4.0	40
May 1941 to September 1958		no longer earn interest	40
SAVINGS NOTES			
October 1968 to October 1970	4 yrs. 6 mos.	4.0	30
May 1967 to September 1968		no longer earn interest	30

Adapted from "Guaranteed Minimum Rates," Bureau of the Public Debt, U.S. Savings Bond Marketing Office.

Table 5.6

Example of October 1986 Series EE Bond

A	B	C	D	E
Row Number	Date of Increase After Initial Purchase of October 1986	Value based on 7.5% for first ten years, 4% for second ten years	Value based on 6.11% average variable rate over twenty years	Value based on 5.9% average variable rate over twenty years
1		500.00	500.00	500.00
2	Apr/87	518.75	515.28	514.75
3	Oct/87	538.20	531.02	529.94
4	Apr/88	558.39	547.24	545.57
5	Oct/88	579.33	563.96	561.66
6	Apr/89	601.05	581.19	578.23
7	Oct/89	623.59	598.94	595.29
8	Apr/90	646.97	617.24	612.85
9	Oct/90	671.24	636.10	630.93
10	Apr/91	696.41	655.53	649.54
11	Oct/91	722.52	675.55	668.70
12	Apr/92	749.62	696.19	688.43
13	Oct/92	777.73	717.46	708.74
14	Apr/93	806.89	739.38	729.65
15	Oct/93	837.15	761.97	751.17
16	Apr/94	868.54	785.25	773.33
17	Oct/94	901.11	809.24	796.14
18	Apr/95	934.91	833.96	819.63
19	Oct/95	969.96	859.44	843.81
20	Apr/96	1006.34	885.69	868.70
21-ten yrs	Oct/96	1044.08	912.75	894.33
22	Apr/97	1064.96	940.63	920.71
23-eleven yrs	Oct/97	1086.26	969.37	947.87
24	Apr/98	1107.98	998.98	975.83
25	Oct/98	1130.14	1029.50	1004.62
26	Apr/99	1152.74	1060.95	1034.26
27	Oct/99	1175.80	1093.37	1064.77
28	Apr/2000	1199.32	1126.77	1096.18
29	Oct/2000	1223.30	1161.19	1128.52
30	Apr/2001	1247.77	1196.67	1161.81
31	Oct/2001	1272.72	1233.22	1196.08
32	Apr/2002	1298.18	1270.90	1231.37
33	Oct/2002	1324.14	1309.73	1267.69
34	Apr/2003	1350.62	1349.74	1305.09
35-seventeen yrs	Oct/2003	1377.64	1390.97	1343.59
36	Apr/2004	1405.19	1433.47	1383.22
37-eighteen yrs	Oct/2004	1433.29	1477.26	1424.03
38	Apr/2005	1461.96	1522.39	1466.04
39-nineteen yrs	Oct/2005	1491.20	1568.90	1509.29
40	Apr/2006	1521.02	1616.83	1553.81
41-twenty yrs	Oct/2006	1551.44	1666.22	1599.65

Chapter 6

TIMING ISSUES
AND MATURITY PERIODS

▶ *Common Misconceptions*
▶ *Timing Issues at Purchase*
▶ *Timing Issues at Redemption*
▶ *Timing Issues at Exchange*
▶ *Timing Issues at Final Maturity*
▶ *What Does "Maturity" Mean?*
▶ *Quick Tips on Timing and Maturities*

How important is timing with savings bond transactions? The government pockets more than $150 million a year at the expense of bond owners who have unknowingly failed to address timing issues related to bond redemption. As you know, whether it's stocks, mutual funds, real estate, or the like, timing is crucial to many financial transactions. Savings bonds are no exception and, as you are about to learn, they are an excellent example of how "timing" is everything.

Common Misconceptions

Once again, sorting the truth from the fiction can help you wisely manage a savings bond investment.

Misconception #1: *It does not matter when you cash a bond.*

Yes, it most certainly does. If you ignore timing issues, you can say goodbye to up to six months of interest on most bonds.

Misconception #2: *All bonds increase in value at the same time.*

Dangerous assumption. Each bond has a unique increase date. Most bonds increase semi-annually; however, Series EE bonds purchased between March 1, 1993, and April 30, 1995, increase monthly up to the fifth year. And EE bonds purchased May 1997 and after increase monthly.

Many people mistakenly think that the increase occurs every May and November because that is when the market-based rates are published. Others think that the increase occurs every March and September because that is when the redemption tables are published. Those events have no connection to the actual date a particular bond will increase in value.

Misconception #3: *All bonds increase in value on the issue date and six months later.*

No. This misconception is particularly damaging to owners who hold older Series E bonds. Over 60% of the series E bonds that are still earning interest increase in value at a time other than the issue date (and again six months later). Nothing on the bond tells you when the increase will occur. See Tables 6.3 and 6.4, pages 72 and 73, at the end of this chapter, to learn when each bond will increase in value.

Misconception #4: *Timing is not important when exchanging for HH bonds.*

It sure is. Many bond owners exchange their Series E, EE, or Savings Notes (SN) for HH bonds so that they can receive current income. The same timing issues that apply to the redemption of bonds also apply to an exchange. Choosing when to exchange can make a significant difference in the client's overall financial picture. See "Timing an Exchange" (page 108) for more information.

Timing Issues at Purchase

A bond's issue date is the first day of the month in which it was purchased (assuming that the funds used to purchase the bond were available to the bank the month in which it was bought). Therefore, purchasing bonds late in the month is best because they will begin to earn interest from the first day of the month in which they were purchased.

Timing Issues at Redemption

Deciding when to cash a bond rests solely with the bond owner. The bank's role is to supply the bond owner with the correct redemption value on the day that the bond is redeemed. The bond owner—not the bank—is responsible for making certain that the timing of a redemption is in their best interest. The following true story illustrates the importance of timing at redemption.

A recently retired high school counselor owned U.S. Savings Bonds. He had cashed several $1,000 bonds purchased in the 1950s which had not yet reached final maturity. Each of his bonds was valued at over $5,000. He thought that bonds increased in value every month and that it did not matter when they were cashed.

The result was that this man forfeited up to $175 on each bond he cashed. Upon cashing ten bonds in this manner, his loss approached $1,000 to $2,000. Guess who was smiling all the way to the Federal Treasury?

A difference of even *one day* can mean the loss of hundreds or thousands of dollars to the bond owner. Cashing a bond one day before an interest increase results in missing out on six months' interest for most bonds. Seldom is the best time "accidentally" selected when bonds are randomly redeemed.

How do I know when a bond will increase?

Each bond has a unique increase pattern. Many older bonds increase at intervals that do not coincide with the issue date and six months later. See Tables 6.3 and 6.4 at the end of this chapter for the increase dates.

Exceptions: Any Series EE bond purchased between March 1, 1993, and April 30, 1995, will increase in value monthly for the first five years (thereafter they will increase in value semi-annually). This change in the bond program accompanied the drop in the guaranteed interest rate from 6% to 4%. Also, any Series EE bond purchased May 1997 and after will increase in value monthly.

Once the correct month is identified, on which day should a bond be cashed?

The increase always occurs on the first business day of the month. A bond will hold that value until the next scheduled increase, either the next month (for bonds that increase monthly) or six months later (for bonds that increase semi-annually).

The same amount of money will be received whether a bond is redeemed on the first business day of the month or the last. **Note:** The date stamped on a bond does not alter this principle. This is illustrated on the bond in Figure 6.1.

Figure 6.1

Series EE Savings Bond

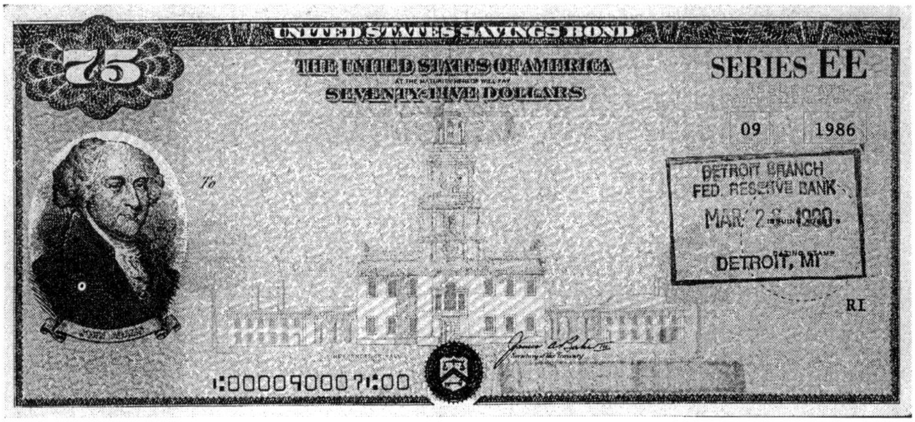

The date stamped on this bond is March 28, 1990. Even if the stamp date was April 10, 1990 or May 30, 1990 the bond would still increase the first day of the month for each month that an increase is due. The issue date (top right-hand corner) is September 1986. This bond will increase September 1st and March 1st. (**Note**: **Not all bonds increase on the issue date and six months later.**)

Timing Issues at Exchange

To exchange, an investor takes the value of a Series E or EE bond or SN at the time of redemption and rolls it over into an HH bond rather than accept the redemption value in cash. (This is often done to continue tax deferral on the interest income of older bonds and also to receive a semi-annual interest payment from the new HH bonds.)

A hypothetical example will serve to illustrate that an investor can lose money if he or she does not consider the timing of their exchange. Suppose an owner has $50,000 in E bonds that they want to exchange for HH bonds because they want the semi-annual interest payments and the 4% interest rate. (The author is not suggesting that this is the best alternative. See Chapter 9, page 103, "Exchanging for HH Bonds," for more considerations.) Assume the overall portfolio is growing at a 6% rate and no thought is given to the timing of the exchange. In a typical case, $750 to $1,500 would be forfeited by not investigating the best time to exchange. This is money that could have purchased an additional HH bond. If the forfeiture is $1,000, the bond owner not only missed the extra principal of an additional HH bond, but if held for ten years, that HH bond would have netted an additional $400 in interest ($40 a year for ten years). The loss now approaches $1,500.

Again, refer to Chapter 9, "Exchanging for HH Bonds," for exchange strategies and the selective redemption alternative.

Timing Issues at Final Maturity

When a Series E or EE bond or SN reaches final maturity (the point at which the bond stops earning interest), it will receive the last increase on the first day of the month in which the bond stops earning interest. For instance, a bond purchased July 1963 will receive its last increase July 1, 2003. No additional value will be added to the bond after that date.

Sometimes the final increase will be for a period less than six months. Many clients will recall that bonds purchased prior to December 1965 used to have an odd number of years and months to final maturity. Final maturity on these bonds has since been changed to an even forty years. For instance, a July 1963 bond originally had a final maturity date of thirty-seven years and nine months from the date of purchase. Now this same bond will reach final maturity in forty years—July 2003. This bond's semi-annual increases occur every April and October. It will receive an increase in April 2003 and again in July 2003—only three months later. The final increase is the only time when an E bond increase will not occur semi-annually.

A Series E bond issued in 1964 will earn interest longer than a Series E bond issued in 1966. Why?

A puzzled investor wrote this in reference to the bond statement she had ordered from The Savings Bond Informer, Inc.:

My bonds are Series E, purchased from 1965 to 1979. The statement gives the date that interest earnings would stop as 30 years from the date-of-purchase. I was under the impression that the bonds would earn interest for 40 years. Please explain if there is an error in the statement.

The report that this bond owner received was 100% correct. Bonds that she thought would earn interest for forty years (those purchased December 1965 and after) are only going to earn interest for thirty years. Another bond owner stated:

It really surprised me that thirty-three of my 200 bonds had stopped earning interest. My bank didn't tell me anything about this. I didn't realize the "30-year, 40-year thing."

Most of your clients don't realize the "30-year, 40-year thing" either.

Note: Any E bond forty years old or older has stopped earning interest. At the end of 1995, thirty-year-old E bonds (issued December 1965 and after) began to reach final maturity, thirty years from their issue date. This means that at the time of writing, bonds issued in 1966 and 1967 have stopped earning interest, while those issued in 1962 and 1963 are still earning interest.

Which Bonds Have Stopped Earning Interest?

As of December 1998, the following bonds are no longer earning and/or paying interest:

- Series E bonds issued from 1941 to December 1958
- Series E bonds issued from December 1965 to December 1968
- Series H bonds issued from 1952 to December 1968
- Freedom Shares/Savings Notes issued from May 1967 to December 1968

Table 6.1

Final Maturity

Series & Issue Date	Final Maturity (Total number of years bond will earn interest)
SERIES EE	
1/80 to present	30 years
SERIES E	
12/65 to 6/80	30 years
5/41 to 11/65	40 years
SAVINGS NOTES	
5/67 to 10/70	30 years
SERIES H	
2/57 to 12/79	30 years
SERIES HH	
1/80 to present	20 years
SERIES I	
9/98 to present	30 years

Adapted from Final Maturity Schedule, BPD, U.S. Savings Bond Marketing Office.

Exchanging for HH Bonds at Final Maturity

Time is of the essence. Do not wait too long. Once a bond stops earning interest, a bond owner has a one-year grace period within which to exchange it for an HH bond. However, the bond will earn no interest from the date of final maturity until the exchange. If the bond is held more than one year beyond final maturity, the only option is to redeem it. See Chapter 9 for information on exchanging for HH bonds.

What Does "Maturity" Mean?

Rules for Bonds Issued Prior to May 1995

Bonds carry three different maturities: original maturity, extended maturity, and final maturity.

Original Maturity is the maximum amount of time it will take a bond to reach face value at the guaranteed interest rate. This date is set at purchase, regardless of when the bond actually reaches face value. So the original maturity is similar to a minimum guaranteed rate that many annuity contracts have.

For example, an EE bond purchased in 1994 has an original maturity period of eighteen years. The guaranteed interest rate is 4%. If this bond ends up with an average market-based interest rate of 5%, it will reach face value in about fourteen years. However, the original maturity period will still be eighteen years. This means that the guaranteed rate of 4% will not change until the bond enters an extended maturity at the end of the eighteenth year.

Extended Maturity periods are always ten years long, except for the last one, which can be less. An extended maturity period begins when a bond reaches the end of the original maturity period. Bonds issued prior to May 1, 1995, will take on a new guaranteed rate as they enter their extended maturity period. Each time a bond enters an extended maturity period, the guaranteed interest rate for that bond becomes whatever the current guaranteed rate is at that time. A bond may have more than one extended maturity period. See Table 6.2 (page 71) for clarification.

Final Maturity is the date after which the bond will no longer earn interest. Why is this knowledge critical? Bond owners have sometimes been counseled to redeem bonds when they reach "maturity." Maturity has been incorrectly defined as "reaching face value." Consequently, bond owners cash bonds that would have continued to earn interest for another ten or twenty years. They also have to declare the full amount of interest on their tax return in the year of redemption. This hurts people who are only a few years from retirement: They declare the interest income when they are most likely in the highest tax bracket of their lives.

Review an example of how the three uses of "maturity," as described above, would work on an EE bond purchased in November 1986. See Table 6.2 (page 71), the third line under Series EE.

A bond purchased in November 1986 will earn interest for thirty years. At the guaranteed rate of 6%, the bond will reach face value in twelve years. (**Note:** If this bond earns more than 6%, it will reach face value in less than twelve years. The original maturity period, however, is still twelve years.) At the end of twelve years, the bond will enter a ten-year extended maturity period. At the end of this extended maturity period, the bond will be twenty-two years old. Since a bond purchased in November 1986 earns interest for thirty years, the last extended maturity period will only be eight years. This bond reaches final maturity thirty years from the purchase date, November 2016.

Table 6.2 provides the original maturity and extension periods for Series E and EE bonds and SNs.

Why All Bonds Are Not Created Equal

The original maturity period of a bond can range anywhere from fifty-four months to eighteen years. The variance is a result of different interest rates and purchase prices at the time of issue. As previously stated, some bonds earn interest for thirty years and others for forty years. In Table 6.2, note that a bond with an original maturity period of eight years, eleven months (purchased May 1959) will have a maturity schedule of three ten-year extensions and a final extension of one year, one month.

Each time a bond enters an extended maturity period, the guaranteed interest rate for that bond becomes whatever the current guaranteed rate is at that time. A bond purchased in January 1986 had an original maturity period of ten years and a guaranteed rate of 7.5%. Since the guaranteed rate was 4% on January 1, 1996, this bond now has a guaranteed rate of 4% for the next ten years.

Reminder: The average market-based (variable) rate can be a factor on any bond five years or older. See Chapter 5, "Understanding Interest Rates."

Maturity Periods for EE Bonds issued after April 1995

EE bonds purchased after April 1995 have an interesting new twist. A bond will receive a one-time catch-up increase to face value if the bond has not yet reached face value by year seventeen. In essence that guarantees a minimum rate of about 4.12% if the bond is held for seventeen years.

The original maturity period for bonds issued under these rules is seventeen years. These bonds will continue to earn interest for a full thirty years from the issue date. Thus an original maturity of seventeen years, an extended maturity period of ten years, and a second extended maturity period of three years.

What rate of interest will be earned after original maturity? The Treasury Department has not committed itself to a specific interest rate structure or pattern beyond seventeen years at the time of writing. While none of the bonds issued under the new rules will reach the seventeen-year mark until 2012, this will be an important issue for bond owners to watch.

Author's Note: The original maturity period for bonds under the new rules is significant in the unlikely event that the seventeen-year catch-up is necessary. It is also significant because the Treasury could assign different interest rates and/or interest rate structures to bonds as they enter extended maturity periods. It would make sense for a bond to earn interest at 90% of the five-year Treasury yield for each six-month period as it enters an extended maturity period, but that is not a sure thing. The final maturity period is important as always, because the bond will not earn any more interest after that date.

The number of people who relate stories of misinformation and financial loss to The Savings Bond Informer, Inc. are evidence enough: Knowing each stage a client's bonds will go through is essential to the planning process.

Quick Tips on Timing and Maturities

- Your client can forfeit hundreds (and in some cases, thousands) of dollars by cashing or exchanging bonds even ***one day*** before the interest accrual date.
- Most bonds have a unique increase accrual pattern that may or may not coincide with the issue date and subsequent six-month anniversary date.
- Series EE bonds purchased between March 1, 1993, and April 30, 1995, increase in value *monthly* for the first five years.
- Bond owners will receive the same amount whether they cash on the first day of the month that interest is credited to a bond or the last. Therefore, it is better to cash sooner in the month rather than later.
- An investor has only a one-year grace period to make an exchange after a bond stops earning interest.
- The best strategy for an investor is to purchase bonds late in the month since interest accrues from the first day of the month.
- Most bonds carry three different maturity periods which can affect the rate of interest the bond is earning—original, extended, and final.

Table 6.2

Guide to Extended and Final Maturity Periods

Issue Date	Original Maturity Period	First Extended Maturity Period	Additional Extended Period	Additional Extended Period	Additional Extended Period	Final Maturity (total number of years bond will earn interest)
SERIES EE						
5/95 to present	17 years	10 years	3 years			30 years
3/93 to 4/95	18 years	10 years	2 years			30 years
11/86 to 2/93	12 years	10 years	8 years			30 years
11/82 to 10/86	10 years	10 years	10 years			30 years
5/81 to 10/82	8 years	10 years	10 years	2 years		30 years
11/80 to 4/81	9 years	10 years	10 years	1 year		30 years
1/80 to 10/80	11 years	10 years	9 years			30 years
SERIES E						
12/73 to 6/80	5 years	10 years	10 years	5 years		30 years
6/69 to 11/73	5 years, 10 months	10 years	10 years	4 years, 2 months		30 years
12/65 to 5/69	7 years	10 years	10 years	3 years		30 years
All Series E bonds purchased after November 1965 will earn interest for 30 years						
6/59 to 11/65	7 years, 9 months	10 years	10 years	10 years	2 years, 3 months	40 years
2/57 to 5/59	8 years, 11 months	10 years	10 years	10 years	1 year, 1 months	40 years
All Series E Bonds over 40 years old have stopped earning interest.						
SAVINGS NOTES						
5/67 to 10/70	4 years, 6 months	10 years	10 years	5 years, 6 months		30 years

Table 6.3

Interest Accrual Dates for Series E Bonds

Month of Issue May 1952 to January 1957	Interest Accrual Dates	Month of Issue February 1957 to May 1959	Interest Accrual Dates
January	March & September	January	June & December
February	April & October	February	July & January
March	May & November	March	August & February
April	June & December	April	September & March
May	July & January	May	October & April
June	August & February	June	November & May
July	September & March	July	December & June
August	October & April	August	January & July
September	November & May	September	February & August
October	December & June	October	March & September
November	January & July	November	April & October
December	February & August	December	May & November

Month of Issue June 1959 to November 1965	Interest Accrual Dates	Month of Issue December 1965 to May 1969	Interest Accrual Dates
January	April & October	January	January & July
February	May & November	February	February & August
March	June & December	March	March & September
April	July & January	April	April & October
May	August & February	May	May & November
June	September & March	June	June & December
July	October & April	July	July & January
August	November & May	August	August & February
September	December & June	September	September & March
October	January & July	October	October & April
November	February & August	November	November & May
December	March & September	December	December & June

Month of Issue June 1969 to November 1973	Interest Accrual Dates	Month of Issue December 1973 to June 1980	Interest Accrual Dates
January	May & November	January	January & July
February	June & December	February	February & August
March	July & January	March	March & September
April	August & February	April	April & October
May	September & March	May	May & November
June	October & April	June	June & December
July	November & May	July	July & January
August	December & June	August	August & February
September	January & July	September	September & March
October	February & August	October	October & April
November	March & September	November	November & May
December	April & October	December	December & June

Adapted from "Interest Accrual Dates," SBD 2082, U.S. Government Printing Office, 1993.

Table 6.4

Interest Accrual Dates for Series EE Bonds and Savings Notes

SERIES EE		SAVINGS NOTES	
Month of Issue January 1980 to April 1997*	Interest Accrual Dates	Month of Issue May 1967 to October 1970**	Interest Accrual Dates
January	January & July	January	January & July
February	February & August	February	February & August
March	March & September	March	March & September
April	April & October	April	April & October
May	May & November	May	May & November
June	June & December	June	June & December
July	July & January	July	July & January
August	August & February	August	August & February
September	September & March	September	September & March
October	October & April	October	October & April
November	November & May	November	November & May
December	December & June	December	December & June

Adapted from "Interest Accrual Dates," SBD 2082, U.S. Government Printing Office, 1993.
* Series EE Bonds purchased from March 1993 to April 1995 will increase in value monthly for the first five years, semi-annually thereafter. All EE Bonds issued May 1997 and after will increase in value monthly.
** Savings Notes stop earning interest after 30 years.

Chapter 7

PURCHASING U.S. SAVINGS BONDS

▶ *Which Bonds Are Currently Available?*
▶ *When Is the Best Time to Purchase Bonds?*
▶ *Where and How Can Bonds Be Purchased?*
▶ *Who Can Buy U.S. Savings Bonds?*
▶ *Purchase Limitations*
▶ *How Should Bonds Be Registered?*
▶ *Purchasing for Special Occasions*
▶ *Bond Investment Growth with Systematic Purchase*
▶ *Bond Series That Can No Longer Be Purchased*
▶ *Quick Tips on Purchasing*

How many people purchase U. S. Savings Bonds? Although sales have slowed significantly since 1992, more than $7 billion were sold in 1995 and over $5 billion in 1996 and 1997. Of the many Americans who purchase each year, approximately 7 million do so through payroll deduction, a systematic purchase strategy.

This chapter will describe the purchase process. The discussion of interest rates and timing issues is limited to new issues of U.S. Savings Bonds. (See Chapters 5 and 6 for details on older bonds.)

Which Bonds Are Currently Available

There are three types of bonds currently available: Series EE, HH, and the new I bond. Each series has a very different purpose.

- **The Series EE bond is an interest accrual bond.** The interest it earns becomes part of the value of the bond. At redemption, the bond owner receives the purchase price plus all the interest earned.

- **The Series HH bond is a current income bond.** As the name suggests, this bond pays an interest payment to the bond owner every six months. The HH bond will always be worth the face value at redemption.

- **The Series I bond (Inflation Protection Bond) is an interest accrual bond.** The interest it earns becomes part of the value of the bond. At redemption, the bond owner receives the purchase price plus all the interest earned.

The greatest distinction between the three, however, is that only Series I and Series EE bonds can be bought for cash. HH bonds can be obtained only by exchanging Series E or EE bonds or Savings Notes or by reinvesting eligible H bonds. For this reason, the bulk of this chapter will deal with the Series EE and I bond. (Additional information on HH bonds is provided in Chapter 9.)

Are EE and I bonds a good investment? In the following information you will find a list of characteristics for both types. Then, an examination of some basic pros and cons will help you think through your position and provide arguments for your opinion.

Series EE Bond Characteristics

- It is purchased at half the face value: A $100 bond costs $50.

- It is guaranteed to reach face value in seventeen years or less.

- The original maturity period is fixed at seventeen years.

- If a bond is cashed in within the first five years, three months of interest is forfeited. This penalty is new to the bond program and was introduced in May 1997.

- A new market rate will be assigned to the bond at each six-month compounding period. The first rate assigned to a bond, if purchased between November 1, 1998, and April 30, 1999, is 4.60%. For current rate information on new purchases of Series EE bonds, call 1-800-4USBOND.

- The bond will earn interest for a total of thirty years from the date of purchase.

- The EE bond is an interest accrual security. This means interest is added to the value of the bond periodically. The bond will increase in value monthly and interest is compounded semi-annually.

- The interest earned is tax-deferred. A bond owner may elect to report interest annually; however, most bond owners do not report interest until they redeem the bonds. (See Chapter 14 for more tax information.)

- Interest earned is subject to federal tax, but exempt from state and local taxes. A 1099-INT is provided to the party redeeming the bond by the agency that cashes the bond.

- When specific guidelines are met, the bonds may be tax-free for qualified educational expenses. (See Chapter 11.)

- The following denominations are available: $50, $75, $100, $200, $500, $1,000, $5,000, and $10,000. If a client purchases bonds through payroll deduction, the minimum denomination they may buy is $100.

- The purchase limit is $15,000 ($30,000 face value) per person per calendar year. (See "Purchase Limitations," page 84.)

The Pros and Cons of Purchasing Series EE Bonds

The Pros of Purchasing EE Bonds

1. No-load to purchase or redeem (no fees to buy or sell bonds).

2. Purchasers can start with as little as $25.

3. The first new market rate for EE bonds purchased November 1, 1998 to April 30, 1999, is 4.60%. Current rates may beat savings accounts and are generally competitive with certificates of deposit, or money market funds, although not as liquid for the first six months. Call 1-800-4USBOND for interest rate information for new purchases.

4. They are fully guaranteed by the United States government.

5. There is no penalty for redemption before maturity, if held at least five years.

6. The interest is exempt from state and local taxes.

7. The principal is secure (though the interest income is modest).

The Cons of Purchasing EE Bonds

1. Bonds must be held for six months (no liquidity for six months; some exceptions in extreme emergencies do apply).

2. Purchase limitations of $15,000 per person per year apply, although this can be exceeded by adding co-owners. (Read about purchase limitations later in this chapter.)

3. The market interest rate may be much lower than an investor's expectations or needs.

4. It may take twelve to eighteen years to reach face value at current market rates. If the average of the market rates is 6% during the original maturity period, then the bonds would reach face value in approximately twelve years. This may not meet a client's investment goals for doubling their money.

5. Interest is subject to federal tax.

6. The real rate of return (after taxes) may not meet a client's investment objectives. Consider a client in the 28% tax bracket who buys a series EE bond that has an average interest rate of 5%, for a time period when inflation averages 2.5%. Your client would realize a real rate of return of about 1% after taxes.

Series I Bond Characteristics

- It is purchased at face value: A $100 bond costs $100.

- If a bond is cashed in within the first five years, three months of interest is forfeited. This penalty is the same as the EE bond penalty enacted for purchases May 1997 and after.

- A fixed interest rate will be assigned to a bond at purchase. An inflation adjusted rate is added to the fixed rate every six-months to create the earnings rate for that six-month period. Thus the earnings rate is comprised of two parts. The new fixed rates and the inflation adjusted rate will be announced each May and November. The inflation adjusted rate is based on the CPI-U (Consumer Price Index-Urban Consumers) for a six-month period. The first fixed rate assigned to a bond, if purchased between November 1, 1998 and April 30, 1999, is 3.3%. When combined with the inflation adjusted rate, the result is an initial interest rate of 5.05%. For current rate information for new purchases of Series I bonds, call 1-800-4USBOND.

- The bond will earn interest for a total of thirty years from the date of purchase.

- The I bond is an interest accrual security. This means interest is added to the value of the bond periodically. At redemption the investor receives the purchase price plus the interest. Interest is added to the bond monthly and compounded semi-annually.

- The interest earned is tax-deferred. A bond owner may elect to report interest annually; however, most bond owners do not report interest until they redeem the bonds. (See Chapter 14 for more tax information.)

- Interest earned is subject to federal tax, but exempt from state and local taxes. A 1099-INT is provided to the party redeeming the bond by the agency that cashes the bond.

- When specific guidelines are met, the bonds may be tax-free for qualified educational expenses. (See Chapter 11.)

- You may purchase the following denominations: $50, $75, $100, $200, $500, $1,000, $5,000, and $10,000. The $200 and $10,000 will not be available until May 1999.

- The purchase limit is $30,000 (twice that of the EE bond) per person per calendar year. (See "Purchase Limitations," page 84.)

The Pros and Cons of Purchasing Series I Bonds

The Pros of Purchasing I Bonds

1. No-load to purchase or redeem (no fees to buy or sell bonds).

2. Purchasers can start with as little as $50.

3. The first interest rate for purchases made November 1, 1998 through April 30, 1999, is 5.05%. Current rates may beat savings accounts and will always exceed the inflation rate. Call 1-800-4USBOND for interest rate information for new purchases.

4. They are fully guaranteed by the United States government.

5. There is no penalty for redemption before maturity, if held at least five years.

6. The interest is exempt from state and local taxes.

7. The principal is secure (though the interest income is modest).

The Cons of Purchasing I Bonds

1. Bonds must be held for six months (no liquidity for six months; some exceptions in extreme emergencies do apply).

2. The interest rate may be much lower than an investor's expectations or needs.

3. It may take twelve to twenty years to reach face value at current interest rates. If the earnings rate (combination of fixed and CPI-U index) averages 6%, then the bonds would double in approximately twelve years. This may not meet a client's investment goals for doubling their money.

4. Interest is subject to federal tax.

5. The real rate of return (after taxes) may not meet a client's investment objectives. Consider a client in the 39% tax bracket who buys a series I bond that has an average interest rate of 7% (made up of a fixed rate of 3.4% and an inflation rate of 3.6%). In a time period when inflation averages 3.6%, they would realize a real rate of return of less than .75% after taxes when cashing their bonds.

Whether savings bonds are the right choice will depend on each client's specific financial situation and goals.

When Is the Best Time to Purchase Bonds?

The best time to buy bonds is late in the month. Why? Whenever a person buys a bond, they begin to earn interest as of the first day of the month in which it was purchased. Therefore, even if you purchase on the twenty-fifth or thirtieth of the month, you earn interest as of the first business day of that month. This means that an investor can use his or her money elsewhere until late in the month, then invest in the EE and I bond, and be credited with interest as of the first day of the month.

Caution: If your client buys late in the month, the funds must be readily available to the bank. Cash, a cashier's check, or a check drawn on the bank that one is purchasing through are readily available funds. A check from a money market account, out-of-state, is not because it may require a hold period. If a bond is purchased on the last day of the month with an out-of-state check, the bond owner will likely receive an issue date as of the following month, because that is when the funds will be available to the bank for purchase.

Where and How Can Bonds Be Purchased?

U.S. Savings Bonds can be applied for in-person or through the mail by several different means:

- Most commercial banks

- Some savings & loans

- Some credit unions

- All Federal Reserve Banks (FRB)

- Many companies via the Payroll Savings Plan

- Via the internet: download the purchase application at www.savingsbonds.gov

Banks, Savings & Loans, Credit Unions, and Federal Reserve Banks

While the Series I and EE savings bond can be applied for in-person at thousands of institutions around the country, it is best to call first. Some banks in certain areas of the country no longer sell or service U.S. Savings Bonds.

Clients may also call or write to a FRB for a bond purchase application. Via mail, send a completed application, with a check, to the FRB in your region. (A listing of FRBs is given in Chapter 18.) If a personal check is sent, the bond will be mailed after the check clears.

The institutions that do sell bonds will provide a Purchase Application for Series I and EE bonds (Figure 7.2, page 90, is a copy of the EE bond purchase application). The following information will be needed:

- ✓ Name or names to appear on bond

- ✓ Social Security number of the first person named on bond

- ✓ Mailing address

- ✓ Number of bonds to be purchased

Upon receiving an application, the bank or institution will forward it to a regional FRB for processing. The bond should be mailed to the address supplied within one to two weeks.

Important to note: In the past, investors received their bond the day it was purchased. During the early 1990s, the government converted to a Regional Delivery System. This means local banks no longer have the actual bond in stock. They simply take an application and forward it to the FRB for processing. If buying a birthday or holiday gift, advise clients that it takes up to three weeks for delivery. In lieu of the bond, most banks have a certificate that they offer indicating that a bond has been purchased and is "on the way" as seen in Figure 7.1.

Figure 7.1

Gift Certificate

Payroll Savings Plan and EasySaver

Millions of Americans buy U.S. Savings Bonds through payroll deduction. If this method of purchase interests your client, have them check with the Human Resources, Personnel, or Payroll departments of their company. If the company has a program in place, they will have the necessary forms.

In the fall of 1998 the government introduced EasySaver, a new option for systematic savings. Now bond owners can sign up for automatic purchase of series EE or I bonds through automatic withdrawal from their checking or savings account. For applications bond owners should call 1-877-811-SAVE or visit the government site at www.easysaver.gov.

Who Can Buy U.S. Savings Bonds?

The information in the following section has been taken, and in some cases adapted for your convenience, from "The Book on U.S. Savings Bonds." Persons eligible to buy and hold bonds inscribed in their names include:

- Residents of the United States, its territories and possessions, and the Commonwealth of Puerto Rico

- Citizens of the United States residing abroad

- Civilian employees of the United States, or members of its Armed Services, regardless of residence or citizenship provided they have a Social Security number

- Residents of Canada or Mexico who work in the United States, but only if the bonds are purchased on a payroll deduction plan and the owner provides a Social Security account number

A person who is not previously listed may, nevertheless, be designated as co-owner or beneficiary of a bond "whether original issue or reissue" unless that person is a resident of an area where the Treasury restricts or regulates the delivery of checks drawn on U.S. funds. Contact your FRB for current information. Such persons who become entitled to bonds by right of inheritance or otherwise will not have the right to reissue, under Treasury regulations, but may hold the bonds without change of registration with the right to redeem them when their area of residence changes or current restrictions are lifted. For full details see Treasury Circular, PD Series 3-80, Section 353.6.

Series EE bonds may be bought by individuals, corporations, associations, public or private organizations, fiduciaries, and other investors in their own right. Bonds purchased by a public or private organization cannot have a co-owner or beneficiary listed on the bond. Likewise an individual bond owner cannot list an organization of any type on a savings bond as their co-owner or beneficiary.

Author's note: This means that you cannot list a charity, church, pet cemetery, or any other organization on a bond as co-owner or beneficiary.

An Intriguing Exception: Gifts to the United States

Believe it or not, some persons buy bonds with the intent that upon their death the bonds will become a gift to the United States. This may be done by designating the United States Treasury as either the co-owner or beneficiary. Purchasers should be advised that these bonds may not be reissued to change such designation, the only exceptions are Series EE or HH bonds on which the Treasury has been designated as beneficiary.

Author's note: Let's review the math on this one. Based on the fact that the outstanding debt of our nation is over $5.5 trillion (1998 figures, I always have to increase the number from previous editions of the book), and the total dollars of outstanding bonds is approximately $180 billion, if all bond owners gift their bonds to Uncle Sam, and we all die tomorrow (in which case we won't care about the debt), we will have covered less than 3.3% of the national debt.

Purchase Limitations

The maximum purchase allowed for Series EE bonds is $15,000 per person per calendar year ($30,000 face value). This means that a bond owner can buy $15,000 on December 30th and another $15,000 on January 2nd. This would use the limitations for each year in which Series EE were bought. However, if a couple purchase in the spouse's name with "or" being the other spouse, they may now buy double that amount—$30,000 (60,000 face value) per year. (They are combining their individual limitations of $15,000.) Want to invest another $15,000? An investor can buy with his son or daughter as a co-owner and use his or her $15,000 limitation.

The maximum purchase allowed for Series I bonds is $30,000 per person per calendar year.

Caution: Remember that anyone named as a co-owner on a bond can cash that bond. Clients should give careful consideration to whom they name as co-owner on any bond. For divorce-related considerations, consult Chapter 14.

Why are there limitations on the amount one can purchase? Originally, the intent was to keep the bond program directed toward the individual investor. Limitations keep large blocks of money from one entity from entering and exiting the bond program. For instance, a company cannot buy $10 million of U.S. Savings Bonds. It is strange that the limits have not been raised since 1980. It would seem logical that they be adjusted upward every five to ten years, especially since the government, from all indications, could use the extra money (or has used the extra money).

How Should Bonds Be Registered?

U.S. Savings Bonds are registered securities. This means that the name of the person or entity entitled to the bonds is printed on the face of the bond.

The three most common forms of registration are single ownership, co-ownership, and owner with beneficiary.

Single Ownership

As the name implies, only one person is listed on the bond as owner.

S.S. # 123-45-6789
John S. Anybody
123 Bond Ave.
Interest, NY 11001

Co-ownership

Two persons are listed on the bond as co-owners. Either party can cash the bond without the other party's consent. Co-ownership means equal ownership. Upon the death of one co-owner, the remaining co-owner becomes the sole owner of the bond. The bonds can be reissued to remove the deceased party's name and to add a new co-owner or beneficiary.

S.S. # 123-45-6789
John S. Anybody
123 Bond Ave.
Interest, NY 11001

OR Mary B. Anybody

Beneficiary

This form of ownership allows for one owner and one beneficiary to be listed on the bonds. The owner may cash the bond at any time (after the first six months). The beneficiary may cash the bonds only after providing a death certificate of the owner. The beneficiary is listed as the "POD" (Pay on Death). This does not mean that the bond must be cashed upon the death of the owner; however, the bond cannot be negotiated by the person named as POD until the owner is deceased. The registration appears as follows:

S.S. # 123-45-6789
John S. Anybody
123 Bond Ave.
Interest, NY 11001

POD Mary B. Anybody

The maximum number of names on a bond is two, regardless of the form of registration. You cannot have two co-owners and a beneficiary.

Purchasing for Special Occasions

Bonds now take up to three weeks to be delivered. Thus clients must plan ahead when buying for special occasions (birthdays, holidays, graduations). If they do get stuck purchasing a bond a few days before the important occasion, the bank can provide a certificate of purchase, indicating that a bond is on the way.

The purchase application will ask for the Social Security number of the first-named party on the bond. If that number is not known, the purchaser may use his or her own number. However, this means that the purchasers number will appear on the bond. This does not create any tax liability for the purchaser, since the person who redeems the bond is required to supply his or her Social Security number at the time of redemption. The person redeeming the bond is supposed to get the 1099-INT. However, the fact that the purchaser's Social Security number is on the bond may lead some bank tellers to incorrectly assign the 1099-INT to that number. The best bet is to call the recipient's family and obtain the correct Social Security number.

The purchase application also asks for a "mail to" address. If when buying a gift the purchaser lists their name and address under "mail to," then their name and address will appear on the bond. (Bonds are mailed in window envelopes.) Thus, although there will be three names on the bond, only the first-named party and the designated co-owner or beneficiary are entitled to it. The "mail to" person is not entitled. This will inevitably cause some confusion down the road but it is unavoidable under the present system.

Note: The bank should not be listed as the "mail to" address. If this happens, the bank name and address will appear on the bond.

Gift Giving

If your clients give bonds as gifts, they may pose the question to you, "Are savings bonds a good gift?" The author is asked this question at least a dozen times a month. This represents a chance to demonstrate your savings bond savvy. Support your position with facts that they can relate to such as:

> "Yes, for $25 bucks it is a nice conservative investment and will provide a neat reminder of the gift giver some day."

or

> "No, at approximately 5% it will take almost 15 years to double the money. Other options will provide more for Junior's college fund."

Bond Investment Growth with Systematic Purchase

Millions of Americans have used bonds to build or supplement their savings. Table 7.2 (page 91) illustrates what can be expected under several different scenarios. The table outlines projected savings at interest rates of 4%, 5%, 6%, and 7%. The 4% interest rate is the guaranteed minimum for eighteen years on Series EE bonds issued from March 1993 to April 1995. The 6% interest rate is the guaranteed minimum for twelve years on Series EE bonds issued from November 1986 to February 1993. Current issues of Series EE bonds do not have a guaranteed rate, and rates in the 1990s have ranged from 4 to 6%.

Bond Series That Can No Longer Be Purchased

In addition to oceanfront property in Iowa, your clients should avoid anyone who tries to sell the following series of bonds: They are no longer being sold.

Table 7.1

Bond Series No Longer For Sale

Series	Issue Period	Comment on Final Maturity
Series A to D	March 1935 - April 1941	All Series A to D bonds have stopped earning interest.
Series E	May 1941 - June 1980	Some, but not all, Series E bonds have stopped earning interest. See page 66 for details.
Series F & G	May 1941 - April 1952	All Series F & G bonds have stopped earning interest.
Series H	June 1952 - Dec. 1979	Series H bonds over 30 years old have stopped paying interest.
Series J & K	May 1952 - April 1957	All Series J & K bonds have stopped earning interest.
Savings Notes	May 1967 - October 1970	Savings Notes will stop earning interest 30 years from the date of purchase, some have already reached final maturity.

Adapted from "The Book on U.S. Savings Bonds," p.8.

If your client owns Series A to D, F, G, J, or K bonds, contact your regional FRB or the BPD for disposition instructions. Chapter 18 lists the appropriate addresses and telephone numbers.

Quick Tips on Purchasing

- There are three bonds available today: Series EE, HH, and I.
- Only Series EE and I can be bought; Series HH must be exchanged for.
- The best time to purchase bonds is late in the month.
- Savings bonds can be applied for in-person, through the mail, or online. Here are common purchase avenues: most banks, some savings & loans, some credit unions, all FRBs, a payroll savings plan and the new EasySaver program.
- To fill out the Purchase Application, investors will need: name or names to appear on the bond, Social Security number of the first person named on the bond, mailing address, and number of bonds to be purchased.

- The purchase limitation for Series EE bonds is $15,000 per person, per calendar year ($30,000 face value). The purchase limitation for Series I bonds is $30,000.
- The three most common forms of registration are single ownership, co-ownership, and owner with beneficiary.

Figure 7.2

Purchase Application for
Series EE Bonds

PD F 5263
Dept. of the Treasury
Bur. of the Public Debt
(Revised February 1991)

ORDER FOR SERIES EE U.S. SAVINGS BONDS

OMB No. 1535-0084
Expires 9-30-91

PLEASE FOLLOW THE INSTRUCTIONS ON THE BACK WHEN COMPLETING THIS PURCHASE ORDER.

1. **OWNER OR FIRST-NAMED COOWNER** (Bonds registered to)

   Name

   Soc. Sec. No.   —   —

2. **BONDS TO BE DELIVERED "CARE OF"** (Do not complete this section unless name is different from the owner or first-named coowner in section 1 above.)

   Mail to:

3. **ADDRESS WHERE BONDS ARE TO BE DELIVERED**

   (NUMBER AND STREET OR RURAL ROUTE)

   (CITY OR TOWN)   (STATE)   (ZIP CODE)

4. **COOWNER OR BENEFICIARY** Coownership will be assumed if neither or if both blocks are checked (See #4 on back).
   The following person is to be named as   coowner   beneficiary

   Name

5. **BONDS ORDERED**

Denom.	Quantity	Issue Price	Total Issue Price	FOR AGENT USE ONLY
$ 50		X $ 25.00	= $	
$ 75		X $ 37.50	= $	
$ 100		X $ 50.00	= $	
$ 200		X $ 100.00	= $	
$ 500		X $ 250.00	= $	
$ 1,000		X $ 500.00	= $	
$ 5,000		X $ 2,500.00	= $	
$ 10,000		X $ 5,000.00	= $	
TOTAL ISSUE PRICE OF PURCHASE		$		AFFIXED AGENT STAMP CERTIFIES THAT TOTAL AMOUNT OF PURCHASE IS CORRECT

6. **DATE PURCHASE ORDER AND PAYMENT PRESENTED TO AGENT**

   (MO.)   (DAY)   (YR.)

7. **SIGNATURE**

   PURCHASER'S SIGNATURE

   (   )

   PURCHASER'S NAME, IF OTHER THAN OWNER OR FIRST-NAMED COOWNER. (Please print)   DAYTIME TELEPHONE NUMBER

   STREET ADDRESS (If not shown above)   CITY   STATE   ZIP CODE

SEE INSTRUCTIONS FOR PRIVACY ACT AND PAPERWORK REDUCTION ACT NOTICE

FRB COPY

Table 7.2

Systematic Purchase Pattern

Estimated Value of Savings Bond Investment at the End of...

	Five Years		Ten Years		Twenty Years		Thirty Years	
	4%	5%	4%	5%	4%	5%	4%	5%
Save $25/month, purchase $150 of EE bonds every six months	$1,642	$1,680	$3,644	$3,831	$9,060	$10,110	$17,107	$20,398
Save $50/month, purchase $300 of EE bonds every six months	$3,284	$3,361	$7,289	$7,663	$18,120	$20,220	$34,215	$40,797
Save $100/month, Purchase $600 of EE bonds every six months	$6,569	$6,722	$14,578	$15,326	$36,241	$40,441	$68,430	$81,595
Save $200/month, Purchase $1,200 of EE bonds every six months	$13,139	$13,444	$29,156	$30,653	$72,482	$80,883	$136,861	$163,189
Save $500/month, Purchase $3,000 of EE bonds every six months	$32,849	$33,610	$72,892	$76,633	$181,205	$202,207	$342,154	$407,974

The calculations in the above table are based the following assumptions:

1. The bond purchaser will save money at an even monthly rate and will purchase bonds twice a year. A monthly purchase pattern will result in a slightly higher final value.
2. That the interest rates used to calculate future values will be consistent over the time period the calculations were made.
3. The money invested is the purchase price of the bonds, not the face value. Thus the term purchase $300 of bonds every six months means $300 purchase price, $600 face value for EE bonds.
4. The guaranteed interest rate for Series EE bonds purchased March 1, 1993 to April 30, 1995 is 4 percent for the original maturity period. There is no guaranteed rate for Series EE bonds purchased after April 30, 1995. Call 1-800-USBONDS for rate information on current purchases.

Note: This table does not guarantee a specific return on any investment you make. Market conditions and rules governing the savings bond program may change without notice. Obtain current rate information and complete details before making any investment.

Table 7.2 cont.

Systematic Purchase Pattern

Estimated Value of Savings Bond Investment at the End of...								
	Five Years		Ten Years		Twenty Years		Thirty Years	
	6%	7%	6%	7%	6%	7%	6%	7%
Save $25/month, purchase $150 of EE bonds every six months	$1,720	$1,760	$4,031	$4,242	$11,310	$12,682	$24,458	$29,478
Save $50/month, purchase $300 of EE bonds every six months	$3,439	$3,519	$8,061	$8,484	$22,620	$25,365	$48,916	$58,955
Save $100/month, Purchase $600 of EE bonds every six months	$6,878	$7,038	$16,122	$16,968	$45,241	$50,730	$97,832	$117,910
Save $200/month, Purchase $1,200 of EE bonds every six months	$13,756	$14,076	$32,244	$33,936	$90,482	$101,460	$195,664	$235,820
Save $500/month, Purchase $3,000 of EE bonds every six months	$34,392	$35,194	$80,611	$84,839	$226,203	$253,650	$489,160	$589,550

The calculations in the above table are based the following assumptions:

1. The bond purchaser will save money at an even monthly rate and will purchase bonds twice a year. A monthly purchase pattern will result in a slightly higher final value.
2. That the interest rates used to calculate future values will be consistent over the time period the calculations were made.
3. The money invested is the purchase price of the bonds, not the face value. Thus the term purchase $300 of bonds every six months means $300 purchase price, $600 face value for EE bonds.
4. The guaranteed interest rate for Series EE bonds purchased March 1, 1993 to April 30, 1995 is 4 percent for the original maturity period. There is no guaranteed rate for Series EE bonds purchased after April 30, 1995. Call 1-800-USBONDS for rate information on current purchases.

Note: This table does not guarantee a specific return on any investment you make. Market conditions and rules governing the savings bond program may change without notice. Obtain current rate information and complete details before making any investment.

Chapter 8

REDEEMING U.S. SAVINGS BONDS

- ▶ *Considerations Prior to Redemption*
- ▶ *Cashing Can Be Taxing*
- ▶ *Who Is Eligible to Cash a Particular Bond?*
- ▶ *Where Can Bonds Be Cashed?*
- ▶ *Watch Out for These Errors*
- ▶ *Quick Tips on Redemption*

Many investors have held their savings bonds for a long period of time. It does not make sense to collect bonds for twenty years and then suddenly cash them all on the same day without careful analysis. In addition to knowing how and when to cash, being aware of which bonds to redeem and the resulting tax consequences will enable you to help your client get the maximum return on his or her investment and avoid costly mistakes. The following true stories illustrate this.

Help Your Clients Avoid This

John was a blue-collar worker who purchased bonds regularly through the Payroll Savings Plan. His family knew he was buying bonds, but they never *realized how many he had until after his death. They were surprised to find 180 savings bonds. Those advising John's wife suggested that she cash the bonds. She did just that. Late in November she redeemed 180 bonds, worth a total of almost $60,000. What she was not told, and what she did not realize, was that 30 of the bonds were due to increase December 1st. Thus, by holding the bonds only a few more days, she could have pocketed an additional $300 to $375. Not only that, holding another specific group of 30 bonds until January 1st would have netted her another $300 to $375. As with most bond owners, she did not realize how important it is to time the redemption of savings bonds. To further complicate matters, Joan was not advised about the tax consequences. Over $40,000 of the $60,000 was reported as interest income when cashing the bonds. Because all the bonds were cashed in one year, it was all reported as income on that year's return. By selectively cashing some of the bonds in November and December, and doing other bonds in January, she would have spread the liability over two years.*

Help Your Client Profit Like This

Betty works for a local school district. She saved her money, much of it in savings bonds, and planned to purchase a condominium. She had only eight bonds, but each had a face value of $10,000. In June, Betty found a condominium she liked; she signed a purchase agreement and the closing was set for September. She was not sure whether to cash her bonds immediately or wait until nearer the closing date. To address her question, she chose to have her bonds analyzed. She discovered that six of the bonds, with a redemption value of $50,000, were due to increase September 1st. By waiting until September to cash the bonds, she would receive $1,500 more than if she cashed them in June. She also discovered that the remaining two bonds had increased in value June 1st, and would not increase again until December. She cashed those last two bonds immediately and put the money into an interest-bearing account. Betty was thrilled to have the extra $1,500. Before learning about her bonds, she had planned on just cashing them all during June or July.

Considerations Prior to Redemption

Selective Redemption

Implementing the practice of "selective redemption" is the only wise alternative to randomly redeeming large groups of bonds. It is based on a simple premise: *At a given point in time it may make more sense to cash one particular bond rather than another.* It is the key to helping your client maximize his or her return.

Chapters 5 and 6 ("Understanding Interest Rates" and "Timing Issues and Maturity Periods") explain that each bond carries a unique set of information. Tracking the bonds, whether you do it yourself or secure the services of a reputable reporting service, such as The Savings Bond Informer (Figure 2.1, page 18), enables you to analyze the data for each bond. It provides a means for comparing the data and determining which bonds to redeem at any given point in time. (If you have a completed bond statement, you may want to refer to it during this discussion.)

There are several factors to consider when evaluating bonds:

1. What rate of interest applies to each bond?

2. When do each of the bonds increase in value?

3. What is the accrued interest on each bond?

4. What is the value of each bond?

5. How much interest-earning life is left in each bond?

6. What is the projected future performance of each bond?

It is important to note that you and the bond owner may place a different priority on the above questions. For one bond owner, minimizing the amount of interest income that will have to be reported may be highest objective (#3). For another, keeping bonds that have the longest life left may be most important (#5). For yet another, the priority may be in keeping the bonds that are paying the highest rate of interest and redeeming the bonds paying a lower one (#1 and #6).

The Sound of Opportunity Knocking

Bonds that have stopped earning interest are currently valued at over $5.3 billion. And the national average suggests that about 3% of the bonds your clients hold fall into this category.

You should be looking for the following bonds: Any Series E bond that was issued November 1965 and before will earn interest for 40 years. So, as of December 1998, any bond issued December 1958 and before has stopped earning interest. Any bond issued December 1965 and after will earn interest for 30 years. This means that bonds issued December 1965 through December 1968 have also stopped earning interest as of the December 1998. Each month two more issue dates are added to this group. For example, in January 1999, bonds issued January 1959 and January 1969 will stop earning interest. In February 1999, bonds issued February 1959 and February 1969 will also cease earning interest.

Remember, your clients are not sent any reminder telling them that their bonds no longer earn interest, nor do they receive any tax information at final maturity. **Finding these bonds can make you the hero.**

The Best Time of the Month to Cash Bonds

Always encourage your clients to cash bonds early in the month. If a bond is due to increase in July and it is redeemed July 1, the bond owner will be credited with the July increase. If they hold that same bond until July 30, the bond owner will receive the same amount as they would have on July 1. Hence, Uncle Sam had free use of their money for twenty-nine days.

The Best Time of Year to Cash Bonds

If your client is thinking of redeeming bonds toward the end of a calendar year, you may want to consider having them wait until after January 1. That way they will have one additional year before they must report the interest. In certain cases it makes sense to redeem some bonds at the end of one year and more bonds at the beginning of the next. This will spread the tax liability over two years.

A Penalty for Cashing Savings Bonds?

Any Series EE or I bond purchased May 1997 or after is subject to a three-month interest penalty if the bond is cashed before it is five years old. There is no penalty for cashing once the bond is five years old. There is no penalty for cashing bonds purchased prior to May 1997.

Limits on How Much Can Be Cashed

Bond owners can encounter problems cashing bonds if their bank is not an authorized paying agent for the government. Banks that are authorized to cash bonds can limit "non-bank" customers to $1,000 (redemption value) per person per day. If your client encounters this problem, contact your regional FRB (Chapter 18) for instructions on sending the transaction directly to the FRB.

Cashing Can Be Taxing

Many bond owners do not realize that cashing a Series E and EE bonds and Savings Note/Freedom Share (SN) creates a taxable event. The interest income earned on a savings bond is deferred until the bond is cashed or reaches final maturity, whichever comes first. In most cases, owners of Series E and EE bonds and SNs have not reported interest earnings prior to redemption. Thus, when the bond is redeemed, the owner creates a taxable event. The one exception is when a person has chosen to report interest earned on an annual basis. (See Chapter 14, "Taxation Issues for U.S. Savings Bonds," for more information on that option.)

The bank that redeems the bond has two basic responsibilities related to the 1099-INT. First, they must provide a copy of the 1099-INT to the person who redeemed the bond. Some banks do this on the spot; others mail all 1099-INT forms at the end of the year (only interest payments totaling more than $10 need to be reported). Second, they must report the interest earned, name, and Social Security number for each transaction to the IRS. This is normally done in one file at the end of the year.

When a Series E or EE bond or SN is redeemed, the bank will require that the person redeeming the bond supply his or her Social Security number. The bank will not (or should not) automatically use the number printed on the bond.

Advise your clients of the tax consequences when cashing bonds. Recommend that the 1099-INT be kept with their tax papers for that year. If an investor throws it away or misplaces the 1099-INT, it can be replaced, although this becomes a challenge during tax season.

Conflicting Government Rules

Regarding interest responsibility, the rules outlined in IRS and Treasury Department literature and what really happens when banks report interest income are not exactly "in sync." The Treasury Department publication "Legal Aspects of U.S. Savings Bonds" (1993, page 4) states that "the principal owner" (defined as "the person whose funds were used to purchase the bonds") bears the tax liability. However, the data collection and reporting systems are not set up to support this statement. In reality, the person who redeems the bonds receives the 1099-INT. Thus, if John Q. Public bought a bond with his son as the co-owner and his son redeems the bond, the bank will ask for the son's Social Security number and will issue the 1099-INT to the son. The IRS has no idea whose funds were used to purchase the bonds; they expect the son to report the interest that the bank reported under his Social Security number. The IRS rules state that the person receiving the 1099-INT should then issue a 1099 to the principal owner and to the IRS. However, in the years that the author has worked with bonds, he has never met a single bond owner who was aware of this IRS rule. (This topic is covered in more detail in Chapter 14.)

Important: Make a note of the interest earned on your client's bonds at the time of redemption. Put this note (or the copy of the 1099-INT, if the bank supplied one) with the client's tax papers for that calendar year. Many bond owners cash bonds early in the year and forget that they have interest income to report. The bond owner may lose, misfile, or not remember having received a 1099-INT, and fail to report the interest on their annual tax return. The IRS, however, makes a habit of making sure the bond owner remembers. The bank supplies them with a copy of the same 1099-INT information that the bond owner receives. The IRS does a simple computer check to see if the amount reported matches the amount they think should have been reported. If the numbers don't match, a bond owner becomes a likely candidate for some personalized attention from the IRS.

Tax Dollars Go Here

Who gets a cut? Interest earned on bonds is subject to federal tax but is exempt from state and local tax. In some cases, if the bond qualifies for the education feature, the interest might even be tax-free. (Refer to the educational feature guidelines in Chapter 11.)

Who Is Eligible to Cash a Particular Bond?

A person cashing a bond needs to have valid identification. At least one piece of the following identification is necessary for redemptions under $1,000 in cases where the bond owner is not known by the bank:

General
- ✓ Current driver's license
- ✓ State identification card
- ✓ Employer identification card

Governmental
- ✓ Armed Forces identification card
- ✓ United States passport
- ✓ Federal employee identification card

The type of identification and specific requirements depend on the dollar amount of the transaction and how familiar the bank is with the bond owner. Have your client call the bank before they go to see if there are any additional requirements. Typically, the bank is the big loser if bonds are cashed by a person who is not entitled. For that reason, bank personnel are required to ensure that the person redeeming a bond is who they say they are.

In Chapter 7, various options for registering a bond are presented. The registration choice made when the bond was purchased determines who is eligible to redeem the bond.

If the bond is in one name only, and that person is living, he or she is the only person who can cash the bond. (Some exceptions may apply in power of attorney cases. However, a local bank will not redeem in power of attorney cases; those bonds must be forwarded to the Bureau of the Pubic Debt for a ruling.)

If the bond is in co-ownership form, either co-owner may cash it without the other's consent. The person cashing the bond will supply his or her Social Security number and will receive a 1099-INT for interest earned.

If the bond is registered in one name with another person listed as the beneficiary, then only the first-named party may cash the bond. Upon the death of the first-named party, the beneficiary may cash the bond. A death certificate for the first-named party is required for a beneficiary to cash a bond.

For rulings regarding personal representatives of an estate, call your regional FRB.

The person submitting bonds for redemption is required to sign the back of each bond. When there are numerous bonds and it would be impractical for the bond owner to sign them all, a PD F 1522 is available (Figure 8.1, page 102) to list all the bonds and the bond owner need sign only once. Read the instructions thoroughly before attempting to use this form.

Where Can Bonds Be Cashed?

All Federal Reserve Banks (FRB) can redeem savings bonds, although the Bureau of the Public Debt (BPD) may handle some cases that require legal rulings. Bonds may be redeemed at thousands of commercial banks across America and at some savings & loans and credit unions, as well.

The easiest place to start is with the client's local bank, but *call* first. Ask the bank if they redeem U.S. Savings Bonds. If they do not, try another bank.

Remember that the bank's role is to give your client the money due to him or her when a bond is presented for redemption. The bank is not required to provide advice on timing issues. It is the responsibility of the bond owner to choose the right time to submit a bond for redemption.

Many financial advisors are uncomfortable with sending clients to a bank because the bank may have their own financial advisors "pitching" products at their client. Form PD 1522 can be used for clients cashing in a lot of bonds and the signature needs to be certified only once (by a bank) instead of on each bond. The form and the bonds can then be sent directly to a Federal Reserve Bank for processing. Call your regional Federal Reserve Bank for complete instructions.

Watch Out for These Errors

The author talks with clients of The Savings Bond Informer, Inc. on a daily basis. The following is a summary of bond owners' experiences resulting in three key areas to "watch out for" when redeeming bonds.

1. **Banks do occasionally provide incorrect redemption values.** This can happen when a teller reads the wrong number on a chart or takes the wrong issue date to value the bond. How do you know your client got the right amount? Double-check their work. Chapter 18 outlines some of your options for obtaining detailed redemption information. Encourage clients to take a current bond statement with them when cashing the bonds to ensure that they are getting the correct amount.

2. **Tellers sometimes tell a bond owner that bonds are still earning interest when they are not.** This has become more prevalent with the thirty-year bonds that have stopped earning interest. Two types of mistakes have been reported. In the first, a teller assumes that all Series E bonds are good for forty years. If that were true, no bond issued in the 1960s would have stopped earning interest. Second, and more common, tellers do not properly read the tables and date ranges for thirty-year bonds. Thus they arrive at an inaccurate conclusion, not because the government table is wrong, but because their interpretation of the table is wrong. Any Series E bond purchased December 1965 and after will stop earning interest thirty years from the date of purchase.

3. **Banks can overstate the amount of the 1099-INT.** This confusion can result from the fact that interest earned on bonds is broken out between bonds issued prior to 1990 and those issued after 1989. When calculations are done manually, mistakes can be made.

A woman had $120,000 of bonds with $61,000 of accrued interest. She cashed in all her bonds and the bank issued a 1099-INT for over $84,000. Had she not had an independent verification of her holdings, she would not have known that her 1099-INT was overstated by $23,000. That would have resulted in an additional unjustified tax bill of almost $7,000.

Quick Tips on Redemption

- Before advising a client to cash bonds, provide a bond statement (analysis) and be familiar with the specific tax consequences of the transaction. To maximize a client's return, implement the principle of selective redemption.

- Look for the 3% of your clients' bonds that may have stopped earning interest.
- Encourage clients to cash a bond early in the month that interest is credited to the bond.
- There are certain cases in which you will want to advise a client to wait beyond the end of the fiscal year to cash bonds.
- Observe in whose name(s) a bond is registered before advising a client to redeem it.
- If your client would rather not deal with a local bank, have them complete form PD 1522 and send it to the FRB that services your client's state.
- Prepare your client to verify redemption values before accepting the redemption value from a bank.

Figure 8.1

Request for Payment PD F 1522

PD F 1522
Department of the Treasury
Bureau of the Public Debt
(Revised October 1992)

FOR FEDERAL RESERVE BANK USE ONLY
TRANSFER MONTH & YEAR _____ / _____
FISCAL AGENT CODE _____

SPECIAL FORM OF REQUEST FOR PAYMENT OF
UNITED STATES SAVINGS AND RETIREMENT SECURITIES
WHERE USE OF A DETACHED REQUEST IS AUTHORIZED

OMB No. 1535-0004
Expires 10-31-94

IMPORTANT: Follow instructions in filling out this form. You should be aware that the making of any false, fictitious or fraudulent claim to the United States is a crime punishable by imprisonment of not more than five years or a fine up to $250,000, or both, under 18 U.S.C. 287 and 18 U.S.C. 3571. Additionally, 31 U.S.C. 3729 provides for civil penalties for the maker of a false or fraudulent claim to the United States of an amount not less than $5,000 and not more than $10,000, plus treble the amount of the Government's damages as an additional sanction.
PRINT IN INK OR TYPE ALL INFORMATION

I am the owner or person entitled to payment of the following-described securities which bear the name(s)
of _____ and hereby request payment.

_____
(This line for use in case of partial redemption only. See paragraph 4 of Instructions.)

SERIAL NUMBER	ISSUE DATE	SERIAL NUMBER	ISSUE DATE	SERIAL NUMBER	ISSUE DATE

(If space is insufficient, use continuation sheet, sign it, and refer to it above. PD F 3500 may be used for this purpose.)

_____ OR _____
Social Security Account Number   Employer Identification Number

Sign in ink in presence
of certifying officer ▶ _____

Daytime Telephone Number _____
Address
(For delivery of check) _____
              (Number and street or rural route)   (City or town)   (State)   (ZIP Code)

I CERTIFY that the above-named person, whose identity is well-known or proved to me, personally appeared before me this _____ day of _____, 19 _____, at _____
                                                                    (City)   (State)
and signed the above request, acknowledging the same to be his/her free act and deed.

(OFFICIAL STAMP
OR SEAL)

_____
(Signature and title of certifying officer)
_____
(Address)

(SEE INSTRUCTIONS ON REVERSE)

SEE INSTRUCTIONS FOR PRIVACY ACT AND PAPERWORK REDUCTION ACT NOTICE

Chapter 9

EXCHANGING FOR HH BONDS

- ▶ *HH Bonds: What They Are and How They Work*
- ▶ *If Your Client Already Has HH Bonds*
- ▶ *Points to Consider Prior to Advising on Exchange*
- ▶ *Where and How to Exchange Bonds*
- ▶ *Tax Consequences of an Exchange*
- ▶ *Timing an Exchange*
- ▶ *Are HH Bonds Right for Your Clients?*
- ▶ *Selective Redemption: A Proven Alternative to Exchanging*
- ▶ *The New Rules Do Not Affect H/HH Bonds*
- ▶ *Additional Technical Guidelines Regarding Registration and Exchange*
- ▶ *Quick Tips on Exchange*

Investors want to know if they should they keep their E and EE bonds or exchange them for HH. On the one hand, current income, tax deferment on the bonds being surrendered, and direct deposits of interest payments may tempt them. On the other hand, the guaranteed interest rate of only 4% (as of January 1999), with no upside potential for ten years and no tax deferment of the yearly interest income, may outweigh the positives.

HH Bonds: What They Are
and How They Work

Series HH bonds are called "current income bonds." As the name suggests, these bonds produce an interest income stream that is paid to the bond owner every six months. Many Series H bonds are still earning interest (for thirty years from date of issue), although the issuing of new Series H bonds ended in December 1979. The HH bond replaced the Series H bond in January 1980.

Series HH bonds cannot be purchased for cash. They are only available through the exchange of Series E, EE, and Savings Notes/Freedom Shares (FSs/SNs). They can also be obtained through the reinvestment of Series H bonds that have reached final maturity.

HH bonds come in denominations of $500, $1,000, $5,000, and $10,000. Bond owners must have a minimum redemption value of $500 from any combination of bonds they wish to exchange. Since the HH bond pays interest every six months, the bond is always worth its face value upon redemption.

HH bonds obtained through exchange as of March 1, 1993, will pay a guaranteed interest rate of 4%. The interest is paid semi-annually via direct deposit to the bank account of the bond holder's choice. This rate is fixed for the first ten years. For the second ten-year period, the bonds will earn the guaranteed rate that is in effect the day they enter the extended period. The market-based rate does *not* apply to HH bonds. The total life of the HH bond is twenty years. See Table 9.2 (page 117) for interest rates for H and HH bonds.

All H and HH bonds that are still paying interest have an initial maturity of ten years. H bonds receive two ten-year extensions for a total life of thirty years. HH bonds receive one ten-year extension for a total life of twenty years. Many bond owners are surprised (and disappointed) that the bonds pick up the current guaranteed rate in effect each time a new ten-year extension is started. This new rate stays in effect for the full ten-year period. Retirees on fixed incomes, who exchanged for bonds in the mid-1980s at 7.5%, have been upset to find that the semi-annual interest payment they are used to has been cut almost in half (to 4%) as their HH bonds enter a new ten-year extension in the mid-1990s. because no notice is sent, they suddenly start receiving smaller payments. See Table 9.2 (page 117) for Series H and HH bond interest rates.

If Your Client Already Has HH Bonds

The following is an HH bond:

Figure 9.1

Series HH Bond

Here is what you can know by looking at the bond:

1. The bond is worth its face value. If the bond pictured above were cashed, the bond owner would receive a check or direct deposit for $500.

2. The first interest payment will occur six months after the exchange. Interest payments thereafter will always be on the anniversary of the issue date and six months later. In this example, the bond owner receives the interest payments every July 1st and January 1st. If cashed before an interest payment the owner will forfeit up to six months of interest.

3. When the investor cashes the bond, he or she will receive a 1099-INT for the amount of deferred interest printed on the face of the bond—$175 in this example. This is reported as interest income and subject to federal tax, but exempt from state and local tax. When this bond was issued, the funds likely came from Series E or EE bonds. The value of the E or EE bonds was a combination of the purchase price and the accrued interest. This accrued interest from the old bonds is "rolled" into the HH bond, and thus is part of the HH bond face value. However this interest has never been reported, so cashing an HH bond causes this amount to become taxable income. Because deferred interest was part of the redemption value ($500), the bond owner will not receive additional dollars.

4. If the bond is an HH bond, it will stop paying interest twenty years from the issue date. (See top right-hand corner.)

5. If the bond was issued May 1989 or after, the client is receiving direct deposit of the interest payments. If issued prior to that date he or she may be receiving a check or direct deposit.

6. As of the date of this publication, all HH bonds are paying either 4% or 6%. There is no market rate. Table 9.2 on page 117 will provide the rate structures as of the date on the table.

How to Know the Amount of Deferred Interest

If an investor chooses to defer the accrued interest from the bonds they exchanged, the amount deferred will be printed on the face of the HH bonds. (See the example on page 105.)

For instance, consider a bond owner who exchanges $20,000 (redemption value) of Series E bonds for Series HH bonds. Of that $20,000, the purchase price was $6,000 and the interest accrued was $14,000. The bond owner receives two $10,000 HH bonds. On the face of each HH bond is a statement similar to the following:

> Deferred interest $7,000 on Savings Bonds/Savings Notes exchanged for this bond and included in its issue price is reportable for federal income tax purposes, for the year of redemption, disposition, or final maturity of this bond, whichever is earlier.

The $7,000 mentioned on the two bonds adds up to the $14,000 of accrued and deferred interest. When the bond owner redeems the HH bonds, he will receive $20,000 and a 1099-INT for $14,000 in interest income.

Points to Consider Prior to Advising on Exchange

Bond owners must hold Series E, EE, and SNs at least six months before the bonds are eligible for exchange. At final maturity (i.e., the date the bond stops earning interest), the investor has one year to exchange for HH bonds. One year past final maturity the bonds are no longer eligible for exchange.

An investor may defer reporting interest earned on Series E, EE, and SNs until the HH bonds received in exchange are redeemed, disposed of (for example, taxable reissue), or have reached final maturity, whichever comes first. The deferred interest will be reported to the bond owner and to the IRS at the time the HH bonds reach such a taxable event. Since HH bonds have a total life of twenty years, bond owners can receive up to twenty years of additional tax deferment when they exchange to HH bonds.

The semi-annual interest payments from HH bonds must be reported as interest income. This interest is subject to federal income taxes, but exempt from state and local taxes.

Unlike Series EE bonds which have a purchase limit, clients may exchange for an unlimited dollar amount of HH bonds. (Refer to Chapter 7, "Purchasing U.S. Savings Bonds," for additional information on purchase limits.)

If your client wants to exchange a substantial dollar amount, consider having them request smaller denominations of HH bonds, such as $500 or $1,000 instead of $10,000. Why? At a later date, he or she may want to cash a few thousand dollars here or there and will be better able to select the exact number of bonds needed. An investor can, however, cash part of a $10,000 bond and have the remainder reissued; needless to say, this requires more paperwork.

Where and How to Exchange Bonds

The exchange process is a simple transferal of the value of E or EE bonds into HH bonds. This transaction can be handled at most commercial banks. If your client's bank handles the redemption of savings bonds, they should be familiar with the exchange procedure.

The redemption value of the bonds presented for exchange need to be recorded on PD F 3253 (Figure 9.2, page 116). The bank will do this, but if you want to double-check their calculations, see Chapter 18 for options. The value of the bonds presented for exchange will probably not exactly match the $500 increments of HH bonds. Investors may add money up to the next $500 increment, or they may take money back, to bring the amount down to the next $500 increment. You may want to make your client aware that this is his or her choice, not the bank's. If your client chooses to receive money, thus rounding down to the nearest $500 denomination of HH bond, some or all of the money received is interest from the old bonds. This amount will be reported as interest income for the year in which the exchange takes place and a 1099-INT will be issued.

The PD F 3253 includes an authorization for the direct deposit of interest payments to an account at the financial institution of the bond owner's choice. The direct deposit feature has been required for all HH bonds issued since October 1989.

Tax Consequences of an Exchange

Because most bond owners do not report the interest accruing on their E and EE bonds annually, they must report it when the bonds are redeemed. When exchanging for HH bonds, the investor has the options of (a) reporting all interest accrued for the bonds presented for exchange, or (b) deferring the reporting of the interest until the HH bond is cashed, reaches final maturity, or is disposed of so as to create a taxable event. By electing to defer interest reporting, a bond owner may receive up to twenty years of additional deferment (the life of an HH bond is twenty years).

The option of whether to report or defer accrued interest is the bond owner's choice, not the bank's. Your client should not be assigned an option without his or her consent.

Removing the principal co-owner (who is living) upon an exchange can result in a taxable event for that person. When you consider removing any living party upon an exchange, consult a Federal Reserve Bank to determine whether the type of re-registration requested would result in a taxable event (the issuance of a 1099-INT). Generally, removing the second named co-owner or beneficiary will not result in a taxable event (unless that person, although named second is actually the principal owner of the bonds).

Timing an Exchange

Since most E and EE bonds and SNs increase in value semi-annually, exchanging right after a semi-annual increase will maximize the amount available for exchange. Tables 6.3 and 6.4, pages 72 and 73, provide the dates of increase for E and EE bonds.

The investor will receive an interest payment every six months after the initial exchange. If the exchange is made in January, the interest payments will arrive every July and January. Thus, if your client wants payments twice a year, all exchanges should be transacted in the same month. (It is more than likely that this will not maximize the timing on the bonds being presented for exchange.) Or if a client prefers to receive an interest payment every month, the exchange requests can be spread over a consecutive six-month period. This will insure that an interest payment will be received twelve months of the year.

Are HH Bonds Right for Your Clients?

Here is where the specific vocation of the financial professional will probably impact the response. The author has yet to meet a financial professional who felt that a 4% rate (that is not tax-free and is fixed for ten years) is a "good" deal. Fee-based advisors may be more apt to consider the deferral aspects and the income stream (though the income stream at 4% is not going to "wow" anyone). Those who are commission-based or who derive their fees from bringing assets under management are anxious to show how much better than this rate they can do.

Before you write off HH bonds as unacceptable under any conditions, consider the following:

Sam Johnson has over $20,000 of bonds that will reach final maturity in 1998 (bonds from both 1958 and 1968). He has $16,000 of accrued interest in these bonds. He is in the 28% tax bracket and one year away from retirement. After retirement, he anticipates that he will be in the 15% tax bracket.

If he cashes now, his tax liability would be $4,480, leaving him $15,520 to reinvest in another option. If he exchanges for HH bonds, holding them for one or two years, he can cash out and be taxed at the lower bracket of 15%. The result would be a tax liability of $2,400. This would leave him with $17,600 to reinvest.

This represents a return of over 10% on his money (over 14% if we count the interest payment he receives) for a one-year period.

Your client may be aware that exchange at final maturity will offer up to twenty years in which to time the redemption to suit his or her specific situation.

To summarize, each bond owner's situation is unique. A case can be made for or against HH bonds, depending on the variables that impact it.

Selective Redemption:
A Proven Alternative to Exchanging

Helping a bond owner to study their options can be profitable for both of you. The information presented in this section is intended to provide you with a system that will maximize the return on a savings bond investment.

At some point, a bond owner will be either cashing or exchanging for HH bonds. Given the changes in the guaranteed interest rate implemented by the government in March 1993, it is important to understand the consequences of these actions.

Millions of Americans bought savings bonds with the intent of exchanging them for HH bonds to supplement their retirement income. This strategy was more attractive when HH bonds paid 6%. However, on March 1, 1993, HH bonds began paying only 4%. Here is what most bond owners fail to realize:

1. Many of their E and EE bonds still have a guaranteed rate of 6%. Exchanging would result in forfeiting 2% of interest on many bonds.

2. When a bond owner exchanges during the 4% rate period that was enacted March 1, 1993, that 4% rate is locked for ten years. Even if rates increase after the exchange for HH bonds they remain at 4% for the first ten years. A HH bond may be cashed after six months; however, the bond owner then has to report any interest that was deferred from the E or EE bonds at exchange—which is probably what prompted them to exchange in the first place.

What is selective redemption? Selective redemption is a process wherein the investor chooses which bonds to redeem or exchange based on interest rates and timing issues. When bonds are to be cashed or redeemed, the goal is to divest the lower-paying interest bonds and hold on to those earning higher rates. Selective redemption is *not* grabbing a handful of bonds and redeeming or exchanging with no forethought.

How does it work? Let's suppose your client was going to exchange for HH bonds. To use selective redemption instead of exchanging, they would cash bonds that would equal the dollar amount that would have been received in interest had they exchanged for HH bonds. This allows the majority of the E and EE bonds to be retained at the higher rates of interest. When selecting which E and EE bonds to cash, choose those that are earning the lowest rate of interest.

One advantage of this strategy is that it puts off the exchange decision for an indefinite period of time. Thus, *if* rates on savings bonds increase in 2000 or 2001, the bond owner could then exchange for HH bonds at the new higher rate, which would be in effect for the next ten years.

Consider this example. A bond owner has Series E bonds with a redemption value of $10,000. If he exchanges the E bonds for HH bonds, he will receive one $10,000 HH bond that is paying 4%. The annual interest earned on that bond is $400. The entire $400 will be reported as interest income for tax purposes.

Instead of exchanging his bonds, this bond owner uses the selective redemption system. First, he determines the exact interest rate that applies to each of the bond's. He learns that some of his bonds are earning 4% and most of them 6%. On average he is earning about 5.8% on his Series E bonds. After identifying the bonds earning 4%, he decides to cash a few of them and receives approximately $400.

Table 9.1

Comparison of Exchange and
Selective Redemption

AFTER ONE YEAR...	EXCHANGING FOR HH BONDS	SELECTIVE REDEMPTION
Value of remaining bonds:	$10,000	Approximately $10,180
Proceeds:	$400 from interest payments	$400 from redemption
Tax consequence:	All $400 is interest income	$400 minus original purchase price of E bonds is interest income
Future options:	Locked in at 4% for ten years, have to cash HH bonds if bond owner wants to exercise other options.	Can continue selective redemption for an indefinite period, or can exchange to HH bonds at any time if the HH bond rate is increased to more attractive level. Keeps options open.

In this example, selective redemption resulted in an even flow of dollars (redemption proceeds) to the bond owner and an increase in the bond holdings by $180. The actual numbers will vary in each case. The primary numbers that may make this option attractive are the interest rates on the E and EE bonds. If the guaranteed rates are 6%, then selective redemption makes a lot of sense.

To effectively use this strategy, you need to know the exact interest rates, values, and timing issues for each bond and how long those rates will be in effect. Chapter 18 outlines the options for obtaining this information for your client's bonds.

If a bond has reached final maturity, the only options are to redeem or exchange (exchange is possible only if the bond is less than one year past final maturity).

The New Rules Do Not Affect H/HH Bonds

Both sets of new rules for EE bonds—implemented May 1, 1995, and again on May 1, 1997, have no impact on new or old issues of H or HH bonds. H/HH bonds have never been affected by the market-based rates and this is still the case. The new I bond rules do not affect the H/HH bonds. The I bond is not eligible for exchange to HH bonds.

Under the current rules that apply to H/HH bonds, any future announcements of a change in the guaranteed interest rates would affect H/HH bonds as they entered extended maturity periods. For more information on extended maturity periods, see Chapter 6.

Additional Technical Guidelines Regarding Registration and Exchange

The remainder of this chapter is fairly technical; some of this information has been adapted from The Department of Treasury, The Bureau of the Public Debt's (BPD) publication, "The Book on U.S. Savings Bonds."

There are some situations where bond owners have reported the interest on their bonds and SNs annually. These bonds and SNs may also be exchanged for Series HH bonds.

When further deferment of tax liability is elected in the exchange, the rules on the registration of the bonds are as follows:

1. If the accrual bonds and SNs are registered in single ownership or beneficiary form, the person named as owner must also be named as owner or first-named co-owner on the HH bonds. A beneficiary may be added, changed, or removed or a co-owner may be added to the registration.

2. If the accrual-type bonds and SNs are registered in co-ownership form, the "principal co-owner" (the one whose funds were used to purchase the bonds and SNs) must be named as owner or first-named co-owner on the HH bonds. The other co-owner could be changed or removed or a beneficiary added. If both co-owners shared equally in the purchase or received them jointly as gifts of a legacy, the registration on the Series HH bond must name both persons as co-owners.

3. If the owner or "principal co-owner" of the older bonds and SNs is deceased, and there is a surviving beneficiary or co-owner, the latter must be named as owner or first-named co-owner on the HH bonds. The person submitting the bonds and SNs for exchange must submit evidence

establishing entitlement (for example, the beneficiary must furnish proof of death of the registered owner). Another co-owner or beneficiary could be named.

Advice on how to resolve difficult situations can be obtained from the BPD. (See Chapter 18 for address and phone number.)

Who May Request Exchange and Changes in Registration

The Owner. The term "owner" means: (1) the registered owner of a security registered in single ownership or beneficiary form, whether or not a natural person, or (2) a beneficiary or co-owner named on a security with a deceased owner or co-owner. The beneficiary would be required to furnish proof of the owner's death. An owner may request the exchange and have the HH bonds issued in his or her name in any authorized form of registration permitted under the Department of the Treasury Circular, Public Debt Series 3-80, provided he or she is owner or first-named co-owner.

The Co-owner. A "principal co-owner" is one who (1) purchased the securities with his or her own funds, or (2) received them as a gift, legacy, or inheritance, or as a result of judicial proceedings, and had them reissued in co-ownership form, provided that he or she received no contribution in any manner from the other co-owner for being so designated. (Those processing the exchange subscription form PD F 3253 are not required to go beyond a person's certification on such form that he or she is the principal co-owner of the securities presented.)

The principal co-owner of the securities presented for exchange must be named as owner or first-named co-owner on the Series HH bonds and his or her Social Security number must be provided.

Co-owners Who May Request An Exchange

Either co-owner may request an exchange, that is, if there is no change in registration and the HH bond is to be registered in exactly the same way as the securities surrendered.

If a tax-deferred exchange is requested, the Social Security account number of the "principal co-owner" (whose name must be shown first in the inscription) must be used for bonds to be inscribed in the names of two persons as co-owners.

If the principal co-owner is not the person requesting the exchange, the principal co-owner must complete Form W-9 to certify the correctness of his or her Social Security account number and that he or she is not subject to backup withholding. In such cases, the co-owner requesting the exchange must also strike the statement on PD F 3253 above his or her signature that he or she is the principal co-owner.

Only the principal co-owner may request an exchange if the HH bonds are to be registered differently from the securities surrendered. Such HH bond registration may be in any form permitted by Department of the Treasury Circular, Public Debt Series 3-80, but must include the principal co-owner as the owner or first-named co-owner.

Legal Representative (Named in Registration on the Bond)

A legal representative means the court-appointed (or otherwise qualified) person, regardless of title, who is legally authorized to act for the estate of a minor, incompetent, aged person, absentee, et al. The legal representative would be required to show full title and provide appropriate identification. Legal representatives of an estate may not conduct exchanges, but should request distribution on PD F 1455 so that persons entitled to the estate may do so.

More Than One Form of Inscription Requested

Subject to the limitations stated above, a subscriber may request that the HH bonds be issued in several inscriptions. A note to that effect should be made on the face of the form with the additional inscriptions recorded, together with the appropriate amounts for each, on the back of the blue (A) copy of Form PD F 3253. The person authorized to request the exchange must execute the requests for payment on the bonds.

HH bonds may be useful under specific circumstances. "To exchange, or not to exchange?" Only you and your client can answer that!

Quick Tips on Exchange

- HH bonds are the only savings bonds available that pay interest (currently 4% annually) to the bond owner at six-month intervals.
- Series H bonds that are less than thirty years old are still paying interest.
- Series E, EE, and SNs must be held for six months before they can be exchanged.
- Bonds that have reached final maturity are eligible for exchange only during the first twelve months following final maturity.
- Request form PD F 3253 for the client who wishes to exchange.

- In some cases the net yield on existing bonds may be higher than the client anticipated and should, therefore, be checked out prior to an exchange.
- Selective redemption is a method that can be used as an alternative to exchanging to HH.
- Investors have two options for handling the interest upon exchange: they can (a) report the interest at the time of exchange or (b) defer the interest until they cash the HH bond or until the HH bond reaches final maturity.
- Exchanging right after a semi-annual increase will maximize the amount available for exchange.
- Any future change in the fixed interest rate will only affect outstanding H and HH bonds as they enter extended maturity periods.

Figure 9.2

Exchange Application (PD F 3253)

PD F 3253
Department of the Treasury
Bureau of the Public Debt
(Revised March 1990)

EXCHANGE APPLICATION FOR U.S. SAVINGS BONDS OF SERIES HH
Please follow the attached instructions and use worksheet when completing the form

OMB No. 1535-0005
Expires 9/30/91

1. For Federal income tax purposes, I _____ (a) wish to defer reporting _____ (b) will report this year or have reported the interest earned on my bonds/notes surrendered in this exchange transaction.

2. $.	3. $.	4. $.	5. $.	6. $.
Redemption Value	Interest Earned	HH Bonds To Be Issued	Payment Returned	Interest Deferred

7. Number Of Each Denomination		$500		$1,000		$5,000		$10,000
FRB USE ONLY Increment On Each Bond								
Bond Serial Numbers								

8. REGISTRATION INFORMATION

OWNER OR FIRST-NAMED COOWNER (Bonds registered to)

TAXPAYER
IDENTIFICATION NO.: _____ — _____ — _____ -- OR -- _____ — _____

Social Security Number   Employer Identification Number

NAME:

NUMBER AND STREET
OR RURAL ROUTE:

CITY / TOWN: STATE: ZIP CODE:

COOWNER OR BENEFICIARY (OPTIONAL). Coownership will be assumed if neither block is checked. The following person is to be named as _____ coowner _____ beneficiary. See reverse for additional registrations.

NAME:

Delivery Instructions for HH
bonds (if different than above): _____

9. DIRECT DEPOSIT AUTHORIZATION (Read instructions before completing this section).

NAME(S) ON
DEPOSITOR ACCT.: _____

ROUTING/
TRANSIT NO.:

DEPOSITOR
ACCT. NO.:

TYPE OF ACCOUNT: CHECKING   SAVINGS

I request that semiannual interest payments on Series HH/H bonds purchased prior to October 1989 and bearing the above taxpayer identification number also be deposited directly to this account. **If neither block is checked, yes will be assumed.**   YES   NO

10. Under penalty of perjury, I certify that I am the owner or principal coowner of any savings bonds and notes submitted herewith; that the number shown on the form is my correct taxpayer identification number; and that I am not subject to backup withholding either (i) because I have not been notified that I am subject to backup withholding (as a result of a failure to report all interest and dividends) or (ii) because I have been notified by the Internal Revenue Service that I am no longer subject to backup withholding, unless I check this block: _____ I am subject to backup withholding.

Daytime
Telephone No.: _____ Serial Number of one savings bond/note surrendered in this exchange: _____

Applicant's Signature: _____   Date _____

11. FINANCIAL INSTITUTION AUTHORIZATION AND CERTIFICATION

NAME, ADDRESS, AND TELEPHONE NO.:

As representative of the financial institution named in this Item, I certify that the account name(s) and number shown in Item 9 are correct and that the financial institution agrees to receive and deposit the semiannual interest payments on the Series HH bonds issued pursuant to this form in accordance with applicable regulations.

PAYMENT METHOD:
_____ Charge Reserve Account *   _____ Check

* ABA NUMBER: _____

Payment Stamp

(Authorized Signature)   (Date)

FRB USE ONLY   CASE NO.: _____   A. Federal Reserve Bank Copy

Table 9.2

Interest Rates For Series HH and H Bonds

(Valid for September 1998 only)

Issue Date	Original Maturity Period	Guaranteed Through Current Maturity Period	Date Next Extension Begins	Life of Bond
SERIES HH				
March 1993 to Present	10 years	4.0%	March 2003 to ...	20 years
October 1988 to February 1993	10 years	6.0%	October 1998 to February 2003	20 years
March 1983 to September 1988	10 years	4.0%	Currently in final extension	20 years
January 1980 to February 1983	10 years	6.0%	Currently in final extension	20 years
SERIES H				
October 1978 to December 1979	10 years	6.0%	October 1998 to December 1999	30 years
March 1973 to September 1978	10 years	4.0%	Currently in final extension	30 years
October 1968 to February 1973	10 years	6.0%	Currently in final extension	30 years
June 1952 to September 1968		0.0%	Bonds have reached final maturity	30 years

Adapted from Department of Treasury, Bureau of the Public Debt, U.S. Savings Bond Marketing Office.

Chapter 10

RECOVERING LOST BONDS

▶ *Replacement Is Possible*
▶ *Filing a Lost Bond Claim Form*
▶ *Non-Receipt Claims: Getting What They Paid For*
▶ *Time Limitations on Claims or Reading the Fine Print*
▶ *Bonds Found after a Replacement Has Been Issued*
▶ *Quick Tips for Recovering Lost Bonds*

Through a series of seminars that the author has conducted for the American Association of Retired Persons (AARP), a common concern was mentioned repeatedly. It goes something like this: "When I was in the service I remember getting those bonds, but I don't know what happened to them. I assume they are gone forever and I'm out of luck." If a client has bonds or even thinks that he or she has had bonds that have vanished or been destroyed, this section may help more than any lottery—but watch out, there is some "fine print."

Replacement Is Possible

Any validly issued Bond that is lost, stolen, destroyed, mutilated, or not received will be replaced either by a substitute Bond bearing the same issue date or by a check for the current redemption value, provided sufficient information and evidence in support of a claim is supplied.

—"The Book on U.S. Savings Bonds"

U.S. Savings Bonds are not like cash. If you lose money, you stand very little chance of regaining it. Savings bonds, however, are a registered security. The government maintains records on all bonds that have been issued and will research those records for legitimate requests *free of charge*. There are two ways that the government classifies missing bonds:

1. **Bonds received and subsequently lost:** The bond owner received the bond, but at some point in time the bond was lost, stolen, or destroyed.

2. **Bonds purchased but never received:** A bond was purchased, but the purchaser never received it.

Filing a Lost Bond Claim Form

If your client wishes to locate his or her lost bonds the first step is to get a copy of PD F 1048 ("Application for Relief on Account of Loss, Theft or Destruction of United States Savings and Retirement Securities"; Figure 10.1, page 125). This form is available from four sources: the Federal Reserve Bank that services your area; the Bureau of the Public Debt, whose phone number is 1-304-480-6112; the government's web site at www.publicdebt.treas.gov; and commercial banks. If you attempt to obtain the form from your bank, call first to make sure they have it in stock.

Note: Only requests from persons who are entitled to research the bonds will be honored. While you can secure the proper form and assist a client in its completion, the bond owner's signature or the signature of his or her legal representative is required.

The cover page of PD F 1048 has specific instructions for its completion and return to the BPD. The time it takes to research the bonds will be reduced if the serial numbers of the bonds and the Social Security numbers of the people named on the bonds have been provided. **Very important:** In some cases the bonds may not be located if this information has not been provided. Allow up to a month or more for a response from the BPD.

> If a robbery, burglary, or theft is involved, a copy of the police report should be furnished if the Bonds total $1000 (face amount)

or more. Furnishing serial numbers will help speed replacement of the Bonds.

—"The Book on U.S. Savings Bonds"

A Nice Surprise for Those Who Have Lost Bonds

The person who loses bonds and then has them replaced is in for a nice surprise. The replacement bonds will carry the same issue date as the lost bonds. This means that if the bonds have not yet reached final maturity, they continued to earn interest the entire time they were lost.

Non-Receipt Claims: Getting What They Paid For

If a Bond is not received by its purchaser or a person designated by the purchaser to receive it, the buyer should contact the organization or institution which accepted the purchase application....

—"The Book on U.S. Savings Bonds"

Now that the FRB Regional Processing Sites are issuing the majority of bonds, researching bonds that were purchased but never received has been streamlined.

In a case where the Bond was acquired through a Payroll Savings Plan and issued by a Federal Reserve Bank, the purchaser's employer should be informed. The Federal Reserve Bank should be notified immediately by the organization or institution through which the Bond was purchased. The Federal Reserve Bank will complete all of Part I of the claim form PD F 3062 ("Claims for Relief on Account of Loss, Theft, or Destruction of United States Savings Bonds After Valid Issue But Prior to Receipt by Owner, Co-owner or Beneficiary"). Federal Reserve Banks are expected to keep issue information for six months after Bonds are issued and provide it on a claim form for the purchaser. The remainder of the form should then be completed and signed by all persons named on the missing Bond. Both parents should sign on behalf of a minor registrant who is too young to sign, and a court-appointed representative should sign on behalf of the estate of a deceased or incapacitated person named on the missing Bond.

If one or both parents cannot sign on behalf of a minor, or if there is no representative appointed for an estate, contact your

Federal Reserve Bank. Once completed and signed, the claim form should be sent to the servicing Federal Reserve Office which issued the Bond. If a Bond was not received and more than six months have passed since that Bond was issued, the servicing Federal Reserve Bank should be contacted for instructions.

—"Adapted from "The Book on U.S. Savings Bonds"

Time Limitations on Claims or Reading the Fine Print

If the records show that the Bonds have been redeemed, the claim usually will be denied unless someone other than the owner or co-owner has cashed the Bonds. In such cases, an investigation of the payment may be appropriate. However, **a Bond for which no claim has been filed within ten years of the recorded date of redemption is presumed to have been properly paid.** Film records of paid Bonds are maintained for ten years following the recorded redemption date. In addition, **no claim filed six years or more after the final maturity of a Bond will be considered unless the claimant can supply its serial number.**

—"The Book on U.S. Savings Bonds"

This last line is critical. Series E bonds of the 1940s and 1950s reach final maturity forty years from the date of purchase. If you want to file a claim on a Series E bond that is over forty-six years old, you must have the serial number. In addition, we now have Series E bonds that have been issued December 1965 and after that are thirty-year bonds. Bonds issued in 1966 and 1967 have already stopped earning interest, so the "six-year" clock is ticking. Once six years beyond the final maturity date, the government will only do research if a serial number is supplied.

Author's note: There seems to be a growing trend within the bond program to restrict legitimate bond owners from claiming their bonds, based on rules made to ease internal operations. Sure, researching old bonds is a time-consuming effort. But since the government saves over $250 million a year, perhaps some of the savings could be used to locate bond owners. A lot of time and effort (money) has been devoted into developing the web site and offering the sale of bonds on-line. Why not devote the same amount of resources to helping Americans recover what is rightfully theirs, instead of passing more rules and guidelines to restrict access to funds? As previously stated, the government is holding over $5.3 billion of Americans money and using this money interest-free. If any company tried the same with a financial product, they would be subject to considerable government regulation and scrutiny.

Swiss banks are being rightfully chastised and held accountable for returning money that they acquired from victims of World War II. What about returning the money to the Americans who helped finance the war?

Most bond owners from the 1940s and 1950s did not record the serial numbers of each bond they owned. Therefore they have no recourse on lost bonds that are six years beyond final maturity. Is that just?

Another growing trend: Recently upon inquiring about a lost bond claim form, the author was told that the BPD only searches by Social Security numbers not by name (for bonds purchased after 1973). This presents a problem for investors who received bonds as gifts and subsequently lost their bonds. Their own Social Security number may not appear on the bonds, and they may not remember who gave the gift. If a bond search is limited to Social Security numbers and/or serial numbers, the BPD may not locate legitimate claims where the bond owner can supply neither.

Bonds Found after a Replacement Has Been Issued

If a lost Bond is found after a substitute or a check has been issued, the owner must return the original Bond immediately to the Savings Bond Operations Office, with a full explanation.

—"The Book on U.S. Savings Bonds"

Important note: When you replace a bond, the original bond becomes the property of the United States. If the original is recovered, it must be surrendered for cancellation. Sometimes heirs get excited when they discover bonds hidden in a relative's house, only to learn that the bonds had been replaced years ago and the replacements subsequently cashed.

However, the proof offered by the BPD that older bonds have either been replaced and/or cashed is not always convincing. Several stories have been sent to the author where bond owners have been left without bonds and without recourse when instead of offering documentation for proof, the bond owner was required to "take the governments word for it."

Although most who file lost bond claims will find their situation resolved satisfactorily, the author has encountered several who have not. Some of their stories are told so you can advise your clients about the importance of accurate record keeping and the need to do a periodic inventory of bond holdings. See Chapter 4, page 35 for a list of items your client should record for each bond owned and page 36 for a record keeping form on which to record it. Advise them to keep an inventory of their bonds in one place and the actual bonds in another, like a safe deposit box.

When in doubt, encourage your client to fill out the form and have the research done. He or she may be unaware of bonds that were purchased in their name by another person. The worst case scenario is that the bonds to which your client thought he or she was entitled are not found. While it takes a little time to file a claim, it costs nothing and could pay off big.

Quick Tips for Recovering Lost Bonds

- Lost bonds can be researched by the government free-of-charge.
- To have bonds replaced, a lost bond claim form (PD F 1048) must be filed.
- A PD F 1048 may be obtained from a bank, the FRB that services your area, the BPD (1-304-480-6112) or downloaded from the government's web site at www.publicdebt.treas.gov.
- Once six years beyond the final maturity date, the government will only research bonds if a serial number is supplied.
- It is important that an owner record key data on each bond including the Social Security number that is listed.
- Chapter 4, page 36, has a record keeping sheet that you can give to each client who owns bonds.
- For bonds cashed over ten years ago, the BPD will provide no evidence of the signature used to cash the bond.

Figure 10.1 **Lost Bond Claim Form (PD F 1048)**

PD F 1048
Department of the Treasury
Bureau of the Public Debt
(Revised May 1991)

OMB No. 1535-0013

APPLICATION FOR RELIEF ON ACCOUNT OF LOSS, THEFT OR DESTRUCTION OF UNITED STATES SAVINGS AND RETIREMENT SECURITIES

IMPORTANT: Follow instructions in filling out this form. You should be aware that the making of any false, fictitious or fraudulent claim to the United States is a crime punishable by imprisonment of not more than five years or a fine up to $250,000, or both, under 18 U.S.C. 287 and 18 U.S.C. 3571. Additionally, 31 U.S.C. 3729 provides for civil penalties for the maker of a false or fraudulent claim to the United States of an amount not less than $5,000 and not more than $10,000, plus treble the amount of the Government's damages as an additional sanction.
PRINT IN INK OR TYPE ALL INFORMATION

INSTRUCTIONS

("Bonds" in these instructions refers to savings bonds, savings notes, retirement plan bonds and individual retirement bonds.)

1. This form should be filled out and signed in ink.

2. (a) If the bonds are registered in the name of only one person as owner, whether or not another person has been named as beneficiary, the owner should execute Part I. If the bonds are registered in the names of two persons as coowners, Part I must be signed by both coowners and sworn to or affirmed by the one having knowledge of the facts concerning the loss, theft or destruction, except as indicated in (b). If it is not convenient for both coowners to join in one application, each should submit a separate application. If the bonds are registered in beneficiary form, the beneficiary will be required to execute PD F 1048-1, unless the beneficiary signs Part II of this application. (If any person named on the bonds is deceased, a certified copy of the death certificate must be submitted.) If the registered owner is deceased, the beneficiary should complete and sign Part I.

   (b) MINOR OWNERS, COOWNERS, OR BENEFICIARY NOT UNDER LEGAL GUARDIANSHIP. A minor owner, coowner, or beneficiary not under legal guardianship should execute this application if, in the opinion of the officer before whom the minor appears for that purpose, the minor is of sufficient competency and understanding to comprehend the nature of the transaction. Otherwise it should be executed on the minor's behalf by both parents if living, *and*, in the event the minor does not reside with either parent, also by the person who furnishes the minor's chief support. The minor's social security account number should be furnished. If any parent is unable to sign on behalf of any such minor for any reason, a statement should be provided explaining the reason why this parent is unable to sign, whether or not this parent would have had access to the bonds and whether it is believed that this parent may now have possession of the bonds.

   (c) OWNER DECEASED OR UNDER LEGAL DISABILITY. If there is a legal representative in the case of (1) a deceased owner not survived by a coowner or beneficiary, (2) a minor owner or coowner, or (3) an incapacitated owner or coowner, Part I should be executed by the representative. The representative should submit a court certificate or certified copy of letters, under seal of the court, showing that the appointment is still in force, unless his/her name and official capacity appear on the bonds, in which case no evidence of the appointment will ordinarily be required. If there is no legal representative in the case of a deceased owner or incompetent owner, the Department of the Treasury should be fully informed as to the facts so that further instructions may be given.

3. *If any person other than the applicant had custody or possession of the bonds at the time of loss, theft or destruction or has firsthand knowledge of the circumstances under which the bonds were lost, stolen or destroyed, the applicant should have such person furnish a statement on Part II of this form or a separate supporting affidavit. If the space provided in Part II is not sufficient in any particular case, the statement should be continued on a separate sheet which should be attached hereto.*

4. Part I (and Part II when required by Instruction 3.) must be signed before an authorized certifying officer or before a notary public or other officer authorized by law to administer oaths for general purposes. Authorized certifying officers are available at banking institutions, including credit unions, in the United States, and as further provided in the current revisions of Department of the Treasury Circular No. 530 and Public Debt Series, Nos. 1-63, 1-75 and 3-80. A certifying officer must impress or imprint the seal or stamp which he/she is required to use in certifying requests for payment. A notary public or similar officer must impress his/her official seal and show the expiration date of his/her commission.

5. If any investigation of the loss or theft was made by the police or other local law enforcement agency or by any insurance, transportation or similar business organization, please attach to this form a copy of the report of such agency.

6. Ordinarily a substitute bond or check will be issued as soon as practicable after the Bureau of the Public Debt receives a report of the loss, theft or destruction. However, if its records disclose that the bonds have been cashed and it becomes necessary to refer the case to the United States Secret Service for investigation, substitute bonds or a check will not be issued until the investigation is completed.

7. The application and correspondence relating thereto should be sent to the Bureau of the Public Debt, Parkersburg, West Virginia 26106-1328.

8. The applicant should make and retain a copy of this form, or some other statement, with other important papers. This record should serve as a reminder to the applicant and to others who may have occasion to take care of the applicant's affairs that when relief is granted on account of lost, stolen or destroyed bonds, the original bonds become the property of the United States and must be surrendered to the Department for cancellation if they are recovered.

Figure 10.1 **Lost Bond Claim Form (PD F 1048)** continued

PART I

The undersigned hereby severally affirm and say that the following-described bonds have been lost, stolen or destroyed and that the information given herein is true to the best of their knowledge and belief: (If application is made on account of destroyed bonds, any charred, scorched or undestroyed pieces should be submitted herewith.)

ISSUE DATE	DENOMINATION (FACE AMOUNT)	SERIAL NUMBER	INSCRIPTION (Please type or print names, including middle names or initials, social security account number, if any, and addresses as inscribed on the bonds.)

(If space is insufficient, use a continuation sheet, sign it, and refer to it above. PD F 3500 may be used for this purpose.)

1. Are you the registered owner of the bonds? _____ If so, go to number 6., unless a minor is named on the bond with you. If a minor is named on the bond, go to number 5.

2. If you are not the registered owner, in what capacity are you acting? _____
    (See Instruction 2.)

3. If you are acting as guardian or legal representative, have you been court appointed? _____
    [See Instruction 2. (c)]

4. What is your relationship to the registered owner? _____

5. If you are acting on behalf of a minor for whose estate there is no court-appointed guardian or other representative and the minor is not of sufficient competency and understanding to complete the questions in this application, answer the following questions: [See Instruction 2. (b)]

    (a) What is the minor's age _____ , Social Security Number _____ and your relationship to the minor? _____

    (b) Does the minor live with you? _____ If not, give the name and address of the person with whom he/she lives _____ .

    (c) If you are not the father or mother of the minor, who furnishes his/her chief support? _____
    _____

6. (a) Were the bonds (1) lost? _____ (2) stolen? _____ (date of theft) _____ or (3) destroyed? _____
        (See Instruction 5.)

    (b) On what date was this discovered? _____

    (c) Who had them last, and for what purpose? (See Instruction 3.) _____

    _____

    _____

126

Figure 10.1 **Lost Bond Claim Form (PD F 1048)** continued

(d) Give the result of inquiry made of other persons as to their knowledge of the loss, theft or destruction of the bonds. (E.g., who, besides you, had access to the bonds, where were they last placed, and on what date were they last seen?) _____

_____

_____

(e) List any identification documents (i.e., driver's license) lost or stolen with the bonds. _____

_____

7. (a) Has the owner, or anyone on the owner's behalf, received reimbursement from any source on account of the loss, theft or destruction of the bonds? _____

(b) If any reimbursement has been received, explain fully. _____

_____

_____

8. Do you wish: (a) bonds _____ or (b) a check _____ ? If you wish a check and the bonds are in the names of living coowners, state the name of the coowner to whom the check is to be drawn. Otherwise, the check will be drawn to both coowners and the entire interest reported under the first-named coowner's social security number.

_____

(Series EE and HH savings bonds are not eligible for payment until six months from their issue dates.)

9. Mail bonds or check to: Name _____

Address _____
   (Number and street or rural route)   (City or town)   (State)   (ZIP Code)

We, the undersigned, hereby severally petition the Secretary of the Treasury for relief as authorized by law, and if such relief is granted, hereby acknowledge that the original bonds shall thereupon become the property of the United States. Upon the granting of relief, we assign all our right, title and interest in the original bonds to the United States and hereby bind ourselves, our heirs, executors, administrators, successors, and assigns, jointly and severally: (1) to surrender the original bonds to the Department of the Treasury should they be recovered; (2) to hold the United States harmless on account of any claim by any other parties having, or claiming to have, interests in these bonds; and, (3) upon demand by the Department of the Treasury, to indemnify unconditionally the United States and to repay to the Department of the Treasury all sums of money which the Department may pay on account of the redemption of these original bonds, including any interest, administrative costs and penalties and any other liability or losses incurred as a result of such redemption. The undersigned hereby consent to the release of any information contained herein, or regarding the bonds described herein, to any party having an ownership or entitlement interest in these bonds.

Signature _____   Signature _____
           (Name)   (Name)

Home
Address _____   Home
Address _____
       (Number and street or rural route)   (Number and street or rural route)

(City or town)   (State)   (ZIP Code)   (City or town)   (State)   (ZIP Code)

☐☐☐ – ☐☐ – ☐☐☐☐   ☐☐☐ – ☐☐ – ☐☐☐☐

      Social Security Account Number   Social Security Account Number

☐☐☐ – ☐☐☐ – ☐☐☐☐   ☐☐☐ – ☐☐☐ – ☐☐☐☐

      Daytime Telephone Number   Daytime Telephone Number

THE CERTIFICATION AT THE TOP OF THE NEXT PAGE MUST BE COMPLETED. SEE INSTRUCTIONS 2. (a) AND 4. ON PAGE 1.

127

Chapter 11

THE EDUCATIONAL FEATURE OF SERIES EE AND I BONDS

▶ *Common Misconceptions*
▶ *What the Advertising Didn't Tell Them*
▶ *Conditions for Qualifying for the Tax-Free Status*
▶ *Record Keeping for the Educational Feature*
▶ *Will the Current Interest Rates Be Enough?*
▶ *Pros and Cons of the Educational Feature*
▶ *An Alternative for Reducing the Tax Burden*
▶ *Two Ways Bond Owners Lose Out On the Tax-Free Feature*
▶ *Quick Tips on the Educational Feature*

What you have heard is true: The largest single expenditure you will ever make, other than buying a home, will most likely be your child's college tuition. By the first decade of the twenty-first century, if recent inflation rates hold, four years at an in-state public institution will cost at least $86,000, and four years at a private college will total about $163,000.

—Janet Bamford, "The Class of 2013," *Sesame Street Parents* (September 1994), pp. 52-55

With educational costs skyrocketing, many parents are paying increased attention to investment options to pay their children's future tuition. This is certainly true in the author's state, whose public universities have announced average tuition hikes of 5% to 10% in recent years. The educational feature of the Series EE bond received a lot of media attention in the past. A closer examination will enable you to assess whether it is right for your clients.

Common Misconceptions

"*Tax-Free for Education.*" In the early 1990s, you probably heard the radio advertisements pitch the sale of EE bonds for the purpose of saving for a college education. Here are the most common misunderstandings.

Misconception #1: *All bonds are now tax-free if used for education.*

No. There is an abundance of misinformation on this point. Only Series EE bonds purchased after December 31, 1989, are eligible, and then only if *seven* other conditions have been met. A complete list of the conditions is presented later in this chapter. The new Series I bond may be used tax-free for education provided the same conditions that apply to the EE bonds are met.

Misconception #2: *I must buy the bonds in my child's name so I can use them tax-free for education*.

No. If a bond is purchased in a child's name, that bond is eliminated from being eligible for the tax-free educational feature. But buying bonds in the child's name is not necessarily a bad idea, as you will see later in this chapter. If you have a client that has already registered their bonds in the child's name because someone gave inaccurate information, the bonds can be retitled. Call your regional Federal Reserve Bank (see Chapter 18, "Where to Get Help"), explain the situation, and ask for the appropriate reissue form. The transaction may be forwarded to the Bureau of the Public Debt (BPD) for approval and processing. The request should be honored in light of the many people who were given wrong information about how the bonds should be registered.

Misconception #3: *I'm buying bonds in the name of my grandchildren so they can use the tax-free educational feature*.

No. Grandparents have to purchase the bonds in the name of the *parents* of their grandchildren to qualify the bonds for the tax-free educational feature. This could be risky business in some families: The parents may not honor the wishes of the grandparents concerning the intent of the bonds. Since they are named on the bonds, the parents are free to negotiate the bonds at their own discretion. However, if properly used by all involved, this can be a way for grandparents to contribute to their grandchildren's education.

Misconception #4: *At the time of purchase, I have to declare that the bonds will be used for education.*

No. A bond owner never has to declare intent with any bond purchase. They can buy the bonds with the intent of using them for education and then change their mind. Cashing them for another purpose means they forfeit the opportunity for the bonds to be "tax-free for education," but there are no additional penalties or hidden fees (unless purchased after April 1997 and cashed within the first five years).

What the Advertising Didn't Tell Them

Many who bought bonds because "they are now tax-free for education" were unhappy to learn that they did not know "the rest of the story." And they are not alone.

What is the "rest of the story?" Your client needs to know the conditions that must be met to qualify for the tax-free status.

Conditions for Qualifying for the Tax-Free Status

There are eight conditions that must be met in order to qualify for the tax-free feature of EE and I bonds (yes, I bonds are also eligible for the tax-free status if all the same conditions are met). The conditions, as given in the government publication, "U.S. Savings Bonds: Now Tax-Free for Education," are:

1. Only EE and I bonds purchased after December 31, 1989, qualify.

2. The bonds must be registered in the name of either one or both of the parents. The child cannot be listed on the bond as owner or co-owner. However, the child can be listed on the bond as the POD (pay on death, i.e., beneficiary) recipient.

3. The parents must be at least twenty-four years of age when purchasing the bonds. (**Author's note:** Let's see... sixteen years old to drive, eighteen

years old to vote, and twenty-four years old to buy bonds tax-free.... You gotta love this country.)

4. The income of the parents *in the year the bond is cashed* will determine whether the bond is exempt from federal tax. (U.S. Saving Bonds are always exempt from state and local taxes.) In 1990, this was set at $60,000 for a married couple filing jointly and $40,000 for a single parent. A partial tax break was available (up to $90,000) for a married couple filing jointly. These income limits are indexed to inflation each year. The 1998 income limits are set at $78,350 for a married couple filing jointly and $52,250 for a single parent. A partial tax break is available (up to $108,350 for a married couple filing jointly or up to $67,250 for a single parent). Contact the BPD for the income limits in future years. (See Chapter 18 for the address and phone number.)

5. Bonds must be redeemed the same year that the bond owner pays his, her, or their child's educational expenses to an eligible institution.

6. The only expenses to which bonds can be applied are tuition and fees. Room, board, and books do not qualify.

7. Educational institutions that are eligible include colleges, universities, technical institutes, and vocational schools located in the United States.

8. The interest on bonds that qualify for the educational feature can be excluded from federal income tax only if the redemption proceeds (interest and principal) are less than or equal to the qualifying tuition and fees paid during the year. If the value of the bonds cashed is greater than the eligible tuition and fees, a proportional amount of the bond interest is exempt. That is, if the tuition and fees total $5,000, yet you redeem $20,000 of eligible bonds, only 25% of the interest income can be excluded from federal income tax. It is very important to note that it is total redemption proceeds (interest and principal) are used in the calculation. This can have chilling effects on the "tax-free" status that the client thought they would enjoy. See the case study at the end of the chapter for an illustration.

Additional rule for married couples: Couples who wish to use the educational feature tax exclusion must file a joint return.

Author's note: Prepaid tuition plans can qualify for the tax-free feature due to a 1997 tax law change.

Record Keeping for the Educational Feature

According to the BPD, bond owners should keep specific records on EE and I bonds that qualify for the educational feature. For each bond your clients should have the following:

✓ Serial number
✓ Face value
✓ Issue date
✓ Date of redemption
✓ Total proceeds received (principal and interest)

In addition, they will need to document:

✓ The name of the educational institution that received payment
✓ The date the expenses were paid
✓ The amount of qualified expenses

Forms 8815 and 8818 are both appropriate IRS forms for recording your transaction. Figures 11.1 and 11.2 provide copies of these forms. You may order the forms from the IRS by calling 1-800-829-3676.

To avoid duplication in record keeping, please note that several of the items mentioned above are already a part of your client's bond records if you followed the suggestions in Chapter 4.

Will the Current Interest Rates Be Enough?

Good question. And here is where the debate really heats up. The author is neither a financial planner nor a financial advisor, but he has heard plenty of views on whether interest rates on bonds will "cut the mustard."

The interest rate on Series EE bonds as of November 1998 is 4.60%. That rate is good for only six months and future rates are unknown. At 5%, a bond will take over fourteen years to reach face value (that is, double). This means if Junior is four years old and somehow makes it through high school by age eighteen, the bonds purchased at his fourth birthday will be worth double the purchase price by the time he starts college. Um...not exactly bowled over yet?

For a person in a 28% tax bracket, a tax-free yield of 5% is equivalent to a taxable yield of approximately 7%. Since savings bonds are also exempt from state and local taxes, a tax free yield of 5% would be equal to a taxable yield of approximately 7.5% for a person in the 28% federal tax bracket and 5% state tax bracket.

If inflation stays at 2% to 3% and figuring the tax-free yield, savings bonds will most certainly outperform CDs and money market funds as savings alternatives—and certainly beat doing nothing at all.

Remember, though, that interest rates will not be constant under the new rules. The rates will fluctuate up and down, tied to five-year Treasury yields. If the rates average 6%, your client's money will double in twelve years. If the rates average 4%, your client's money will double in eighteen years. If the rates average 7%, your client's money will double in a little over ten years.

Table 11.1

Time Period to Double Investment

Constant Interest Rate Compounded Semi-Annually	Approximate Number of Years for Investment to Double in Value
3%	24 years
4%	18 years
5%	14.4 years
6%	12 years
7%	10.3 years
8%	9 years
9%	8 years

Table 11.2 (page 141) shows how much a person can expect to save for college by using savings bonds in a systematic savings program. Please note that on line one, projections at 4% were guaranteed as a minimum for bonds purchased March 1993 to April 1995. As you can see in the last column, it will take a savings of $250 a month for eighteen years at an interest rate of 5% to reach $86,000—the cost projected for four years of college in-state in the first decade of the next century.

Pros and Cons of the Educational Feature

Pros

1. Bonds can be used for the educational expenses of a husband, wife, or children. They are not limited to children only.

2. If not used for education, there is no additional penalty; the interest earned on the bond is simply not eligible for federal tax exemption.

3. Bonds can be used at an eligible school (see item #7, page 132) of the bond owner's choice, in-state or out-of-state.

4. There is no set window or time frame for enrollment—anytime after December 31, 1989 will do.

5. Bond owners may invest as little as $25 or as much as $15,000 per person, per year for the EE bonds, and as little as $50 or as much as $30,000 per person on the I bonds. You can buy the limit of both in the same year. Full faith and credit of the U.S. government back the bonds.

6. There are no commissions or fees for entry or exit.

7. The bonds are easily purchased through payroll deduction (at participating companies) or from most local banks.

Cons

1. The interest rate may be unattractive to you and your client and be inconsistent with the client's investment goals.

2. The unknown factor of having the tax-free status determined by the investor's income in the year the bond is redeemed may not justify the trade-off on the potential return. This is especially true if the client's income is already near the established level and you expect it to outpace inflation. (See case study #1, page 136.)

3. Record keeping, although not too onerous, is the responsibility of the bond owner.

An Alternative for Reducing the Tax Burden

There is an alternative to using bonds for education with a reduced tax burden. In fact, it may prove to be more of a guarantee than waiting fifteen years to see if your client's income allows them to qualify for the tax-free status.

A bond owner can shift the tax liability to their children by buying the bonds in the children's name. The parent can appear as a beneficiary on the bond, but not as a co-owner. If the bonds are registered this way they will not be eligible for the educational feature described earlier.

In choosing this alternative, the bond owner should annually report the interest income of the bonds. If the child's total income is under $650 (this is the limit for 1997; check with IRS for annual adjustments), the child pays no taxes on the interest earned. And because the interest is reported annually, most of it will have been reported by the time the bonds are redeemed.

To use the annual reporting method, the investor must file a return the first year to show intent to use this method. He or she must also file a return any year the child's income exceeds the limit set by the IRS. Because many tax laws change every year, this method should be monitored against any future changes.

Advise your client: If they choose to report interest annually, they should clearly understand how to avoid double taxation. When cashing the bonds, a 1099-INT will be issued for all the interest dating back to the date of purchase. The amount previously reported can be deducted from the 1099-INT amount on the tax return. Failure to deduct the amount previously reported will result in double taxation of some of the interest.

Two Ways Bond Owners Lose Out on the Tax-Free Feature

Case Study #1: *Income Outpaces Indexed Income Numbers*

Jill and Sam have two children, ages four and six. Savings bonds look like an interesting option for college savings, especially the tax-free part. Because their income is $68,000 in 1997 (Sam worked for a car company and Jill worked without pay as a stay-at-home mom) — below the limits established for qualifying for the tax-free feature at that time—they move ahead with their plans.

Over the years they invest more than $120,000 in savings bonds resulting in over $70,000 in accrued interest by the time their eldest is ready for her first year of college. In the meantime, the income guidelines have been adjusted about 2% each year.

In the year 2002, Jill goes back to her former career as a public relations director and the family income doubles. By the time their eldest goes to college, they are earning over $150,000 annually—too much to qualify for the tax-free feature. Not only do they not qualify for the tax-free feature, but all the interest they earned (if the bonds were cashed and used for education) will be taxed at a bracket even higher than the bracket they were in when the bonds were purchased.

The tax bill amounted to over $20,000 for this family—taxes that they thought would not have to be paid on "tax-free" savings bonds.

Case Study #2: *Misunderstanding How the Calculations Are Done*

A client is in a 28% tax bracket. She thinks the tax-free feature of EE bonds will provide significant savings for her child's education. However, she gets started a little late and has only three years to save before Junior heads to college.

For three years she invests $30,000 a year into the EE bonds receiving an average return of 5% that results in a total value approximately $99,200. Since Junior goes to college at the end of the third year, she cashes all the bonds with the expectation that, since his tuition and fees are $10,000 and the total interest earned on the bonds is only $9,200, that the interest will all be tax-free.

However, the actual calculations prove to be quite painful because she is unaware of two things: (1) investors are required to report the total redemption value on their IRS forms, and (2) that this value is compared to the actual tuition and fees. Should the total redemption value exceed the tuition and fees (as it does in this case), only a portion of the interest earned will be tax-free.

Let's examine the calculations.

Abbreviated version IRS form 8815 for tax year 1998

Line 2.	Tuition and fees	$10,000
Line 3.	Minus nontaxable scholarships or grants	0
Line 4.	Subtract line 3 from line 2	$10,000
Line 5.	Total proceeds from all eligible bonds cashed (using total proceeds hurts the client)	$99,200
Line 6.	Interest from eligible bonds cashed	$ 9,200
Line 7.	Is line 4 less than line 5? If yes, divide line 4 by line 5, enter result as a decimal (round to second place)	.10
Line 8.	Multiply line 6 by line 7 (this is where the client is getting shafted)	$ 920.00
Line 9.	Enter modified adjusted gross income	$65,000
Line 10.	Enter $78,250 if filing jointly	$78,250
Line 11.	Subtract line 10 from line 9, if zero or less, skip line 12, enter "0" on line 13, and go to line 14.	
Line 12.		Skip
Line 13.		0
Line 14.	Subtract line 13 from line 8. Enter result.	$ 920.00

Instead of receiving $9,200 tax-free, the actual amount that can be deducted from income is only $920—about 10% of what she thought she would receive.

The unexpected tax bill comes to:

Interest she thought would be tax-free	$ 9,200
Actual interest that is tax-free	$ 927.42
Interest that will be taxed at 28% (or higher)	$ 8,272.58
Unexpected tax due	$ 2,316.32

This woman lost more than $2,300 because she did not understand how the tax calculation would be done. Furthermore, her "tax free" investment proved to be hardly that, with barely 10% of the interest gains actually receiving the "tax free" status.

   If cashed equally over four years then approximately $920 a year or $3,680 total could be tax-free. This still only represents 40% of the interest. Unexpected tax due on $5,520 is still $1,546.

The closer you can get to making the amount of bonds cashed equal to the amount of tuition, the higher the percentage of interest that may be excluded from being taxed.

Quick Tips on the Educational Feature

- Your client may be under the mistaken impression that the EE bonds he or she purchased are tax-free for education.
- An investor must meet eight conditions to qualify for the tax-free status (see page 131).
- Bonds that have been incorrectly registered, and therefore no longer qualify the investor for tax-free status, can be retitled.
- Record keeping is the responsibility of the bond owner.
- Shifting the liability to the children is an alternative for reducing the tax burden.
- Investors who chose to report interest annually should be counseled on how to avoid double taxation.
- Two ways that bond owners lose out on the tax-free feature of the EE bond is (1) when income outpaces indexed income numbers, and (2) when they purchase with expectations that do not take into account how the calculations are done.

Figure 11.1

IRS Form 8815

Form **8815**

Department of the Treasury
Internal Revenue Service

Exclusion of Interest From Series EE
U.S. Savings Bonds Issued After 1989
(For Filers With Qualified Higher Education Expenses)
▶ Attach to Form 1040 or Form 1040A.

OMB No. 1545-1173

Attachment
Sequence No. **57**

Caution: *If your filing status is married filing separately,* **do not** *file this form. You* **cannot** *take the exclusion even if you paid qualified higher education expenses in 1997.*

Name(s) shown on return	Your social security number

1

(a) Name of person (you, your spouse, or your dependent) who was enrolled at or attended an eligible educational institution	(b) Name and address of eligible educational institution

If you need more space, attach additional sheets.

2	Enter the total qualified higher education expenses you paid in 1997 for the persons listed in column (a) of line 1. See the instructions to find out which expenses qualify	**2**
3	Enter the total of any nontaxable educational benefits (such as nontaxable scholarship or fellowship grants) received for 1997 for the persons listed in column (a) of line 1. See instructions	**3**
4	Subtract line 3 from line 2. If zero or less, **stop.** You **cannot** take the exclusion	**4**
5	Enter the total proceeds (principal and interest) from all series EE U.S. savings bonds **issued after 1989** that you **cashed during 1997**	**5**
6	Enter the interest included on line 5. See instructions	**6**
7	Is line 4 **less than** line 5? **No.** Enter "1.00." **Yes.** Divide line 4 by line 5. Enter the result as a decimal (rounded to two places) }	**7** × .
8	Multiply line 6 by line 7	**8**
9	Enter your modified adjusted gross income. See instructions . . .	**9**
	Note: *If line 9 is $65,850 or more ($106,250 or more if married filing jointly or qualifying widow(er)),* **stop.** *You* **cannot** *take the exclusion.*	
10	Enter $50,850 ($76,250 if married filing jointly or qualifying widow(er))	**10**
11	Subtract line 10 from line 9. If zero or less, skip line 12, enter -0- on line 13, and go to line 14	**11**
12	Divide line 11 by $15,000 (by $30,000 if married filing jointly or qualifying widow(er)). Enter the result as a decimal (rounded to two places)	**12** × .
13	Multiply line 8 by line 12	**13**
14	**Excludable savings bond interest.** Subtract line 13 from line 8. Enter the result here and on Schedule B (Form 1040), line 3, or Schedule 1 (Form 1040A), line 3, whichever applies . . ▶	**14**

General Instructions

Section references are to the Internal Revenue Code.

Purpose of Form

If you cashed series EE U.S. savings bonds in 1997 that were issued after 1989, you may be able to exclude from your income part or all of the interest on those bonds. Use Form 8815 to figure the amount of any interest you may exclude.

Who May Take the Exclusion

You may take the exclusion if **all four** of the following apply:

1. You cashed qualified U.S. savings bonds in 1997 that were issued after 1989.

2. You paid qualified higher education expenses in 1997 for yourself, your spouse, or your dependents.

3. Your filing status is any status **except** married filing separately.

4. Your modified AGI (adjusted gross income) is less than $65,850 (less than $106,250 if married filing jointly or qualifying widow(er)). See the line 9 instructions to figure your modified AGI.

U.S. Savings Bonds That Qualify for Exclusion

To qualify for the exclusion, the bonds must be series EE U.S. savings bonds issued after 1989 in your name, or, if you are married, they may be issued in your name and your spouse's name. Also, you must have been age 24 or older before the bonds were issued. A bond bought by a parent and issued in the name of his or her child under age 24 does not qualify for the exclusion by the parent or child. **Bond information may be verified with Department of the Treasury records.**

For Paperwork Reduction Act Notice, see back of form.   Cat. No. 10822S   Form **8815** (1997)

Figure 11.2

IRS Form 8818

Form **8818**	**Optional Form To Record Redemption of Series EE**	
(Rev. March 1995)	**U.S. Savings Bonds Issued After 1989**	
	(For Individuals With Qualified Higher Education Expenses)	OMB No. 1545-1151
Department of the Treasury Internal Revenue Service	▶ Keep for your records. **Do not send to the IRS.** ▶ **See instructions on back.**	

Name		Date cashed
1 (a) Serial number	**(b)** Issue date (must be after 1989)	**(c)** Face value

2	Add the amounts in column (c) of line 1	**2**	
3	Total redemption proceeds from bonds listed above that were issued after 1989. Be sure to get this figure from the teller when you cash the bonds	**3**	
4	Multiply line 2 above by 50% (.50). This is your cost	**4**	
5	Subtract line 4 from line 3. This is the interest on the bonds	**5**	

For Paperwork Reduction Act Notice, see back of form.   Cat. No. 10097L   Form **8818** (Rev. 3-95)

Table 11.2

Using Savings Bonds to Save for Education Expenses

Assumed Interest Rate	Save $50 a month to purchase $300 of bonds every six months. Value after 10 years.	Save $50 a month to purchase $300 of bonds every six months. Value after 18 years.	Save $100 a month to purchase $600 of bonds every six months. Value after 10 years.	Save $100 a month to purchase $600 of bonds every six months. Value after 18 years.	Save $250 a month to purchase $1,500 of bonds every six months. Value after 10 years.	Save $250 a month to purchase $1,500 of bonds every six months. Value after 18 years.
4%	$7,289	$15,598	$14,578	$31,196	$36,446	$77,991
5%	$7,663	$17,190	$15,326	$34,380	$38,316	$85,952
6%	$8,061	$18,982	$16,122	$37,965	$40,305	$94,913
7%	$8,484	$21,002	$16,968	$42,005	$42,420	$105,011

The calculations in the above table are based on the following assumptions:

1. The bond purchaser will save money at an even monthly rate and will purchase bonds twice a year. A monthly purchase pattern will result in a slightly higher final value.

2. That the interest rates used to calculate future values will be consistent over the time period the calculations were made.

1. The money invested is the purchase price of the bonds, not the face value. Thus the term "purchase $300 of bonds every six months" means $300 purchase price, $600 face value. (Remember EE bonds are purchased for one-half the face value.)

2. The guaranteed interest rate for Series EE bonds purchased March 1, 1993 to April 30, 1995 is 4%. Series EE bonds purchased after April 30, 1995, do not have a guaranteed interest rate (see Chapter 5). Call 1-800-USBONDS for interest rate information on new purchases.

Note: This table does not guarantee a specific return on any investment. Market conditions and rules governing the savings bond program may change without notice. Obtain current rate information and complete details before making any investment decision.

Part III

Beyond the Basics

_____ Chapter 12

COMPARING SAVINGS BONDS TO OTHER INVESTMENTS

▶ *What About Those Who Say, "Just Cash Them All"?*
▶ *Which Savings Bond Rate Should Be Used?*
▶ *Evaluating New Bond Purchases*
▶ *Evaluating an Exchange*
▶ *Savings Bonds vs. Savings Accounts, CDs, and Money Market Funds*
▶ *Savings Bonds vs. Treasury Bills, Notes, and Bonds*
▶ *Savings Bonds vs. Your Products*
▶ *Savings Bonds vs. Pork Bellies*
▶ *Quick Tips on Comparison*

As stated in the preface, the author's purpose in writing this book is neither to recommend the redemption nor purchase of savings bonds (although you probably have an opinion). The intent of this chapter is to provide a fair framework within which savings bonds can be compared to other investments.

The person who dismisses all bond holdings because of the possibility of "doing better elsewhere" may fail to take into account the unique nature of an investor's financial position, including their overall asset allocation, risk tolerance, and other intangibles that go into a person's choice of investment vehicles. Before introducing a structure for an equitable comparison, we will take a brief look at what the author considers "bad advice."

What About Those Who Say, "Just Cash Them All"?

The author has conducted hundreds of interviews for radio, television, and print media and has worked with thousands of financial professionals. The vast majority work hard to provide accurate, useful information. Occasionally, however, someone will make a bold statement that is not in the best interest of the bond owner. For example, anyone who says, "you don't need to do a comparison, just cash them all," without reviewing a written analysis of the savings bond holdings is oversimplifying the issue and doing a disservice to the client.

In his book *Savings Bonds: When to Hold, When to Fold and Everything In-Between,* the author advises savings bond owners to ask the following questions:

- Does the person making the suggestion have a vested interest in your action, that is, "cashing all of your bonds?"

- Have they provided you with the specific analysis and data to support their recommendation? (**Note**: The government program, "Savings Bond Wizard," provides only the worth of bonds and so is not a sufficient tool for evaluating bonds. The person who provides only values and then concludes with advice to cash the bonds has not done an analysis.)

- Do they have a systematic plan for redemption that will minimize tax consequences and take advantage of the bond increase date?

The following scenarios reveal how bad advice can be financial damaging:

Scenario #1: A couple purchased $30,000 ($60,000 face value) in bonds in October 1986, locking in a guaranteed rate of 7.5% for ten years. On September 15th, 1996, a "money expert" advises them to cash all the bonds and invest in mutual funds. The advice is followed and the bonds are redeemed that very week. Unfortunately, they just forfeited $2,260 that would have been theirs had the bonds been held for another 15 days (until October 1). If we annualize it, this return equals 90%. Is there a mutual fund that is guaranteed to perform that well? Furthermore, they now have less money to invest in the mutual fund because they cashed just before the bonds were to be credited with an increase.

Scenario #2: Once again, assume that the "money expert" mentioned in Scenario #1 gives the same advice about the October 1986 bonds. In this case, however, the bond owner's tax bracket will be changing next year from 28% to 15% due to retirement. If all of the bonds are cashed now, all of the interest will be taxed in the current bracket of 28%. Had they waited until January 1st to cash, some or all of the interest would have been taxed at 15%. Assuming that half the interest was taxed at 15%, an additional $1,489.06 would have been available to invest in some other "hot" option that was proposed.

This sort of advice is generally born from the fact that the stock market and most mutual funds have consistently outperformed savings bonds over the last decade. Remember, though, timing and tax issues should be considered before advising a client to cash any bond.

Which Savings Bond Rate Should Be Used?

This section examines the three government-published rates and whether each, or any, of these rates offers a reasonable measurement of long-term performance. Since most bond owners are concerned with performance over the next several years, historic data (looking backward) and short-term data (measuring only six-months of performance) are both lacking as useful tools for projections. Here are the most common, government-published (free) rates used to analyze savings bonds and an alternative that measures longer term performance (fee):

- The average annual yield

- The six-month earnings rate

- The guaranteed rate

A fourth source of data will be described at the end of this section (fee-based):

- The Savings Bond Informer Rating System℠

As outlined in Chapter 5, "Understanding Interest Rates," EE bonds bought after April 1995 are governed by a program best identified as "what you see is what you get." But what about older bonds that carry both the guaranteed and average market rate? Which rates should be used to evaluate future earnings? What about the government's new yield tables that show the average annual yield from the date of purchase? What about the yield table that shows the earnings rate for the next six months?

Most people are not as concerned with the next six months' yield as they are with long range projections of how a bond will perform over the next several years or even decades. This is because bonds may be part of a client's retirement savings or the means for funding the educational expenses of a child. The decision centers on whether to stay in for the long term or move on.

It can be debated which interest rates or yields should be used to predict a bond's long-term performance. Since there are many different interest rates and yields published for savings bonds, it is important to examine each in order to determine which would be the best representation of future performance.

It is important to discern the reliability and usefulness of the savings bond data you use. If those who present the data cannot fully describe the context for any given piece of information, or if they are merely feeding back information from government tables, they probably don't understand savings bonds and the information may lead to inaccurate conclusions. Let's examine those rates.

The Average Annual Yield

Let's rule out this one. The average annual yield over the life of the bond is a good historic number. It shows how the bond *has* performed. However it is *not* a good indicator of future performance. This is particularly true of savings bonds. Why? Interest rates in the early 1980s were high compared to today's rates. Thus most bonds over ten years old had a much higher return in the past than they do today. When high returns early in the life of a bond are averaged with low returns late in the life of a bond, the overall average is generally much higher than the bond's current yield. Also, the average annual yield does not account for inflation and thus is a poor representation of the "real rate of return."

The average annual yield is a "feel good" piece of data. It will typically be 50 to 300 basis points higher than the actual current or future performance of most bonds. It is "feel good" data because it may make the bond owner feel good about what "did" happen, but it is of no use in predicting what "will" happen. Here is the problem with this piece of data and how it is often being used to arrive at wrong conclusions.

Wrong Conclusion: The government recently added a new column to the redemption tables that are used by many bank tellers. This column is called the "Average Annual Interest Rate." Because older bonds received high interest rates in the 1980s, the "Average Annual Interest Rate" will often overstate the current performance of a particular bond. The trouble is that many tellers are leading investors to believe that the "Average Annual Interest Rate" is the actual rate they are currently earning on their bonds. (In the fall of 1997, a teller at a bank in Illinois told the author that a bond issued in October 1986 was currently earning 7.34%. That bond was actually earning 4%.)

The Six-Month Earnings Rate

The yield for the next six months is a good short-term indicator in that it projects what return a bond will receive for that six-month period. While this can be helpful for short-term decisions, it can also lead to inaccurate conclusions about long-term performance. It is often a temporary distortion of what the long-term performance will be and may result in an under- or overinflated view of how a bond is performing. Consider the following two examples:

Wrong Conclusion: A bond bought in November 1993 received a flat rate of 4% for the first five years. Once it turned five years old it received a market-rate of 5.22% retroactive to the date of purchase. Because the retroactive feature is all credited on the bond's fifth anniversary, the net yield for the time period including the fifth anniversary will be skewed upward. The government table listed this bond as having a yield of 16.47%. What the data did not say, however, is that the same bond would drop back down to a range of 4% to 5.5% after the five-year catch-up. A bond owner who looks at the yield table, sees a great yield, and decides to hold that bond for the next decade will be disappointed. The future performance of this bond will provide far less than the table indicates due to this one-time "spike."

Another Wrong Conclusion: (This example is similar the previous one, but on the opposite end of the spectrum.) In 1996 the government yield tables revealed that some bonds bought in 1987 and 1988 had short-term yields as low as 2%. Without using this space to detail the reason why, this "dip" was short-term. They returned to a guaranteed rate of 6% for several years before the end of the original maturity. However, a bond owner seeing a low yield, could easily assume that these bonds should be cashed. Bond owners who made that mistake often redeemed bonds that would pay them 6% over the next several years, while keeping bonds that were paying them only 4 to 5%.

Note: Short-term yields are often aberrations (skewed up or down depending on when the data is analyzed) compared to the long-term performance of a bond. They are not an accurate barometer of long-term performance.

The Guaranteed Rate

The best choice of the free options is the government-published guaranteed rate. The guaranteed rate of interest in your current maturity period is just that—a guarantee of the minimum you will earn over the entire maturity period. This is the most conservative estimate of what the bond will return. (Bonds may yield higher returns if the market-based average for a given bond results in a greater redemption value than the redemption value produced by using the guaranteed rates.) Since this rate is guaranteed over the entire maturity period that the bond is in, the author views this information as the best "free source" representation of future performance (until the bond enters the next extended maturity period). This is also the most conservative estimate. Better to err on the side of being conservative in future estimates rather than create an expectation that is never achieved. Here's why: The market rate program received a great deal of fanfare and attention through the 1980s. In fact, the first rate ever published was a whopping 11.09%. Yet due to the complicated way the rates are averaged, no one ever received 11.09% on their bonds. All bonds purchased prior to May 1995 now carry guaranteed rates of either 6% or 4%.

Exceptions: Series EE bonds purchased between March 1993 and April 1995 will receive a retroactive bonus at the end of the fifth year if the market rate average exceeds 4%. The result on those bonds will be a one-time spike in the short-term yield at the end of the fifth year that can produce short-term yields of 10% or more.

The Savings Bond Informer Rating System℠

The Savings Bond Informer Rating System℠ provides a rating for each bond based on a projection of the two-year and five-year future performance. This system takes into account the specific interest rates and timing periods and then assigns a rating specific to each bond. A rating of each bond and a complete description of the rating system is provided with each bond statement prepared by The Savings Bond Informer, Inc. This system reveals exceptions (like spikes and dips) for your review. It also clearly identifies the best and worst performing bonds. There is a nominal cost involved. See page 18 for an example.

If you are using savings bond information that provides a short-term yield without also including the guaranteed floor for the current maturity period and a future rating, you are not getting the full picture.

Evaluating New Bond Purchases

The new rules on Series EE savings bonds are easy to understand: What you see is what you get. Each May and November the government announces a short-term market-based rate for savings bonds. The most recent rate that has been published will be the rate a bond earns for the first six months. Every six months the bond will pick up a new rate that will move up or down depending on market conditions.

Example: A bond bought in May 1997 received a rate of 5.68% for the first six months. In November 1997, a new rate of 5.59% was published and this is what the bond earned for the second six months. In May 1998, a new rate of 5.06% was published and this is what the bond earned for the third six-month period. In November 1998, a new rate of 4.60% was published and the bond will earn that rate until May 1999. The interest rates can be illustrated as follows:

May 1997 to November 1, 1997	5.68%
November 1997 to May 1, 1998	5.59%
May 1998 to November 1, 1998	5.06%
November 1998 to May 1, 1999	4.60%

Under the current system, the new rate published every May and November will always be lower than the average of the five-year Treasury yields for the six months preceding the rate announcement. Why? The government is giving the bond owner 90% of the average rate for five-year Treasury yields.

To evaluate whether clients should buy or not, based on current rates, call 1-800-USBONDS. The recorded line will give you the current market rate that will apply to the bond for the first six months. The problem with evaluating bonds as long-term investments is that without a guaranteed rate clients should no longer tuck a bond away for ten or twenty years and forget about it. Rates should be monitored to determine whether this investment is meeting their expectations. For information on the series I bond and a comparison of EE and I bonds, see Chapter 7.

Evaluating an Exchange

Bond owners are generally unhappy about the rate on HH bonds and this represents another opportunity for those who offer financial advice and alternative products. Thousands of bond owners have complained of the proverbial "rock and a hard place" between which the government has squeezed them with the low 4% rate on HH bonds. This is what they mean. Suppose they have bonds that have reached final maturity and have stopped earning interest. They have a lot of accrued interest that has, to this point, not been reported as interest income and, therefore, not taxed. At final maturity they must either redeem the bonds (which creates a taxable event) or exchange them for HH bonds (which pay only 4%). There is no option to just "hold the bonds." They earn no interest on bonds that have reached final maturity. Adding insult to injury, the IRS makes them report the interest in the year the bonds reach final maturity, whether the bonds are cashed or not. The only exception to this is when the bond owner exchanges for HH bonds. Why does this upset bond owners? Because as long-term investors who have kept their bonds for thirty or forty years, all they are offered is an HH bond paying less than a three-month T-bill (often over 100 basis points less). Some opt for the HH bond to delay reporting the interest, however, many bond owners leave the bond program rather than exchange.

Savings Bonds vs. Savings Accounts, CDs, and Money Market Funds

To conduct a fair evaluation, U.S. Savings Bonds must be compared to other like investments. Investment options can generally be classified into one of three risk categories—high, moderate, and low risk. Opinions about which investments fit into which categories are often the subject of much debate. Most people, however, would agree that savings bonds fit into the latter. Savings bonds are defined in the marketplace with monikers like: secure/safe, conservative, patriotic, government product, liquid, low-risk/low-return. Consider, for example, that no one has ever received less than what they invested in a savings bond. Over time a bond always has a positive return (we are not factoring in inflation-adjusted returns in this discussion). Thus for comparison purposes, savings bonds should be grouped with other conservative, safe investments.

Three other popular investment/savings options can easily fit within the range of conservative investments: savings accounts, certificates of deposit, and money market funds. Table 12.1 (page 155) was completed in the third quarter 1998 and can be used to compare these investments. A blank copy, Table 12.2 (page 156), is included as a worksheet that can be easily updated and used in future evaluations.

Savings Bonds vs. Treasury Bills, Notes, and Bonds

Comparing these government products is sort of like comparing three brothers. They are distinctly different yet they come from the same family. Hence they share certain attributes inherent in government products—safe, conservative, debt-financing instruments. The younger brother, savings bonds, has considerably less freedom than the two older: T-bills and T-notes/bonds can be bought at original issue and venture out into the secondary market. The bottom line is that each of these government products is used to round out the conservative end of millions of Americans' portfolios.

Table 12.3 (page 157) highlights the features of each security and can be easily used for comparisons.

Savings Bonds vs. Your Products

You know the strength and weaknesses of your own product line. And, undoubtedly when financial professionals hear that most bonds are earning between 4 and 6%, their eyes light up. This, they believe, is an opportunity waiting to happen.

You can use the grid at the end of the chapter to insert the savings bond information next to your product. Please allow the author to offer a couple of observations that may spare you a lawsuit or two.

1. Respect the safety (low-risk) factor of savings bonds. Stocks and mutual funds and many other financial products introduce risk and volatility factors that may be unsettling for your clients.

2. Consider suitability. What can or can't the client live with? A client who sleeps well with their savings bond holdings may become an overnight insomniac with even a minor market correction. To build long-term relationships with clients, offer as much attention to the risks and downside of other investment options as to the upside.

Savings Bonds vs. Pork Bellies

For a brief look at the lighter side, compare extremes. The author once worked at the Chicago Mercantile Exchange (the "Merc"), where futures commodities are traded and fortunes are won and lost—sometimes in the same day. Let's examine the commodities market to see how this investment compares with the conservative nature of savings bonds.

*   The place where traders stand to conduct business is called a "pit." The author's experience is that a pit is usually a deep, dark hole from which it is generally difficult to retrieve things, such as…oh, let's say…money.

*   Trades are conducted by hand signals. Many of the hand signals witnessed in the "pit" by the author are those frequently used on the freeway.

*   As you look out onto the trading floor, you see coats of many colors. This conjures up images of the biblical Joseph who was cast into a "pit" and ended up broke and in prison.

What's the point? It's probably a bit safer to buy your pork at the super market. And, of course, lock up any person who suggests that pork bellies carry a risk equivalent to that of savings bond holdings.

Few investments carry the security and backing that savings bonds have. With that security, savings bonds offer a fairly predictable, non-spectacular return.

Quick Tips on Comparison

- Telling clients to cash without providing them a written analysis of their holdings is risky.
- Interest rates, timing issues, tax consequences, risk tolerance, suitability, as well as values must be considered when giving advice on savings bonds.
- The best representation for projecting the long-term performance of bonds purchased prior to May 1995 is The Savings Bond Informer Rating System℠.
- To evaluate whether clients should buy or not, call 1-800-USBONDS for interest rates on new purchases.
- Other conservative investments against which bonds are often compared include T-bills, notes, bonds, CDs, and money market funds.

Table 12.1

Comparing Savings Bonds to
Savings Accounts, CDs, and Money Market Funds

	Series EE & Series I Savings Bonds	Savings Accounts	CDs	Money Market Funds
Federal Tax	Yes, deferred until bond is cashed or reaches final maturity	Yes	Yes	Yes
State Tax	No	Yes	Yes	Yes
Local Tax	No	Yes, if applicable	Yes, if applicable	Yes, if applicable
Minimum Investment	Series EE: $25 for a $50 face value bond Series I: $50 for a $50 face value bond	None, although some accounts have minimum balance requirements	Usually $500, some may be available for lower initial investment	Usually $500, some accounts may be opened for less initial investment
Maximum Investment	Series EE: $15,000 purchase price per person per year Series I: $30,000 purchase price per person per year	None	None	None
Interest Rates	Series EE: 5.06% first six months for bond purchased 5/98 to 10/98 Series I: 4.66% for 9/98 and 10/98	Average of 1% to 3%, depending on bank	Small denomination six-month CDs averaged 4.67% as of 9/9/98 * source Bank Rate Monitor	Averaged 5.19% as of 9/98
Liquidity	Can cash bond anytime after six months, three-month penalty if cashed prior to five years.	Can take money out at any time without penalty, although minimum balance requirements and penalties may apply	Must hold until "official" maturity date or face penalties for early withdrawal	Can usually liquidate at any time without fees or penalty
Safety	Backed by full faith and credit of U.S. government	Are insured up to $100,000 at qualified financial institutions (FDIC insured)	Are insured up to $100,000 at qualified financial institutions	Are usually not insured

Table 12.2

Complete Your Own Comparisons

	Series EE and Series I Savings Bonds	Other Investment Option: _____	Other Investment Option: _____	Other Investment Option: _____
Federal Tax	Yes, deferred until bond is cashed or reaches final maturity			
State Tax	No			
Local Tax	No			
Minimum Investment	Series EE: $25 Series I: $50			
Maximum Investment	Series EE: $15,000 Series I: $30,000			
Interest Rates	Series EE: 4.60% if purchased 11/98 to 4/99 Series I: 5.05% if purchased 11/98 to 4/99			
Liquidity	Can cash bond anytime after six months, three-month penalty if not held five years			
Safety	Backed by full faith and credit of U.S. Government			

Table 12.3

Comparing Savings Bonds to
Treasury Bills, Notes, and Bonds

	Series EE Savings Bonds	Treasury Bills	Treasury Notes/Bonds
Federal Tax	Yes, deferred until bond is cashed or reaches final maturity	Yes, in the year the bill reaches face value (or matures)	Yes, the semi-annual interest payment is subject to federal tax in the year it is received.
State Tax	No	No	No
Local Tax	No	No	No
Minimum Investment	$25 for a $50 face value bond	$1,000, receive a discount after the issue date once purchase price is established	$5,000 for a two-year note, $1,000 for anything longer.
Maximum Investment	$15,000 purchase price per person per year	$1,000,000	$5,000,000
Interest Rates	4.60% first six months for bond purchased 11/98 to 4/99	4.49% as of 12/17/98 for three-month T-bill 4.55% as of 12/17/98 for six-month T-bill 4.51 as of 12/10/98 for one-year T-bill	Most recent auction prior to 12/98 2 yr: 4.625% (11/30/98) 5 yr: 4.25% (11/16/98) 10 yr: 4.75% (11/16/98) 30 yr: 5.25% (11/16/98)
Term	Six months to thirty years	three-month six-month one-year	Two-year, five-year, ten-year thirty-year, other issues may be offered periodically
Liquidity	Can cash bond anytime after six months without penalty	Can sell at any time in secondary market, however there is a commission or fee to sell, and current market conditions will determine the sale price	Can sell at any time in secondary market, however there is a commission or fee to sell, and current market conditions will determine the sale price. May receive more or less than the face value if sold prior to maturity.
Safety	Backed by full faith and credit of U.S. government	Backed by full faith and credit of U.S. government	Backed by full faith and credit of U.S. government
Where to Purchase	Through payroll deduction with many employers, at financial institutions, at Federal Reserve Banks.	Federal Reserve Banks, commercial banks, brokers	Federal Reserve Banks, commercial banks, brokers
Purchase or Redemption Costs	None	None if purchased from a Federal Reserve Bank and held to maturity. If purchased from a bank or broker, fees and/or commissions will apply.	None if purchased from a Federal Reserve Bank and held to maturity. If purchased from a bank or broker, fees and/or commissions will apply.

_____ Chapter 13

SAVINGS BONDS AND RETIREMENT

▶ *Pre-Retirement Issues*
▶ *Retirement Issues*
▶ *How to Help Careful Savers Spend*
▶ *Maximizing Family Wealth*
▶ *Quick Tips on Retirement*

U.S. Savings Bonds: Some of your clients purchased them faithfully for decades before they ever met you. They may represent a portion of their assets that were targeted for retirement, or they may constitute the client's rainy day fund. Regardless of intent, one thing is certain: The holder received no owner's manual outlining the important strategies for maximizing this investment. As retirement nears, however, it is important that they carefully and thoughtfully examine their savings bond investment.

Part of making the most of this investment is to avoid serious pitfalls. Another aspect is to have a systematic plan for the use of the bonds, one based on specific needs and goals. In this chapter we will consider both, in addition to common retirement questions.

Note: The information presented is best utilized by integrating the savings bond portion of a client's investment into an overall strategy for funding their retirement years. This chapter is intended to help you do that.

Pre-Retirement Issues

Let us assume that a client will be retiring in the next two to ten years. What savings bond issues should she be concerned with? Start with the basics:

- How much are the bonds worth now?
- What interest rates are they earning?
- How much deferred interest has not yet been reported?
- When will the bonds stop earning interest?
- How long will the bonds earn interest at their current rates?

All of this information is readily available by ordering a bond statement from The Savings Bond Informer, Inc. (see page 18); some of the information is available by creating a statement yourself (see Chapter 2). Once you have this information, Table 13.2 (page 171) will help you project approximately how much the bonds will be worth by the time the client retires.

Bonds that Stop Earning Interest Before the Client Retires

If bonds reach final maturity prior to retirement, the client will need to decide whether to redeem them or exchange them for HH bonds. Even though the HH bond pays a stingy 4% (at the time of writing), it may still make sense to exchange for them. This is especially true for those in high tax brackets who are close to retirement. If you anticipate that the client may be in a lower tax bracket after retirement, deferring the interest from old Series E and EE bonds could provide a nice tax savings, as demonstrated in the following example:

Sam Jones is 63 years old. He plans to retire in two years. Next year, at age 64, $20,000 of his old Series E bonds will reach final maturity. Of the $20,000 redemption value, approximately $17,500 is deferred interest—income that would have to be reported should he cash the bonds. Since Sam is in a 28% tax bracket, his tax bite would be $4,900 if he cashes them before retirement. Thus he would have only $15,100 to invest or live on after taxes.

Sam anticipates that his income will drop after retirement. He has figured he could take about $4,000 a year in income that would be taxed at a lower rate of 15%. Sam is trying to decide if he should roll over to HH bonds and cash some ($4,000) each year, or if he should cash all the bonds now and reinvest the proceeds in something else.

Table 13.3 (page 172) outlines the options that Sam is considering. Option #2 will provide a higher income stream over the next five years and the greatest amount left to reinvest after taxes (Option #1 equals $15,100 vs. Option #2 which equals $17,375).

Several variables will affect each bond owner's situation. The most significant is, "What is the expected return on the other investment options?"

Common Pre-Retirement Questions

Should I keep investing in bonds?

Examine this question in light of the other investment alternatives (see Chapter 12). The advantages and disadvantages, like those presented for savings bonds, need to be determined for the other investment options. Here are the savings bond pros and cons for the two series currently available, Series EE and Series I.

Advantages

1. Savings bond growth is tax-deferred. Just prior to retirement, the client may be in the highest income period of his life; additional income during these peak earning years will likely be taxed at a higher rate than after retirement. Thus, for most wage earners nearing retirement, tax-deferral is often desirable. It allows the dollars to grow and compound without a tax bite until the bonds are cashed. This is particularly important if you anticipate that your client's tax bracket will shift downward after retirement.

2. Savings can be systematic. The investor may belong to a payroll deduction program and have experienced firsthand the growth of a savings bond portfolio through systematic purchases. For most Americans, a disciplined form of savings beats the "I'll save when I have extra money" approach. (**Note:** The I bond may not yet be available through payroll deduction.)

3. A savings bond investment is liquid; that is, holders can cash bonds anytime after the first six months; they don't have to wait until they are 65 or 70½ or whatever other age the government decides upon. But remember, there is a three-month interest penalty if a bond is cashed prior to five years.

4. The client can purchase as little or as much (almost) as he or she wants: $15,000 per person per calendar year for EE bonds and double that amount for I bonds. See Chapter 7 for more information on purchase options and limitations.

Disadvantages

1. The current interest rate structure does not provide a guaranteed minimum return on EE bonds. The first rate for EE bonds purchased November 1998 through April 1999 is 4.60%. That is good for the first six months only. This rate, always lower than the preceding six-month average of five-year Treasury yields, may not meet investor demands for a reasonable return. The rate changes every six months. The I bond interest rate is based on a fixed rate (3.3% as of November 1998) and a rate that is tied to inflation. The combination of the two provided an initial interest rate of 5.05% on I bonds purchased November 1998 through April 1999. Both rates are reset every May and November. Current rates can be obtained by calling 1-800-USBONDS.

2. Investments in savings bonds are made with after-tax dollars. With several other investment options available through employers, you can invest pre-tax dollars. Investing pre-tax dollars is not currently available with U.S. Savings Bonds.

3. Savings bonds do not receive a stepped-up basis at the time of death. If bonds are passed on to children who are in higher tax brackets, the interest will be taxed at that higher rate when the bonds are redeemed or reach final maturity. (See Chapter 14 for more tax information.)

4. The deferred reporting of interest income, usually an advantage, can also be viewed as a ticking tax bomb. At some point (redemption or final maturity), the bomb goes off and decades' worth of deferred interest has to be reported. Often this causes some or all of the interest to be taxed at a higher rate.

5. The client may have over 50% of their entire portfolio tied up in savings bonds. Further purchases will add even more eggs to a loaded basket. For these clients, diversification, even among other conservative options, should be discussed.

Should I cash my bonds now?

Most taxpayers are in a higher tax bracket during their working years than they will be in retirement. The exception would be a person who has a lower income in the later working years, but who has significant income potential from investments in retirement plans—401(k) plans, Individual Retirement Accounts, and other qualified retirement pension plans. If a taxpayer is in a lower tax bracket in his final working years than he thinks he will be in after retirement, he should consider cashing some bonds while in the lower tax bracket.

It often makes sense to defer income tax if it is anticipated that the income tax rate before and after retirement is projected to be the same or lower.

Throughout this book one theme has been emphasized: Do not cash bonds without first evaluating each and every one. In the evaluation process you learned what each bond is earning. That must be compared with other investment options. Keep in mind that cashing bonds creates a taxable event. Thus, the redemption value minus the taxes due is the amount that truly is available to spend or invest in another option.

Should I convert to HH bonds?

As long as the guaranteed rate on HH bonds is 4%, and E or EE bonds still have interest-earning life left, owners should not exchange for HH bonds. (See Chapter 8 for more on the concept of selective redemption.) HH bonds are paying only 4% and the rate is fixed for the first ten years with no upside potential. If a client exchanges now they also forfeit the opportunity to exchange these same Series E or EE bonds two or three years from now should HH bond interest rates go up to five or six percent.

Can I gift these bonds away?

The real question is, "Can I gift these bonds without a taxable event?" The staple answer is no, with one gray area. To gift bonds to a charity, the bond owner must cash the bonds and then give the money to the charity. Cashing the bonds creates a taxable event. Bonds that are titled to a bond owner cannot just be handed over to a charity or another person. Savings bonds are non-transferable, so the bond owner cannot sign them over to someone else. The one gray area is created by the reporting system used by the IRS to collect data when bonds are cashed. This gray area is outlined in the tax discussion in Chapter 14.

I want to gift bonds to my grandchildren so they can use them tax-free for education. Can I do this?

Sit the client down, and then break the news…the answer is "no" for several reasons. First, only bonds purchased January 1, 1990, and after qualify. Chances are that many of the bonds were purchased prior to that date. Second, the bonds must be registered in the name of the parent or parents of the child. Since the bonds are registered in the grandparent's name, they will not qualify. And, a bond owner cannot simply "get the name changed." Taking grandfather's name off the bond (assuming he is listed first) would normally create a taxable event. For more on the educational feature of savings bonds, see Chapter 11.

I want to systematically convert to HH bonds over the next five years. How can I do that?

As has been stated repeatedly, HH bonds currently earn a rate of 4%. If the investor is still interested, here are some tips for making the exchange.

1. Convert to the lowest denomination of HH bond—$500; this makes the redemption of the holdings easier (much easier than if the money is locked into $10,000 bonds).

2. Identify the increase dates for the E and EE bonds that need to be converted. Time the exchange right after the bonds have been credited with an increase.

3. Since they want to systematically convert some bonds each year for the next five years, pick the bonds with the lowest interest rates and convert them first.

4. Determine if they want an income stream monthly, quarterly, or semi-annually. Remember that HH bonds pay interest every six months (it does not accumulate as with E or EE bonds). Thus, if they want a monthly income stream, bonds should be converted every month for six months in a row.

Retirement Issues

Steps to Managing Bonds in Retirement

Make sure you ask your clients if they own bonds. Financial advisors are often surprised when substantial savings bond holdings ($200,000 to $1,000,000) show up in an estate. Often, they had no idea the client had even one savings bond.

Although the following steps are very basic, they can serve as a good reminder.

Step #1: *Know where the client stands (what they have, what they need, when they need it).*

What they have. Take inventory of their holdings. This should include all assets—house, car(s), 401(k), IRAs, mutual funds, savings bonds, Treasury securities, etc. Although this book will not advise you on how to maximize each of these investment areas, you do need to know which assets are available to convert to income so that you can determine when in the client's retirement (if ever) they will need to cash some bonds.

Chapters 2 and 18 explain how to create or purchase a savings statement of bond holdings. This is an indispensable tool for your financial plan. The statement provides the value of their holdings, the interest rates, and the dates the bonds will change interest rates. It also shows when each bond will stop earning interest.

What they need. The key here is to evaluate what their needs are going to be. This should include both ongoing living expenses and one-time big-ticket items (car, vacations, weddings). Table 13.4 , page 173, can help the client start to think and plan.

When they need it*:* Many people have investments that they do not access until a certain age (65 or 70½). This means the client may have to access the savings bonds, using them as "a bridge" until future income "kicks in." Consider this example:

Mary Johnson and her husband will both retire at the age of 63. They choose not to start withdrawing from their 401(k) until the age of 70½. For seven and a half years, they will need to supplement their income. Fortunately, they own more than $200,000 in U.S. Savings Bonds and they plan to cash about $20,000 a year once they retire. The savings bonds will provide the "bridge" they need to keep a level income stream until they start to withdraw their 401(k) plan.

Step #2: *Make a plan in partnership with the client.*

The author has witnessed bond owners forfeiting thousands upon thousands of dollars because they had no plan for handling their savings bonds. Suddenly one day they decide, for whatever reason, to redeem a substantial portion of their bond holdings. If they do not consider tax issues, timing issues, and interest rates, it is highly unlikely that they will pick just the right bonds to redeem at just the right time.

As you formulate a plan with your client, the following components should be incorporated: tax issues, timing issues, estate planning, and control of the assets (registration issues).

Step #3: *Encourage the client to follow the plan.*

For many clients, you are providing counsel and advise, but they are still "pulling the trigger" on decisions. If they are keeping bonds in their portfolio, then during your scheduled reviews (quarterly or at least annually), see if they are following the decisions you discussed. Savings bonds are unique in that you cannot negotiate the bond on behalf of the client. Thus you need the client to keep you informed of any major changes in strategy with savings bond holdings.

Step #4: *Evaluate the plan and revise as needed.*

Many factors can affect our plans, including the tragic, yet inevitable, loss of a loved one. As a client's circumstances change, keep the plan up to date. Make sure the proper paperwork is available for the client's heirs. Find out who, if anyone, the client wants to be made aware of the savings bond holdings and communicate the necessary information to those who may need to know.

Common Questions From Retirees

The author has conducted dozens of seminars on retirement issues. The lines of people waiting to ask questions after these sessions reveal several things. First, each person has a different scenario; thus they need information specific to their situation. Second, many bond owners make a point of voicing their frustration at not being able to get good answers to their questions (usually they are asking the wrong people; for example, expecting a bank teller to address a retirement tax question). Your clients will be grateful to receive information that you tailor to their specific concerns.

In this section the most common retirement questions and concerns will be examined. If you don't find the answer to your question, please write to the author so that it can be considered for a future edition.

Will cashing in savings bonds cause some or all of my Social Security to be taxed?
Possibly. This often happens when bond owners are in a very low tax bracket: They have little or no income and, as a result, little or no tax. However, they may have a large cache of U.S. Savings Bonds, which has accrued a considerable amount of interest over the years. Redeeming a large number of bonds at one time may cause a substantial portion of their Social Security income to be taxed.

Can I gift the bonds to someone else?
Sometimes investors find they do not need their savings bonds. They have ample income from other investments and they would like the savings bonds to be taken out of their names and given to children, grandchildren, or some other important person. The rules regarding transfer of ownership state: If the principal owner (generally the first-named owner or co-owner) removes his or her name, that creates a taxable event. Thus they cannot just "sign the bonds over, by signing the back of the bond" to the relative of their choice. See Chapters 14 and 15 for more detail.

Is there an automatic stepped-up basis on bonds?
No. See Chapter 14 for more detail.

What tax consequences will my heirs face when they inherit these bonds?
If the interest has not been previously reported (and in most cases it has not), they will inherit the liability for all the interest earned from the date of purchase. See Chapter 14.

Will these bonds end up in probate?
Not if they have a co-owner or beneficiary listed on the bonds and they predecease that person. However, the person who receives the bonds should have the bonds retitled into their name and add a co-owner or beneficiary of their choosing. This way when they die, should their estate go through probate, the bonds will again pass directly to the co-owner or beneficiary they have listed on the bonds.

May I list a charity as the co-owner or beneficiary of my bonds?
No. A "non-natural" entity such as an organization, charity, or trust cannot be listed as a co-owner or beneficiary of a bond.

How to Help Careful Savers Spend

Many an older American has gone to the grave lacking basic necessities in the latter years of their life. Upon examining their assets (which heirs doubt exist), it is discovered that they had numerous savings bonds (and/or other assets). Rather than finding out later what they "could" or "should" have done, assist clients by illustrating what they can spend without depleting their "rainy day fund."

The following true story illustrates how one couple could spend a portion of their savings bond investment without affecting its current value.

A couple in Michigan had over $400,000 in bonds representing half of what they had saved for early retirement. The wife called and was afraid that by cashing some of the bonds they might deplete their holdings. After having her investment analyzed, she discovered that the holdings were growing at over 5% a year. This meant they could redeem $20,000 a year and still have over $400,000 left for retirement.

If they cashed $20,000 a year, this couple wouldn't even touch their principal. If they chose to redeem $50,000 a year over the next ten years, they would still not deplete the entire portfolio. Educate your clients so that the fear of cashing does not keep them from using money that could be helpful to them.

The table below illustrates what could be cashed each year for the next ten, fifteen, or twenty years before bond holdings would be exhausted. The data assumes an earnings rate of 5%.

Remember: To effectively use this strategy, you should get the details on each bond and cash the bonds earning the lowest interest rates first. (See page 18 for an example and the last page of book to order.)

Table 13.1

Redemption at a Fixed Annual Amount

Current Total value of bonds	An annual redemption that will not affect your principal	An annual Redemption that will leave $0 in 10 years	An annual Redemption that will leave $0 in 15 years	An annual redemption that will leave $0 in 20 years
$10,000	$500	$1,295	$963	$802
$50,000	$2,500	$6,475	$4,815	$4,010
$100,000	$5,000	$12,950	$9,630	$8,020
$250,000	$12,500	$32,375	$24,075	$20,050
$500,000	$25,000	$64,750	$48,150	$40,100

Assumptions and Comments:

1. Overall holdings will grow at a constant rate of 5%. Bonds will vary and a specific analysis is recommended before invoking this strategy.
2. Money will be removed at the end of a given year.
3. This is the amount prior to taxes.

While some people won't cash any of their bonds, others rush in and redeem all of them at once.

Oops, the Opposite Extreme

A TSBI client from the Midwest wrote the following letter describing a case of the "panic and do something" method of bond ownership.

We had a close friend who cashed in all his bonds in the year of his retirement, and thus ended up paying a large amount of taxes, because he was so afraid that "he and his wife would not be able to make ends meet." This in spite of the fact that he was to receive a large pension, social security, plus investment income from other sources. We talked ourselves blue in the face, trying to convince him that he should wait and see if he would actually need the money from the bonds. He cashed them all and put the proceeds into a savings account where it is still drawing taxable interest of 3% or less!

For "conservative" people like this who suffer from retirement phobia, perhaps you could stress in your book that it is not a "do it now or never" situation, since savings bonds can be redeemed at least twice a year, or more often.... So the retiree can easily wait until the situation arises where he may actually need the money, and even then it may not be necessary to cash all the bonds at one time.

Well said.

Maximizing Family Wealth

Choosing which asset to liquidate can make a difference when it comes to maximizing family wealth.

A 65-year-old woman has $80,000 of stocks, $40,000 of which is capital gain that will be taxed if sold. She also has $80,000 of savings bonds that have $40,000 of untaxed interest income. Her tax bracket is 28% or less. She would like to sell one group of assets to supplement her retirement plans. The second group of assets will likely be passed on to her heirs.

Prior to 1998 if she were to liquidate either group of assets the federal tax would have been the same. In 1998, due to the new lower capital gains rate, she would pay $8,045 in federal taxes if she cashed the savings bonds and only $5,590 if she sold the stock. In 1998, her taxes would be $2,455 lower if she sold the stock rather than cashing in the bonds. At first glance, this appears to be the best approach and this would be true if these assets were treated the same at her death.

Note: In most states, there would also be tax on the capital gain of the stocks. The treatment of these two assets upon the death of the owner is different and has a significant impact upon family wealth. If this woman leaves the savings bonds to her heirs, they will inherit the liability for all the interest and will be taxed at their own rate when the bonds are cashed. If she leaves the stocks to her heirs, they are liable only for the gain in the value of the stock from the time of her death until the stock is cashed. The $40,000 gain that took place during her life is excused due to the stepped-up basis that the stocks receive. Assuming the heirs are in the 28% tax bracket, they will pay $11,200 more in taxes if they receive the bonds than if they receive the stocks. So the family unit is $8,745 ($11,200 minus $2,455) better off in this case if she cashes the bonds during her lifetime rather than selling the stock. By paying $2,455 more in taxes in 1998, her family will save $11,200 after her death.

As demonstrated, tax issues for savings bonds are unique and very different from those for stocks. The reporting of interest earned on bonds has probably been deferred (that is, it has never been reported and so the bond owner has never paid any tax on the accrued interest). If the holder dies while still in possession of the bonds, the children can, of course, inherit the bonds (unless he or she has named someone else as a co-owner or beneficiary). But, guess what else they inherit? The tax liability. If the interest is not reported on the last return of the deceased, or if it is not reported within the estate, the full amount of interest income becomes a liability to the recipients of the bonds when the bonds are cashed or reach final maturity. Consider another example:

Jonathan Smith, an only child, inherited $50,000 in bonds from his mother. The accrued interest on the bonds was $40,000. At the time of her death, his mom had been in the 15% tax bracket—and had been for the last decade of her life. Jonathan, a successful businessman, was in the 39.6% tax bracket. If the bonds had been cashed during her lifetime, the $40,000 could have been taxed at her 15% rate. (Note: This may have required cashing the bonds over several years to avoid reporting all the income in one year, which would have thrown her into a higher tax bracket.) The tax bill would have been approximately $6,000. If Jonathan cashes the bonds now, his tax rate will be used to calculate the tax, resulting in a bill of $15,840—almost $10,000 more than had his mother cashed the bonds.

From the standpoint of maximizing "family" wealth, it often makes sense to cash bonds in order to utilize the lower tax brackets of older parents.

There is one other strategy for Jonathan to consider. Upon his mother's death, he could disclaim his interest in the bonds (assuming the other heirs are Jonathan's children) and let the bonds be titled directly to his children. Once his children are 14 years old, they can cash the bonds and be taxed at their rate. This may result in an even lower tax bite. See Chapter 16, page 215, for further explanation. Consult with a competent attorney and/or CPA before attempting to invoke this strategy.

Quick Tips on Retirement

- Ask each client if they own bonds. If they do, determine how much they are worth now, the interest rates they are earning, how much deferred interest has not yet been reported, when they will stop earning interest, and how long they will earn interest at their current rates.
- For bond owners in low tax brackets that plan on leaving bonds to heirs in high tax brackets, cashing bonds during the life of the bond owner, rather than passing them on to heirs, can maximize the family wealth.
- Provide documentation for the family of any bond transactions. This will save the family from trying to "piece" together what action was or wasn't taken.

Table 13.2

Projected Value of Bond Portfolio at Retirement

Current Value of Bond Holdings and Average Projected Interest Rate	Value in 3 Years	Value in 5 Years	Value in 10 Years	Value in 20 Years
$10,000 at 4%	$11,262	$12,190	$14,859	$22,080
$10,000 at 5%	$11,597	$12,801	$16,386	$26,851
$10,000 at 6%	$11,941	$13,439	$18,061	$32,620
$25,000 at 4%	$28,154	$30,475	$37,149	$55,201
$25,000 at 5%	$28,992	$32,002	$40,965	$67,127
$25,000 at 6%	$29,851	$33,598	$45,153	$81,551
$50,000 at 4%	$56,308	$60,950	$74,297	$110,402
$50,000 at 5%	$57,985	$64,004	$81,931	$134,253
$50,000 at 6%	$59,703	$67,196	$90,306	$163,102
$100,000 at 4%	$112,616	$121,899	$148,595	$220,804
$100,000 at 5%	$115,969	$128,008	$163,862	$268,506
$100,000 at 6%	$119,405	$134,392	$180,611	$326,204
$250,000 at 4%	$281,541	$304,749	$371,487	$552,010
$250,000 at 5%	$289,923	$320,021	$409,654	$671,266
$250,000 at 6%	$298,513	$335,979	$451,528	$815,509
$500,000 at 4%	$563,081	$609,497	$742,974	$1,104,020
$500,000 at 5%	$579,847	$640,042	$819,308	$1,342,532
$500,000 at 6%	$597,026	$671,958	$903,056	$1,631,019

Table 13.3

Two Options for Cashing Bonds
that Stop Earning Interest Before Retirement

	Option #1: Cash all the bonds when they reach final maturity	**Option #2**: Exchange E & EE bonds for HH bonds, deferring all interest until after retirement. Then cash $4,000 of bonds per year over a five-year period.
Value of bonds at final maturity	$20,000	$20,000
Amount of accrued interest	$17,500	$17,500
Tax bracket	28%	Can take $4,000 a year and be taxed at 15% rate
Current year	Cash in all bonds, all interest is taxed at 28%. Received $20,000 cash. Pays $4,900 in taxes. The net amount left is $15,100.	Roll bonds over to HH bonds, deferring all interest until a HH bond is cashed. HH bonds pay interest at 4% per year.
Years one through five after retirement	$15,100 is put into the investment of choice to produce income. Assume a conservative investment, with a return of 5%.	Cash $4,000 of bonds each year. $3,500 will be treated as interest income and taxed at 15%. Annual taxes to be paid on savings bond interest is $525. Over five years this would be $2,625.
Income stream	$15,100 x 5% = $755 a year	HH bond interest + interest from other investment that pays 5% yr 1 $20,000 $800 + 0 =$800 yr 2 $16,000 $640 + 174 =$814 yr 3 $12,000 $480 + 348 =$828 yr 4 $8,000 $320 + 521 =$841 yr 5 $4,000 $160 + 695 =$855
Amount left at the end of five years	$15,100	$17,375

Important assumptions:
1. The bond owner will spend the income stream that is received each year.
2. In Option #1, after-tax money from bonds after tax is invested at 5%, a different interest rate (higher or lower) would obviously change the income stream.

In Option #2, the bond owner would save $2,275 in taxes by exchanging for HH bonds and creating a systematic redemption pattern over a five-year period. This tax savings is significant provided the other investment option yield is close to the HH bond yield.

Table 13.4

Anticipated Expenses in Retirement

Category	Monthly Cost	Annual Cost
Food		
Utilities		
Rent or Mortgage		
Transportation		
Medical/Dental		
Charitable Giving		
Savings Investment		
Insurance		
Entertainment		
Clothing		
Child Support/Alimony		
Gifts/Presents		
Loan Payments		
Misc.		
Other _____		
Other _____		
Total:		
Big Ticket Expenses	**Estimated Cost**	**Projected Date**
Car		
House/Condo		
Wedding		
Vacation		
Other: _____		

Chapter 14

TAXATION ISSUES FOR
U.S. SAVINGS BONDS

▶ *Common Tax Mistakes*
▶ *How and When to Report Interest Income*
▶ *Who Has to Report Interest Income*
▶ *Tax Concerns When Transferring Bonds*
▶ *Taxes upon Death*
▶ *Watch Out for Double Taxation*
▶ *Federal Estate Tax*
▶ *Gift and Inheritance Taxes*
▶ *Taxes in a Divorce*
▶ *Comments on the 1997 Tax Law Changes*
▶ *Quick Tips on Taxation*

Tax information.... A typical chapter on this exhilarating subject will cure even the worst case of insomnia. And quite frankly, this chapter contains quite a bit of technical information. However, you will find some things that should catch your attention: tax tips; how to avoid tax traps; and information designed to help you recognize options for your clients.

Due to the specific nature of this chapter, there is more technical language here than in other parts of this book. This change in style is necessary to thoroughly address these very important tax issues. The information presented in this chapter relies in large part upon the Internal Revenue Service Publications 17 and 550 and the Department of Treasury, Bureau of the Public Debt (BPD) publications, "Legal Aspects of U.S. Savings Bonds" and "The Book on U.S. Savings Bonds."

Throughout this chapter, whenever possible, a reader-friendly explanation accompanies the technical explanation.

Tax Starter: The interest on U.S. Savings Bonds is subject to federal income tax, but exempt from state, municipal, or local income taxes. (See Chapter 11 for possible exceptions when bonds are used for education.)

Common Tax Mistakes

When evaluating the status of your clients' savings bond holdings, taxation issues should be taken into careful consideration. This will ensure that they receive the maximum total return on their bond investment. Here are the four most common tax mistakes bond owners make:

Mistake #1: *Cashing savings bonds without first considering how much interest income will be reported and how much tax liability must be paid.*

Author's Note: I am amazed at how many calls I receive from financial professionals who need answers to two questions *after* advising a client to cash a large sum of bonds: (1) Did the redemption generate a taxable event? (2) If it did, is it a capital gain? Clients need to be advised prior to the transaction, for their benefit and yours.

Mistake #2: *Gifting or transferring bonds without knowing the tax consequences.*

Mistake #3: *Paying double tax: Unknowingly paying tax again on bond interest that had already been reported by a previous taxpayer.*

Mistake #4: *Lower-income retired persons cashing a large number of bonds in one year, causing a substantial portion of their Social Security benefits to be taxable.*

How and When to Report
Interest Income

In order to determine how interest on savings bonds is taxed, two questions must be answered:

1. Is the taxpayer using the cash basis or the accrual basis of accounting for income tax purposes?

2. What type of savings bond is being analyzed (E, EE, I, SN, H, HH)?

Cash Basis vs. Accrual Basis Accounting

The cash basis of accounting is used by the majority of individuals owning U.S. Savings Bonds. If your client is unsure whether they are on the cash or accrual method, most likely they are on the cash method. A bond owner must expend effort to elect the accrual method; if they have never specifically elected accrual, the cash method is the automatic *default*.

The difference between the purchase price of an E or EE bond and its redemption value is considered interest income under IRS Code. At some point in time, this income will have to be reported. When to include (or report) this interest income as taxable income (on a tax return) becomes an important issue. Interest on Series E and EE bonds and SNs is not paid on an annual or semi-annual basis to the bond holder. Instead, the interest is added to the value of the bond, which is paid when the bond is cashed. This is called interest accrual: The bond value is growing as a result of the interest being added to the value of the bond. The taxpayer on the cash basis method must choose between two methods of reporting interest income:

1. **Deferral**. Defer the reporting of the interest income until the year in which the E or EE bonds or SNs are cashed, disposed of, or reach final maturity, whichever comes first. If the bond owner does nothing, this is the option they have chosen. All the interest accrued will be reported in the year the bonds are cashed or reach final maturity.

2. **Annual Reporting**. Report the interest earned each year as it accrues on the bond.

Deferral Method

If a person has purchased a bond and done nothing about the interest, they have automatically chosen the deferral method. The interest the bond earns causes it to increase in value, but they choose not to be taxed annually on this interest because none has been received in the form of cash. It should be emphasized that when bonds are cashed under this method all the interest earned will be taxable in one year.

For older bonds, this could result in a significant amount of taxable income. There have been many instances when a taxpayer cashed bonds without taking into account the *timing* of the transaction for income tax purposes, looking only at the interest rates and liquidity issues. With proper tax planning, cashing bonds can be timed to minimize tax liability. This is especially important if the taxpayer has had an unusually high- or low-income year.

TAX TRAP: *When a bond reaches final maturity*, it not only stops accruing interest but *any interest accrued is taxable that year*. This is an easy item to overlook since bond owners receive no statement telling them that a particular bond has stopped earning interest. Thus many bond owners unknowingly hold bonds past final maturity. An advisor that is aware of client bond holdings can help clients avoid this trap. If your clients hold bonds that are over three years past final maturity, consult a professional tax advisor for your options.

If they discover this situation after their tax returns for the year have been filed, amended returns should be filed to properly report the bond interest income. It is extremely important to know when their bonds are scheduled to reach final maturity so that they can plan for the tax impact on the interest that has accrued on each bond.

Series E bonds issued before December 1965 reach final maturity forty years after their issue date. Series E bonds issued after November 1965 and all Series EE bonds and Savings Notes reach final maturity thirty years after their issue date. **Note**: A special rule permits further deferral if an E bond or Savings Note is exchanged for Series HH bonds no later than one calendar year after the bond reaches final maturity.

> A $1,000 Series E bond purchased in June 1958 for $750 has a current value of $7,381.20. If the owner has not already reported any of the interest on this bond, the entire difference of $6,631.20 is potentially taxable as interest income in 1998. The only way to avoid liability in 1998 is to exchange it for HH bonds.

TAX TIP: Taxpayers holding Series E bonds that are reaching final maturity should consider whether they want all the interest income taxed in the year of final maturity. If they do not, they should consider exchanging their Series E for HH bonds. The interest on HH bonds is paid every six months and is taxable in the year of receipt. However, the accrued interest on the Series E bonds that have been surrendered will continue to be deferred until the Series HH bonds are either cashed or mature. (See Chapter 9 for details on exchanging.)

Annual Reporting

Under the cash basis method, the bond holder may choose to report the annual increase in the bond's value (the interest income) on each year's tax return, rather than waiting until the bond is cashed or reaches final maturity.

If a taxpayer wants to report interest as it accrues, *all* interest accrued and not previously reported on all Series E and EE bonds and SNs must be included as income for the tax year in which this election is made (that is, the year the bond owner starts to report interest annually). In other words, if a taxpayer chooses this method, it will apply to all the bonds he or she owns. He or she cannot pick and choose which bonds to report annual interest on and which to leave alone. It should be kept in mind that once this method is chosen, an investor must continue to report the interest for all Series E and EE bonds and SNs they own and will own, unless he or she has secured permission from the IRS to change back to the deferral method. (See IRS Publication 17 for rules on changing methods.)

If the taxpayer is in a low tax bracket, it may make sense to be taxed on interest income each year as it accrues. In some situations, little or no tax is paid if the income is reported each year. If all the income is taxed in the year the bonds are cashed or in the year of final maturity, this "bunching" of the interest income may create a significantly higher total tax than if the tax had been paid each year. This would be especially true for a low-income taxpayer who held a large number of bonds which would come due in one tax year.

For example, a seventy-year old single taxpayer has bonds that are increasing in value at $3,000 per year. This taxpayer also has $5,000 of additional taxable interest income and receives $10,000 in Social Security benefits each year. She plans to cash the bonds in ten years.

> *Option 1*: She decides to report as interest income the $3,000 per year as the bonds increase in value. The total federal income tax due each year using 1998 rates and exemptions would total $0 per year, for a total federal income tax of zero for the ten years.

> *Option 2*: She chooses to defer the interest income on these bonds and pick up the whole $30,000 ($3,000 times 10 years) in year ten. The total federal income tax due would then be approximately $6,645, assuming that the tax rates are similar to 1998 rates.

In this simple situation, the difference in total federal income tax between options 1 and 2 is *$6,645*. This is a considerable amount of money. *The time value of money must be taken into account when making this calculation.* If there were taxes in Option 1, they would be paid earlier than in Option 2. In many cases the difference is so great that it is better to report the interest each year, even if it meant a small amount of taxes, rather than to defer it until year ten.

TAX TRAP: In the situation above, part of the tax increase occurs in year ten when all the bond interest income is taxable. A portion of the bond holder's Social Security benefits would become taxable, too, because she has a higher total income. This tax bite has surprised many a taxpayer receiving Social Security. In the example above, $2,380 of the $6,645 additional taxes was due to the fact that

$8,500 of the $10,000 Social Security benefits received that year were taxed at 28% because of the influx of bond interest.

When a bond owner chooses the annual reporting method for a minor, the first year's tax return should report all the interest income accrued through that tax year. In successive years the minor need only file when total income exceeds the IRS level for reportable income. In 1997, a minor who made less than $650 did not need to file (this limit is adjusted annually based on inflation). If your client chooses this method, please pay special attention to the double taxation discussion later in this chapter to ensure that they avoid reporting the interest twice.

Accrual Basis: E and EE Bonds

If the taxpayer has specifically elected the accrual basis for income tax purposes, the interest on E and EE bonds *must be reported as income each year* as the interest accrues.

H and HH Bonds

Interest on Series H and HH bonds is paid semi-annually by check or by direct deposit and must be reported annually for federal income tax purposes.

Who Has to Report
Interest Income

Co-owners

When bonds are held by co-owners, there is often a great deal of confusion as to who is liable for the tax on the interest when the bond is redeemed. The following chart adapted from "Legal Aspects On U.S. Savings Bonds" states the government's position. As discussed in Chapter 8, the actual reporting method used by the banks, Federal Reserve Banks (FRBs), and IRS when documenting Social Security numbers and names to generate a 1099-INT *does not* match the rules outlined on the next page:

Bond Purchaser	Tax Liability
"Dad" buys bond in the names of "Dad" and "Son" as co-owners.	Interest is income to "Dad," the person who contributed the purchase price.
"Dad" and "Son" buy bonds in co-ownership, with each contributing part of the purchase price.	Interest is income to both "Dad" and "Son," in proportion to their contributions to the purchase price.
"Son" and "Daughter" receive bonds in co-ownership as gift from "Dad."	Interest is income to both "Son" and "Daughter": 50% to each co-owner.
"Mom" buys a bond in the name of "Son," who is the sole owner of the bond.	Interest is income to "Son."

If a client buys a U.S. Savings Bond and adds a co-owner, the person whose funds were used to purchase the bond is the person who must pay the tax on the interest. This is true even if the purchaser lets the other co-owner redeem the bond and keep the proceeds.

The problem with this situation is that the organization that redeems the bonds will issue a 1099-INT to the person who redeems the bond despite the fact that, according to IRS rules, the interest is taxable to the co-owner who purchased the bond. Since the redeeming co-owner will receive a 1099-INT at the time of redemption, he or she is supposed to provide the purchaser/co-owner (who is to be taxed) with another 1099-INT, showing the amount of interest that is taxable.

The co-owner who redeemed the bond is called a "nominee." If a taxpayer receives a 1099-INT for interest received as a nominee, he or she should list that amount separately below the subtotal of all interest income listed on Schedule B. That amount should be labeled "Nominee Distribution" and subtracted from the interest income subtotal. This procedure ensures that the bond interest will not be added into the nominee's taxable income on his or her tax return.

Author's note: If the previous section seems confusing, don't be alarmed: It is absolutely confusing. The purpose of this chapter is to inform you of the rules—whether they make sense, are being enforced, or even have the capacity to be enforced. The author is not aware of a single case in which the redeeming, non-purchaser co-owner actually issued a 1099-INT to the first-named co-owner and sent a copy to IRS.

This rule leaves room for shady action, as you may realize. According to this rule, Uncle John buys bonds with his nephew as a co-owner. His nephew cashes the bonds and receives a 1099-INT. The young man then turns around and issues a 1099-INT to Uncle John and reports that same 1099-INT to IRS. Nephew is now "in the money" tax-free. The only drawback may be meeting up with his uncle in the near future.

Tax Concerns When Transferring Bonds

There are many situations when bonds are reissued in a different person's name or are reissued to eliminate, or add, a co-owner's name. The question that is often overlooked by the taxpayer and the financial advisor making these changes is, "Does this change cause tax consequences to any of the parties involved?" The answer could be "yes" or "no," depending on the situation. Any time a change in ownership due to the reissue of bonds is recommended, tax consequences must be considered.

Non-Taxable Event

The general rule is that *a change in the registration of a savings bond that does not change ownership will not result in shifting income tax liability*. Here are some examples when changes *do not* result in the shifting of income tax liability and, consequently, are *not* considered a disposition that requires the owner to report interest income.

1. The original owner who furnished 100% of the funds to purchase the bond has it reissued to name the original owner and another person as co-owner.

2. An original owner who furnished 100% of the funds for the bond's purchase has the bond reissued to eliminate a co-owner's name from the bond.

3. If bonds that two co-owners purchased jointly are reissued to each of the co-owners in the same proportion as their original contribution to the purchase price, neither co-owner has to report, at reissue, the interest earned before the bonds were reissued.

4. The owner can continue to postpone reporting the interest earned if a taxpayer owns Series E or EE bonds and
   a. transfers them to a trust, and
   b. is considered the owner of the trust, and
   c. the increase in value both before and after the transfer continues to be taxable to the owner.

5. If a person who owns Series EE bonds exchanges them for Series HH bonds, and the Series HH bonds are issued in the owner's name and that of another co-owner, the original owner must remain the first named person on the HH bonds.

Taxable Event

What action creates a taxable event? These following situations illustrate when a change in registration will cause the interest to become taxable at the time of the change.

1. If a person buys Series E or EE bonds entirely with his own funds and has them reissued in a co-owner's name alone, this is considered a disposition. In the year of reissue, the original bond purchaser must report all interest earned on these bonds that has not been previously reported.

2. If a person buys Series E or EE bonds entirely with his or her own funds and has them reissued in another beneficiary's name alone, this is considered a disposition. In the year of reissue, the original bond purchaser must report all interest earned on these bonds that has not been previously reported.

3. When a person who owns Series E or EE bonds gives the bonds to another person and reissues the bonds in the recipient's name alone, the reissuance of the bonds causes this to be a taxable situation for the person who makes the gift. Any previously unreported interest would have to be included in the giver's income in the year of the reissue. **Note**: Any interest earned on the bond after the reissue would be taxable to the recipient.

4. If a person transfers Series E or EE bonds to a trust and also gives up all rights of ownership, that person must report all the interest earned through the date of transfer (that has not been previously reported). This interest would be taxable in the year of transfer.

Additional note: Be aware that persons who inherit bonds may create taxable events by removing their names from the bonds. Contact your FRB or a professional tax advisor for more information before taking this course of action.

Taxes upon Death

Many financial professionals and bond owners expect that, as with other investment vehicles, a stepped-up basis applies to U.S. Savings Bonds. This is *not* the case. In fact, there is no automatic stepped-up basis for people who inherit or receive bonds upon the death of another individual (see glossary).

The manner of reporting interest income on Series E or EE bonds after the death of the owner depends on the accounting and income reporting method the decedent had used. If the bonds transferred at death were owned by a person who used the accrual method (or who used the cash method and chose to report the interest each year), the interest earned in the year of death must be reported on that person's final return. The beneficiary, or new owner, of the bonds includes as income only the interest earned after the date of death.

If the decedent had used the cash basis method (and had not reported the interest each year) and had bought the bonds entirely with his or her own funds, all interest earned before death must be reported in one of the following ways:

1. The surviving spouse or personal representative (executor, administrator, etc.) who files the final income tax return of the decedent can choose to include on that return all of the interest earned on the bonds before the decedent's death. The person who acquires the bonds then includes as income only interest earned after the date of death.

2. If Option 1 is not selected, the personal representative can report all of the interest in the estate and have it taxed at estate income tax rates. If this method is chosen, the interest should not be included in the decedent's final return.

3. If the bond owner does not choose either Options 1 or 2, the interest earned up to the date of death is *income in respect of a decedent* and it should not be included in the decedent's final return. *All of the interest earned both before and after the decedent's death is income to the person who acquires the bonds.* If that person uses the cash method and chooses not to report the interest each year, he or she can postpone reporting any of the interest until the bonds are redeemed or reach final maturity, whichever comes first. In the year that the interest is reported, he or she can claim a deduction for any federal estate tax paid for savings bond interest that was included in the decedent's estate.

In summary, the personal representative of the estate actually has three options.

1. Elect to report unreported savings bond interest on the final income tax return of the decedent under Code Section 454(a) of the Internal Revenue Code.

2. Report all of the savings bond interest in the estate. This can be done by electing to report all previously unreported interest in the estate or by reporting the interest as the bonds are cashed in the estate.

3. Distribute the bonds to the residuary beneficiaries (the person or persons entitled to the estate residue, whatever is left over from the estate assets and not specifically designated to a particular entity). In this case, the beneficiaries would report the savings bond interest when cashed or in the year an election is made to report previously unreported interest.

It should be noted that beneficiaries who receive bonds could choose to continue deferring interest or to report interest annually on the bonds they receive.

TAX TIP: To see which option provides the lowest amount of federal income tax liability when a large number of bonds are involved, the tax consequences for all three options must be calculated. If the decedent was in a low income bracket, it often makes sense to include the interest in the decedent's final return. See page 215, Table 16.1, for an example of this calculation.

Watch Out for Double Taxation

Can savings bond interest be double taxed by the Internal Revenue Service? You bet it can! While not intentional, it nonetheless happens due to the confusing nature of the rules. As mentioned earlier, the financial institution that redeems the bond will issue a 1099-INT to the person redeeming it. The 1099-INT shows the difference between the amount the holder receives and the purchase price.

Important note: There are several instances when the 1099-INT may show more interest than the taxpayer is required to include as income on the tax return. This may happen if:

The bond owner chooses to report the increase in the redemption value of the bond each year. The interest shown on his 1099-INT will not be reduced by the amounts previously included as income.

1. The bond owner received a bond from a decedent. The interest shown on his 1099-INT will not be reduced by the interest reported by the decedent before death, or on the decedent's final return, or by the estate on the estate's income tax return.

2. The interest shown on the investor's 1099-INT will not be reduced by the interest accrued prior to a transfer of bond ownership.

3. The bond owner redeems a bond on which he was named as a co-owner but which he did not buy; the person who had purchased the bonds previously reported interest accrued.

TAX TIP: Any taxpayer or personal representative who chooses to include interest on U.S. Savings Bonds in a year other than the year the bonds are redeemed should keep a detailed worksheet showing the years when the interest was taxed, as well as the amount of interest that was previously included as income. They should also keep copies of the federal tax returns (Form 1040 and Schedule B) on which this interest was reported. These records should be safely stored and available to the co-owners and to persons who may obtain the bonds through reissue transactions.

TAX TIP: If your client has received a sizable number of bonds from a decedent and paid tax on the interest for the entire 1099-INT issued, check prior records to see if any of this income had been previously taxed in the decedent's tax returns or in the estate returns. *If this has happened within the past three years, your client may be entitled to a federal income tax refund: They should file amended returns.* Better yet, now that you know what to look for, advise your client how to research the reported interest status of their bonds **before** they cash them.

Federal Estate Tax

In this section, we will provide a brief overview of estate tax rules as they relate to U.S. Savings Bonds. Much of the information in the next few sections is adapted from the Bureau of the Public Debts (BPD) publication, "The Book On U.S. Savings Bonds."

To begin, be aware that the estate is primarily liable for any estate tax that can be attributed to bonds that were owned by the decedent, even if they pass directly to a co-owner or beneficiary. In the event the estate fails to pay the estate tax, the persons receiving the bonds or other property could be required to pay the estate tax.

Determining Bond Values

When savings bonds are included for estate tax calculation purposes, it is important to include the proper value of the bonds. *The proper value is the redemption value of the bond on the date of the owner's death.* An increasing number of executors and attorneys are engaging the services of The Savings Bond Informer, Inc., rather than track down old redemption tables and calculate the value of each bond themselves (see a sample on page 18, ordering information on page 270).

Income Tax Deduction for Federal Estate Tax Paid

Under certain conditions, it is possible for a taxpayer to take a deduction for federal estate tax paid on savings bond interest that was included in a decedent's estate for tax calculation purposes. Assume, for example, that the taxpayer acquired the bonds either as surviving co-owner, beneficiary, or distributee of an estate of a (cash-basis) taxpayer who had not elected to report interest annually. At the time the accrued interest on the bonds is reported as income, the taxpayer would be entitled to claim a deduction on his or her federal income tax return for the portion of the estate tax paid that was applicable as a result of interest accrued during the decedent's lifetime.

It should be emphasized that this is not a dollar-for-dollar offset. It is a deduction that may or may not equalize the taxes, depending on the respective tax brackets of the estate and the income distributee. Computations in this area can be very complicated, and if you need the help of specialist, see the resource section (Chapter 18).

For more information on estate planning considerations, see Chapter 16.

Gift and Inheritance Taxes

Federal Gift Tax

Any one taxpayer who gives more than $10,000 to any other person in a calendar year must file a gift tax return (Form 709). The value of any U.S. Savings Bonds given would be included in this $10,000 computation. The value used for the gift would be the bond's redemption value on the date of the gift. A gift of savings bonds can be made in several ways and is subject to the federal gift tax.

One way to give savings bonds is to purchase the bonds in the name of the person who will receive them (the donee). Another way is to reissue the bonds in the name of the donee. If the value of the bonds given is under $10,000 per year per donee, no gift tax is due. If gifts of more than $10,000 are made in one year to one person, gift tax may be due. *The tax is imposed on the person making the gift*, not the person receiving the gift. (Remember that reissuing bonds to gift them will generate a taxable event to the person giving away the bonds even if the gift is under $10,000.)

A husband and wife may combine their gift tax exemptions to give a third person a total of $20,000 annually. The husband could give $20,000 in savings bonds to the third person without exceeding each spouse's $10,000 annual exemption. Both the husband and wife must consent to the gift splitting by signing gift tax Form 709, which must be filed for the year the gift is given.

Note: Starting January 1, 1999, the annual gift tax exclusion will be indexed annually for inflation.

State Gift Tax

U.S. Savings Bonds may be subject to state gift tax.

State Inheritance Tax

When bond ownership is transferred by the death of one owner, it is subject to state inheritance tax. In the case of co-owned bonds, many states follow the rule applied under the federal estate tax provisions measuring each co-owner's taxable interest by the amount each contributed to the purchase price. Other states view the bonds as held in equal shares by each co-owner and require that one-half of their value be reported as part of the gross estate of the co-owner first to die, regardless of who purchased the bonds. Contact your state's tax authorities for current information.

Taxes in a Divorce

If your client is going through a divorce and owns savings bonds, there are some areas that he or she will need to be advised on. This counsel should come prior to a settlement so that the financial terms of any settlement can account for some of the nuances of the savings bond holdings.

Valuing the Savings Bonds

A current value of the bonds should be used for placing a value on this asset group. The face value or the purchase price should **not** be used. A bond can be worth as little as half the face value or as much as seven times the face value. Ensure that the assets are valued with the "current value" (how much one would receive if the bonds were cashed in).

If your client is going to receive the savings bonds as part of the settlement and is named first on the bonds, having the bonds retitled into his or her name alone or with a co-owner or beneficiary of their choosing will not create a taxable event. The divorce decree should specify exactly which bonds would go to your client.

Negotiating Financial Terms

In negotiating the financial terms of the settlement, the client should note that it is unlikely that the interest has been reported as income yet (it has been deferred). Thus if the bonds were cashed and the client had to pay taxes, the after-tax value could be substantially less than the redemption value enabling an opportunistic attorney to "stick it" to unsuspecting parties in a divorce settlement. However, if your client gets "stuck," there may be a way to fight back (see examples below).

Example #1: The bonds are in the husband's name first with the wife named as the co-owner. The divorce decree has awarded the bonds to the wife. She can choose to say that either she was the principal co-owner (in which case she is responsible for the interest) or that he is the principal co-owner (in which case he is responsible for the interest). If she chooses to say that she is the principal co-owner, the bonds will be retitled to her without an immediate tax event. She can add a co-owner or beneficiary of her choosing. She must be named first on the retitled bonds. Form PD 1938 and a copy of the divorce decree should be sent directly to the BPD.

However, if she says that the husband is the principal owner (and here's where it can get a bit testy), the tax liability up to the point of the divorce will be assigned to him, whether he wants it, likes it, or even knows about it. She will furnish his name, address, and social security number, and the BPD will issue a 1099-INT to him. The bonds will be retitled to her based on the divorce decree.

Watch out for double tax in this situation. When the woman (or the person she has named as co-owner, or beneficiary if she is deceased) cashes the bonds, she will receive a 1099-INT for all the interest back to the date of purchase. She can deduct the amount previously reported (under the former husband's Social Security number). If she fails to deduct the amount previously reported, tax will have been paid twice on the same interest.

Example #2: The bonds are in the husband's name alone. The divorce decree has awarded the bonds to the wife. She should have the bonds retitled as soon as possible. Because the bonds were in the husband's name alone, he is considered the principal owner, and removing his name will create a taxable event for him. She can add a co-owner or beneficiary of her choosing. She must be named first on the retitled bonds. Form PD 1938 (See Figure 14.1, page 193) and a copy of the divorce decree should be sent directly to the BPD.

The tax liability up to the point of the divorce will be assigned to him, whether he wants it, likes it, or even knows about it. She will furnish his name, address, and

Social Security number, and the BPD will issue a 1099-INT to him. The bonds will be retitled to her based on the divorce decree.

Again, watch out for double tax in this situation. When the woman (or the person she has named as co-owner, or beneficiary if she is deceased) cashes the bonds, she will receive a 1099-INT for all the interest back to the date of purchase. She can deduct the amount previously reported (under her former husband's Social Security number). If she fails to deduct the amount previously reported, tax will have been paid twice on the same interest.

A couple in the Midwest divorced. More than $250,000 of bonds were awarded to the wife in the settlement and spelled out in the divorce decree. The bonds had over $200,000 of accrued interest that had not been reported as income up to the time of the divorce. Half the bonds were in the husband's name alone and the other half had his name first, with his former wife named as the co-owner. Upon receiving the bonds, she had them all retitled to remove the husband's name. She chose not to stick the husband with the liability for the bonds issued in co-ownership form (although she could have). She claimed that she was the principal co-owner (although she was named second) and those bonds were retitled without a taxable event. However, the bonds that were in his name alone, were retitled and a 1099-INT was issued to him for all the interest earned on those bonds up to the point of the divorce (he did not know that he was going to receive this 1099-INT). She was thus able to give him a little "parting gift" that cost him thousands of dollars in taxes not negotiated in the settlement.

Watch Out! Protect your client from a little-known operational practice that could cost him or her thousands of dollars. When a bond is retitled due to a divorce decree, the date of the retitling transaction, not the date of the divorce decree, is used for generating the dollar amount to appear on the 1099-INT.

Regardless of which party is your client, explore the savings bond tax consequences so that they can be factored into the settlement.

Comments on the 1997 Tax Law Changes

The Taxpayer Relief Act of 1997 was signed into law on August 5, 1997. It contains the biggest tax cut in more than sixteen years. There is nothing in the law that specifically changes the income taxation of U.S. Savings Bonds interest. However, there are several provisions where deductions and credits begin to be phased out at various adjusted gross income (AGI) levels for individual taxpayers.

When investors cash savings bonds, they increase their adjusted gross income by the amount of the taxable bond interest income. Without proper tax planning, this additional interest income could cause the taxpayer to exceed AGI phase-out limits. A list of the new deductions and credits (which may be affected when cashing bonds) are listed in the chart below. The numbers listed represent the level where AGI phase-out begins.

Table 14.1

1997 Tax Law Deduction and/or Credit Phase-Out Levels

Deduction or Credit Description	Levels at which adjusted gross income phase-out begins	
	Single Taxpayer	**Married Filing Jointly**
Hope credit for higher education	$40,000	$80,000
Lifetime learning education credit	$40,000	$80,000
Higher education loan interest deduction	$40,000	$60,000
Child tax credit	$75,000	$110,000
First time home buyer credit	$70,000	$110,000
Roth & educational IRA's	$95,000	$150,000

One additional factor that effects many investment decisions is the new lower capital gains rate. The maximum capital gains rate (for long-term capital gains) was reduced from 28% to 20%. Taxpayers in the 15% tax bracket may be entitled to 10% capital gains rate instead of the 20% rate. Consult with a tax advisor if you need to determine which rate applies to you. When considering an investment in savings bonds, remember that bond interest will be taxed at ordinary income rates, not at the capital gains rate and the advantages of a lower capital gains rate, are not applicable to bond interest.

For additional information on savings bond tax issues that should be considered in estate planning, see Chapter 16, page 213.

Quick Tips on Taxation

- Interest earned on savings bonds is subject to federal tax, but exempt from state and local taxes.

- When savings bonds are inherited or received due to a retitling, past records should be scrutinized to determine if any interest was previously reported. This can help the bond owner avoid double taxation.

- The redemption value of the bonds as of the date of death is the proper value to use when savings bonds are part of an estate.

- Bond owners who receive social security payments may cause a portion of their social security benefits to be taxed (that may have previously not been taxed) when cashing in a large amount of savings bonds in one year.

- Most bond owners have not reported interest annually, thus they must report the interest when the bond is cashed or when the bond reaches final maturity (exchanging for HH bonds can provide additional deferral).

The information in this chapter is based on current tax laws. Because tax laws are constantly changing, the information in these pages may become obsolete. It is not our intent to offer legal or tax advice. The author strongly suggests that anyone with a specific savings bond tax issue or legal issue consult a competent and experienced professional for advice.

Figure 14.1

Reissue Form PD F 1938

PD F 1938
Department of the Treasury
Bureau of the Public Debt
(Revised December 1996)

REQUEST FOR REISSUE OF UNITED STATES SAVINGS BONDS/NOTES
DURING THE LIVES OF BOTH COOWNERS

OMB No. 1535-0008

IMPORTANT: Before filling out this form, read instructions INCLUDING TAX LIABILITY NOTICE. You should be aware that the making of any false, fictitious or fraudulent claim to the United States is a crime punishable by imprisonment of not more than five years or a fine up to $250,000, or both, under 18 U.S.C. 287 and 18 U.S.C. 3571. Additionally, 31 U.S.C. 3729 provides for civil penalties for the maker of a false or fraudulent claim to the United States of an amount not less than $5,000 and not more than $10,000, plus treble the amount of the Government's damages as an additional sanction.

PRINT IN INK OR TYPE ALL INFORMATION

TO: Federal Reserve Bank

1. We are the coowners of the United States Savings Bonds described in item 6 on the reverse hereof and request reissue thereof in the form set forth in item 3 below to the extent of $_____ (face amount).

2. In support of our request, we hereby severally certify that:
   (The applicable statement(s) below MUST be completed - See General Instruction 1.)

   a. We are related to each other as _____ , AND
   (Give exact relationship)

      i. ☐ desire adjustment of our holdings by reissue of the bonds in the name of one of us as shown in item 3 below.

      ii. ☐ _____ is related to _____
   (Give present coowner's name)   (Give new registrant's name)

      as _____ ☐ a minor ——— years of age
   (Give exact relationship)   ☐ an incompetent

   b. _____ is
   (Give name of minor or incompetent in whose name, or for whose benefit, reissue is requested.)

      i. ☐ The bonds are a gift to the minor under a statute authorizing such gifts.

      ii. ☐ The legal guardian or similar representative has been appointed for the estate of the minor/incompetent.

   c. _____ has married since issue of the bonds.
   (Give present coowner's name)

   d. ☐ We have been divorced or legally separated from each other, or our marriage has been annulled, since issue of the bonds.

   e. _____ whose Social Security Account Number is
   (Name of principal coowner)

   ☐☐☐ – ☐☐ – ☐☐☐☐ , is the principal coowner of the bonds submitted herewith.

   He/she is responsible for any federal tax liability arising from this transaction (SEE TAX LIABILITY NOTICE in the General Instructions for a definition of the term "principal coowner").

   (Failure to furnish the information in item 2e. could cause rejection of the transaction.)

---

3. Registration: _____
   (First name)   ((Middle name or initial)   (Last name)

   _____
   (Number and street or rural route)   (City or town)   (State)   (ZIP Code)

   If a coowner or beneficiary is desired, complete the following line:

                                   ☐ coowner
   _____ as
   (First Name)   (Middle name or initial)   (Last Name)   ☐ beneficiary

4. Social Security Account Number of new owner or new first-named coowner: ☐☐☐ – ☐☐ – ☐☐☐☐

NOTE: If the transaction involves Series H/HH bonds, the new owner or new principal coowner must complete I.R.S. Form W-9, and it must be submitted with this request. (See Detailed Instructions, Item 4-c.)

5. If the new bonds are not to be delivered to address shown thereon, deliver them to:

   _____
   (Name)

   _____
   (Street Address)

   _____
   (City or Town)   (State)   (ZIP Code)

193

Chapter 15

REISSUING U.S. SAVINGS BONDS

- ▶ *Common Reissue Cases*
- ▶ *When Bonds Do Not Need to Be Reissued*
- ▶ *How to Reissue Bonds*
- ▶ *Who Can Help with the Forms: Cost for Assistance*
- ▶ *Which Reissue Transactions Create a Taxable Event*
- ▶ *What Reissue Forms Are Available and From Where*
- ▶ *Where to Send the Reissue Forms*
- ▶ *Quick Tips on Reissue*

"Reissue" is the term used by the Federal Reserve Banks (FRB) and the Bureau of the Public Debt (BPD) to describe a change of registration on a U.S. Savings Bond. The public often uses the word "retitle."

There are literally hundreds of variables that can affect any given reissue case. This chapter will attempt to deal with some of the most common cases and questions, as well as to present resources available to you and the bond owner.

As you will see in the following story, knowing the reissue options is vital to managing a bond investment.

The year was 1992, the state, Arkansas—and no, this story is not about a presidential election. A wife and mother had just suffered the loss of her husband. They had been married for several decades.

Over the years the couple had purchased U.S. Savings Bonds worth more than $200,000. Both of their names were on the bonds as co-owners. After several months, she began to attend to her financial matters and, in the process, took the bonds to her bank to ask what she should do. After listening to her situation, the bank representative told her she "must redeem the bonds."

Cashing the bonds would mean having to report $150,000 of interest income, with a minimum tax bite of over $50,000. Fortunately, this woman sought a second opinion and received an answer that was totally different from what the bank had told her.

A written analysis of this woman's bonds from The Savings Bond Informer, Inc., revealed that her bonds all had over eight years of interest-earning life left. She was listed as a co-owner on the bonds and in *no way* did she have to redeem them. She could simply get them reissued by having her deceased husband's name removed and her name put first, adding the co-owner or beneficiary of her choice. Reissuing, in this case, is not a taxable event. Once bonds are reissued they can be held to final maturity, exchanged for HH bonds which continues the tax deferment, or the bonds can be selectively redeemed over a period of years to spread the tax liability.

When appropriate, reissuing savings bonds can often provide advantageous financial and/or timing options to the bond owner. When seeking answers to reissue questions, never take the verbal advice of anyone without confirming it with an FRB or the BPD. (See Chapter 18 for phone numbers and addresses.)

Common Reissue Cases

There are hundreds of reasons why a bond might need to be reissued. Here are some of the most common:

- ✓ To add a co-owner or beneficiary to a bond that is presently in one name only (see Figure 15.1, page 203, PD F 4000)

- ✓ To change the beneficiary who is presently listed on the bond to co-owner (see Figure 15.1, PD F 4000)

- ✓ To correct an error in the way the issuing agent inscribed the bond

- ✓ To eliminate the name of a deceased co-owner or beneficiary and add another person in his/her place (see Figure 15.1, PD F 4000)

- ✓ To have the bonds retitled into a trust (see Figure 15.2, page 204, PD F 1851)

✓ To remove the name of a living person from the bond (**Note:** This may create a taxable event and may require the consent of the party being removed.)

When Bonds Do Not Need to Be Reissued

U.S. Savings Bonds do not need to be reissued for the following cases.

1. The government will not reissue Series E and EE bonds or Savings Notes for a change of address. The average American moves five to eight times over a thirty- to forty-year period. The address of the bond owner has no bearing on the bond. **Note:** Owners of Series H and HH bonds *are* required to notify the BPD so that interest account records can be updated. Current addresses are needed to deliver the forms 1099-INT to these bond owners.

2. A savings bond does not need to be reissued for a change of name due to marriage. The bond may still be redeemed with proper identification. The person named on the bond will sign her married name, "changed by marriage from," and then sign her maiden name.

3. If a bond is within two months of final maturity it will not be reissued by the BPD. Contact your local FRB if they will be processing your client's reissue as their guidelines may differ slightly.

How to Reissue Bonds

This section will present what is needed when advising clients regarding savings bond reissues. If you choose to have another financial professional handle your client's transaction, this will allow you to "look" over their shoulder.

1. Identify and order the proper reissue form. One of the FRB regional sites or the BPD can assist you. A brief description of each form is given at the end of this chapter.

2. Read the instructions that come with each form. While in small print, they address most of your questions.

3. Complete the form in full. The author suggests working on the form on a weekday during normal business hours, if possible. Then, if you or the client have a question or a quandary, a phone call to the BPD or your regional FRB can be made immediately. (They do not staff their phones

on the weekends or in the evenings.) Be prepared for a lengthy process; most forms require the serial number, issue date, face value, and registration information for each bond.

4. Secure the necessary signature guarantees, certifications, or notarizations.

5. Upon completion of the form, make a photocopy for your client's records.

6. Send the form, the bonds, and any additional paperwork required to the FRB, or take the bundle to the client's bank or your bank and ask that they forward it for you. (See "Where to Send the Reissue Forms," page 201.)

Special note: For most reissue transactions, the bond owner will *not* need to sign the bonds. In all cases, however, the appropriate person(s) must sign the form and their signatures must be certified, guaranteed, or notarized.

Who Can Help with the Forms: Cost for Assistance

The bond owner has several avenues for assistance when completing reissue forms. If doing it themselves, the bond owner can call the appropriate regional FRB site or the BPD. They will answer their questions, but it will be the owner's responsibility to enter the correct information onto the appropriate reissue form. There is no cost for this assistance.

If you and the client would prefer to have someone else complete the paperwork, there are several options.

Commercial Banks. Many banks will complete reissue forms for bond owners. The cost will vary from bank to bank because banks are free to create their own policies regarding what work they will do and how much they will charge. Many banks will not charge a fee to complete the reissue forms, although this may be limited to bank customers. Other banks will charge as much as $5 a bond: $1,000 if you have 200 bonds. Have your client ask for a quote in writing before they let them begin. **Caution:** If the bond holder's bank seldom completes reissue forms, this may not be the best choice. If the bank frequently processes reissue requests and there is no charge, that could be a winning combination.

Financial Professionals. With the increase in personal trusts and total financial planning, many people in the financial professional community provide assistance on reissue forms. As with banks, price and level of service will vary. If you and the client choose another financial professional (attorney, accountant, financial planner, or bank representative) to handle the reissue transaction, ask for a price quote in writing. If they are familiar with bonds, they should be able to estimate the time this task will take and provide a quote.

The Savings Bond Informer, Inc. They will complete all of the necessary paperwork prior to submitting a reissue transaction to the FRB. Call 1-800-927-1901 for a quote. Photocopies of all the bonds to be reissued are required to process the paperwork. **Author's note:** Although this service is not "marketed," it has grown largely as a result of financial professionals' dissatisfaction with the other options available to them.

Which Reissue Transactions Create a Taxable Event

Certain types of reissue transactions generate a taxable event for the bond owner. A detailed review of which transactions create taxable events is covered in Chapter 14, "Taxation Issues for U.S. Savings Bonds."

Holders ask one reissue question with regularity: "Can I remove my name and give my bonds to my grandchildren?" Yes, investors can, but do they want to? The case just described will create a taxable event for Grandpa. If he removes his name, he will have to report all the interest earned on the bonds up to that point in time, even though he will receive no money from the bonds.

Even worse, when a grandchild cashes the bond ten or twenty years later, he or she will receive a 1099-INT for all the interest it ever earned. If they do not know that Grandpa had reported some of the interest, they will report all the interest again. Thus, part of the interest will be taxed twice. (See Chapter 14, page 185, "Watch Out for Double Taxation.")

When reporting interest income from U.S. Savings Bonds, the specific bonds and serial numbers are not listed on the 1099-INT. The IRS has no easy way of knowing or tracking the fact that interest on a particular bond may have been reported twice.

Removing the principal co-owner (normally considered the first-named party, unless evidence can be produced to show otherwise) from a bond while that person is still living creates a taxable event for the principal co-owner.

Beware: A change in policy by the BPD will create problems for many bond owners. The previous operating policy ensured that the bond owner be notified if a transaction were to result in a taxable event. Now the BPD will simply process the transaction, and the investor may be the unhappy recipient of a 1099-INT.

This can be particularly damaging to some older Americans who are unprepared to receive a 1099-INT "after the fact."

What Reissue Forms Are Available and From Where

The following list of Public Debt (PD) forms are available from the five regional FRBs and from the BPD (listed in Chapter 18). Commercial banks may carry some of the forms, particularly the most requested.

PD F 1455
Request by Fiduciary for Reissue of United States Savings Bonds/ Notes

PD F 1851
Request for Reissue of United States Savings Bonds/Notes in Name of Trustee of Personal Trust Estate

PD F 1938
Request for Reissue of United States Savings Bonds/Notes During the Lives of Both Co-owners

PD F 3360
Request for Reissue of United States Savings Bonds/Notes in the Name of a Person or Persons Other Than the Owner (Including Legal Guardian, Custodian for a Minor Under a Statute, etc.)

PD F 4000
Request by Owner for Reissue of United States Savings Bonds/Notes to Add Beneficiary or Co-owner, Eliminate Beneficiary or Decedent, Show Change of Name, and/or Correct Error in Registration

PD F 5336
Application for Disposition—United States Savings Bonds/Notes and/or Related Checks Owned by Decedent Whose Estate is Being Settled Without Administration

Where to Send the
Reissue Forms

A regional FRB or the BPD processes all reissue transactions. Bond owners may submit their transactions to a local commercial bank for forwarding or they can mail directly to the appropriate regional FRB processing site. (See Chapter 18 for address and phone number.)

If the investor's commercial bank is an authorized issuing and paying agent (that means they sell and redeem bonds), they will probably be familiar with the appropriate regional FRB site and thus be willing to forward the transaction. The advantages of this are (1) the bond owner will save postage, and (2) should there be a problem, the bank can verify that the transaction was submitted. The disadvantage is that, in some cases, it may take a little longer to travel through the bank's mailing or delivery system.

The second option is for the bond owner to submit the transaction directly to the appropriate FRB regional processing site. If this option is chosen, it is best to send the transaction by registered or certified mail, return receipt requested. The receipt becomes important in case there is any problem locating the transaction: It will verify that the paperwork reached the FRB. Should special handling or rulings be required for a particular reissue case, the FRB may forward the case to the BPD.

Unfortunately, the need to reissue bonds can come at a time that is less than ideal, that is, after the death of a loved one. If bond owners are counseled to follow the suggestions in this chapter and are patient in pursuing the correct avenues of assistance, reissuing bonds can be a relatively easy, although time-intensive, process.

Quick Tips on Reissue

- Reissuing bonds, when appropriate, can provide advantageous financial and/or timing options to the bond owner.
- Reissuing bonds may or may not create a taxable event.
- Bonds do not need to be reissued for the following: a change of address, a name change due to marriage, or if the bond is within two months of final maturity.
- Reissue forms are available through the FRB and most banks.
- There are three option for having bonds reissued by a third party: (1) commercial banks, (2) other financial professionals, or (3) The Savings Bond Informer, Inc.

- The cost to have bonds reissued varies and, in some cases, can be free. Choose an organization/company that has had experience with this.
- Completed reissue forms can be sent to a regional FRB or the BPD or submitted to a local commercial bank for forwarding.

Figure 15.1

Reissue Form PD F 4000

PD F 4000
Department of the Treasury
Bureau of the Public Debt
(Revised May 1989)

REQUEST BY OWNER FOR REISSUE OF UNITED STATES SAVINGS BONDS/NOTES TO ADD BENEFICIARY OR COOWNER, ELIMINATE BENEFICIARY OR DECEDENT, SHOW CHANGE OF NAME, AND/OR CORRECT ERROR IN REGISTRATION

OMB No. 1535-0023

IMPORTANT: Follow instructions on the reverse in filling out this form. Any person who makes a statement on this form knowing it to be false, fictitious or fraudulent may be fined $10,000 or imprisoned for five years, or both.
PRINT IN INK OR TYPE ALL INFORMATION.

PAPERWORK REDUCTION STATEMENT: The completion of this form by any member of the public is voluntary. However, if completion of the transaction named below is desired, the information on this form must be provided.

To: Federal Reserve Bank
The undersigned hereby presents and surrenders for reissue the following-described United States Savings Bonds.
Total face amount _____

ISSUE DATE	DENOMINATION (FACE AMOUNT)	SERIAL NUMBER	INSCRIPTION (Please type or print names, including middle names or initials, social security account number, if any, and addresses as inscribed on the bonds.)

(If space is insufficient use continuation sheet on page 4, sign it and refer to it above -- or use Form PD 3500 for this purpose.)

I hereby certify that _____ is the principal coowner of any bonds registered in coownership form
(Name of coowner)

submitted herewith and is responsible for any federal tax liability arising from this transaction (SEE TAX LIABILITY NOTICE), and I hereby request that said bonds be reissued in the following form of registration:

Mr. ☐   Mrs. ☐   Miss ☐ _____
(First name)   (Middle name or initial)   (Last name)

Address _____
(Number and street or rural route)   (City or town)   (State)   (ZIP Code)

If a coowner or beneficiary is desired, complete the following line:

With Mr. ☐   Mrs. ☐   Miss ☐ _____ as { ☐ coowner ☐ beneficiary
(First name)   (Middle name or initial)   (Last name)

TAXPAYER IDENTIFYING NUMBERS (See General Instructions, page 3)

☐☐☐ - ☐☐ - ☐☐☐☐   ☐☐☐ - ☐☐ - ☐☐☐☐   ☐☐ - ☐☐☐☐☐☐☐
(S.S. No. - Owner or first coowner)   (S.S. No. - Second coowner or beneficiary)   (Employer Identification Number)

If new bonds are not to be delivered to address shown thereon, give delivery instructions here.

Name _____
Address _____
(Number and street or rural route)   (City or town)   (State)   (ZIP Code)

Reissue is requested for the reason(s) shown below:

┌─────────────────────┐
│ IN ALL CASES │
│ THIS FORM MUST BE SIGNED │
│ ON THE REVERSE SIDE │
└─────────────────────┘

1. ☐ To add a coowner or beneficiary.
2. ☐ To change present beneficiary to coowner.
3. ☐ To eliminate a living beneficiary and reissue the bonds in either single ownership form or with another person as coowner or beneficiary. (For Series E and H bonds and savings notes, the present beneficiary must consent on page 2.)
4. ☐ To reissue in the name of a surviving owner, coowner, or beneficiary or in his/her name and that of another person as coowner or beneficiary. (Proof of death of owner, coowner, or beneficiary named on Series E or H bonds or savings notes, and owner or coowner named on Series EE or HH bonds, must be furnished.)
5. ☐ Change of name by: (a) ☐ marriage   (b) ☐ divorce   (c) ☐ court order   (d) ☐ naturalization   (e) ☐ otherwise
   if (e) is checked, furnish explanation: _____
6. ☐ Correct error in registration. (See specific instruction No. 6) Provide following information:
   (a) The bonds were purchased by: _____
   (b) The funds belonged to: _____
   (c) Explanation of error _____

203

Figure 15.2

Reissue Form PD F 1851

REQUEST FOR REISSUE OF UNITED STATES SAVINGS BONDS/NOTES
IN NAME OF TRUSTEE OF PERSONAL TRUST ESTATE

PD F 1851
Department of the Treasury
Bureau of the Public Debt
(Revised April 1990)

IMPORTANT - Before filling out form, read instructions INCLUDING TAX LIABILITY NOTICE. Any person who makes a claim or statement on this form knowing it to be false, fictitious, or fraudulent may be fined $10,000 or imprisoned for 5 years, or both.
PRINT IN INK OR TYPE ALL INFORMATION.

TO: Federal Reserve Bank

BEFORE FILLING OUT THIS FORM, READ TAX LIABILITY NOTICE ON PAGE 3
(The applicable statement(s) below MUST be completed; see instructions.)

1. I (we) hereby request reissue of the bonds described on the reverse hereof in the form set out in item 5 below to the extent of

   $_____ (face amount).

2. In support of this request, I (we severally) certify that the trust estate described in item 5 below is a personal trust estate as defined in item 1 of the instructions on page 3 of this form, and

   a. ☐ was created by _____
   (Name(s) of owner or both coowners creating trust)

   b. ☐ was created by one coowner, _____
   (Name of coowner creating trust)

   c. ☐ was created by some other person and
      (i) ☐ I am (one of us is) a beneficiary of the trust.   ☐☐☐ – ☐☐ – ☐☐☐☐

      (ii) ☐ _____, a beneficiary of the trust, is related
      (Name)

      to_____ as _____
      (Name of owner or coowner)   *(Give exact relationship)*

3. You must check box a. or b. (SEE "TAX LIABILITY" SECTION OF INSTRUCTIONS):

   a. ☐ I (we) certify that, for federal income tax purposes, I (we) will be treated as owner(s) of the portion of the trust represented by any tax-deferred accumulated interest on the surrendered bonds.

   b. ☐ I (we) certify that, for federal income tax purposes, I (we) will <u>not</u> be treated as owner(s) of the portion of the trust represented by any tax-deferred accumulated interest on the surrendered bonds, and therefore, I (we) <u>will include</u> the tax-deferred accumulated interest in gross income for the taxable year in which the bonds are reissued to the trust. I (we) am aware that a 1099 INT will be issued and the interest will be reported to the Internal Revenue Service by the agent that processes the transaction. The interest which will be reported includes deferred interest on H/HH bonds as well as interest earned on E/EE bonds from the issue date until the date of reissue.

4. _____ is the principal coowner of any bonds registered in coownership
   (Name of coowner)

   form submitted herewith. (A principal coowner is a coowner who (1) purchased the bonds with his or her own funds or (2) received them as a gift, inheritance or legacy, or as a result of judicial proceedings, and has them reissued in coownership form, provided he or she has received no contribution in money or money's worth for designating the other coowner on the bonds.) The above-named principal coowners is responsible for any tax liability arising from the reissue transaction requested hereon and his/her Social Security Account Number is:

   ☐☐☐ – ☐☐ – ☐☐☐☐
   (Failure to furnish this information could cause rejection of the transaction.)

5. Form in which bonds _____
   are to be reissued.   *(Inscription: include name(s) of trustee(s), name(s) of creator(s) or trustor(s) and date of trust's creation)*

   _____
   (Address)

   (Taxpayer Identifying   ☐☐ ☐☐☐☐☐☐☐   ☐☐☐ – ☐☐ – ☐☐☐☐
   Number Assigned to
   Trust)   *(Employer Identification Number)*   *(Social Security Account Number)*

   If the new bonds are not to be   _____
   delivered to address shown   *(Name)*
   thereon deliver them to: _____
                                              (Street Address)

   _____
   (City or town)   *(State)*   *(Zip Code)*

OWNER AND OTHER REGISTRANTS MUST SIGN AND HAVE THEIR SIGNATURES CERTIFIED ON PAGE 2

(1)

204

Figure 15.3

Reissue Form PD F 1455

PD F 1455
Department of the Treasury
Bureau of the Public Debt
(Revised February 1994)

**REQUEST BY FIDUCIARY FOR REISSUE
OF UNITED STATES SAVINGS BONDS/NOTES**

OMB No. 1535-0012

> **"BONDS" AS REFERRED TO
> BELOW INCLUDES SAVINGS
> NOTES WHEN APPROPRIATE.**

> **IMPORTANT:** Follow instructions in filling out this form. You should be aware that the making of any false, fictitious or fraudulent claim to the United States is a crime punishable by imprisonment of not more than five years or a fine up to $250,000, or both, under 18 U.S.C. 287 and 18 U.S.C. 3571. Additionally, 31 U.S.C. 3729 provides for civil penalties for the maker of a false or fraudulent claim to the United States of an amount not less than $5,000 and not more than $10,000, plus treble the amount of the Government's damages as an additional sanction.
> **PRINT IN INK OR TYPE ALL INFORMATION**

TO: Federal Reserve Bank.
The following-described United States Savings Bonds totaling $ _____ (face amount), are surrendered for reissue as indicated below:

ISSUE DATE	DENOMINATION (FACE AMOUNT)	SERIAL NUMBER	INSCRIPTION (Please type or print names, including middle names or initials, social security account number, if any, and addresses as inscribed on the bonds.)

(If space is insufficient, describe additional bonds on back of this form.)

I/We hereby request that the above-described bonds, to the extent $ _____ (face amount), be reissued in the following form:

☐ Mr. ☐ Mrs. ☐ Miss ☐ Ms. _____
(See instructions 2. and 3.)

Address _____
(Number and street or rural route)   (City or town)   (State)   (ZIP Code)

Taxpayer Identifying No.
(See Instruction 4.) ☐☐☐ – ☐☐ – ☐☐☐☐   **OR**   ☐☐ ☐☐☐☐☐☐☐
(Social Security Account Number)   (Employee Identification Number)

NOTE: If the transaction involves Series H/HH bonds, the new owner must complete I.R.S. Form W-9, unless he/she executes a request on a September 1983 or later revision of PD F 4000, and the applicable form must be submitted with this request. (See instructions 2. and 4. (e).) and request that the new bonds be delivered to: _____

Address _____
(Number and street or rural route)

_____
(City or town)   (State)   (ZIP Code)

I/We certify that the person in whose name reissue is requested (in his/her own right or in a fiduciary capacity) is lawfully entitled thereto by reason of _____ and has agreed to such reissue.
(See instruction 5.)

Sign here _____   (____) ____ - _____
(Daytime Telephone Number)

> See **"TAX LIABILITY" in instructions
> as reissue may result in a Federal
> tax liability.**

(Show fiduciary capacity and include reference to estate or trust. See instruction 6.)

_____

_____

I certify that the above-named person, whose identity is well-known or proved to me, personally appeared before me on the _____ day of _____ ,19 ____ at _____ and signed the above request, acknowledging the same to be a free act and deed (and the free act and deed of said corporation).

*(OFFICIAL STAMP
OR SEAL)*

_____
(Signature and official designation of certifying officer)

_____
(Address)

SEE INSTRUCTIONS FOR PRIVACY ACT AND PAPERWORK REDUCTION ACT NOTICE

Chapter 16

TRUSTS AND ESTATE PLANNING

- ▶ *Whose Bond Is It?*
- ▶ *Succession Plans and Retitling*
- ▶ *Q & A about Trusts*
- ▶ *Estate Planning Options—Run the Numbers*
- ▶ *Savings Bond Abnormalities*
- ▶ *Quick Tips on Trusts and Estate Planning*

The increased use of trusts as part of the estate planning process raises a myriad of savings bond questions. This chapter will address many of the trust and estate planning issues involving savings bonds. While not every situation can be covered, the explanations will offer specific questions to ask your clients, options for when and how to report savings bond interest, and registration issues that impact estate planning.

Whose Bond Is It?

A recent caller indicated that they had found 32 bonds in an old photo album. The caller was not named on the bonds and in fact did not know either of the parties listed on the bonds. Is this a case of "finders keepers" or one where the rightful heirs can lay claim to an undiscovered asset?

The person(s) named on the bond is critical to the ownership of the bond. Discovering a lost treasure trove of bonds does not necessarily create a windfall for the finder. Only the person(s) named on the bond (or the legal representative of such) are generally entitled to the bond. In the event that the person(s) named on the bond is deceased, the bond will belong to the estate of the last deceased party. In the example above, the two parties listed on the bond were likely deceased and those handling the estate probably had no idea the bonds existed.

Suggestion: Whenever you are involved in an estate (either planning or settlement), request that the client (or legal representative if the client is deceased) file a lost bond claim form (PD 1048, see Chapter 10). There is no cost to file and this will determine if bonds are owned unbeknown to the client or the estate.

In another example, suppose your client was given bonds by her mother. On the bonds it named the mother and the mother's sister as co-owners. Mother died first and sister died two years later. The estate of sister is entitled to the bonds. Even though mother's money may have been used to purchase the bonds, and even though mother gave the physical bonds to your client, the sister was the sole owner of the bonds when she died and, therefore, her estate is entitled to the bonds.

Generally you must be named on a bond or be the personal representative of the estate of the person entitled to the bond in order to negotiate the bond. If a deceased person has no estate (except for savings bonds) or if the estate has already been settled, contact the Bureau of the Public Debt (BPD) for options. There is a form that heirs can submit to request payment or reissue of bonds that were not specifically designated by a will or other means.

Succession Plans and Retitling

Are the Bonds Titled to Achieve the Client's Succession Plans?

For many bond owners, the inscription on the bonds may not be aligned with their present desires concerning whom they want to receive the bonds. If the bonds were purchased several decades ago, relatives or friends from that time period could be named on the bonds as co-owners or beneficiaries. Now the bond owner may wish to have children or other important persons designated as recipients, rather than those previously named on the bonds. This can present some problems.

For Series EE, a beneficiary can be removed from a bond by the owner without the beneficiary's consent. However, for older Series E and Freedom Shares, a living beneficiary would have to "sign off," relinquishing his or her rights. Obviously, this can lead to some extremely awkward, if not impossible, situations (for instance, persons no longer on speaking terms, etc.). If the beneficiary is deceased, the benficiary's name can be removed by the owner of the bonds using form PD 4000. For all series of bonds, living co-owners can only be removed if they "sign off," relinquishing their rights to the bonds.

Each bond should be examined to determine which parties have a current or future interest in the security.

Who Is the Legal Owner of Each Bond?

U.S. Savings Bonds are a unique investment vehicle. Upon the death of an owner, the new owner is the surviving co-owner or beneficiary listed on the bond. U.S. Savings Bonds are registered securities. This means that the name of the person or entity entitled to the bonds is printed on the face of the bond.

The three most common forms of registration are outlined in Chapter 7, "Purchasing U.S. Savings Bonds": they are single ownership, co-ownership, and owner with beneficiary.

The maximum number of names on a bond is two, regardless of the form of registration. A bond cannot have two co-owners *and* a beneficiary. When registering bonds in a trust inscription or in the name of an organization, you cannot list a co-owner or beneficiary on the bond.

Help your clients by examining how each of their bonds is titled. Is the titling of the bonds consistent with the client's plans for that money?

Q & A about Trusts

The following questions are adapted directly from the BPD publication titled "Questions and Answers about Personal Trusts." Since a Federal Reserve Bank (FRB) or the BPD will normally handle the retitling of bonds into a trust registration, this will acquaint you with their view of what is and is not permissible. Call the BPD at 1-304-480-6112 to order the complete document.

Can United States Savings Bonds be registered in trust form?

Yes, the governing regulations authorize bonds to be registered to various types of trusts on original issue and permit reissue of bonds in the name of the trustee of a personal trust estate. Personal trust estates are defined in the governing regulations as trust estates established by natural persons in their own right for the benefit of themselves or other natural persons in whole or in part, and common trust funds comprised in whole or in part of such trust estates. Bonds registered in the names of individuals may be reissued to a personal trust estate as follows:

a. A bond registered in single ownership form may be reissued during the lifetime of the owner to name as new sole owner the trustee of a personal trust estate which was created by the owner or which designates as beneficiary either the owner or a person related to him/her by blood (including legal adoption) or marriage.

b. A bond registered in co-ownership form may be reissued during the lifetime of both co-owners to name a trustee of a personal trust estate created by either co-owner or by some other person if either co-owner is a beneficiary of the trust or a beneficiary of the trust is related by blood or marriage to either co-owner.

c. A bond registered in beneficiary form may be reissued during the owner's lifetime to eliminate the names of the owner and the beneficiary and to name as new owner the trustee of a personal trust estate which was created by the owner or which designates as beneficiary either the owner or a person related to him or her by blood (including legal adoption) or marriage.

What is the proper form of trust registration for savings bonds?

The governing regulations require that the registration of a bond issued to a trust must include the name(s) of the trustee(s) and an adequate identifying reference to the authority governing the trust. This means that the registration should include the name(s) of the grantor(s) of the trust, the name(s) of the trustee(s), and the date of the trust instrument (the date the trust was created). There are generally two basic forms of registration for personal trusts:

a. When the trustee and the grantor are the same person, bonds are registered "*Trustee's name,*" trustee under declaration of trust dated "*date of trust instrument.*" For example, if Jason Brown created a trust on June 6, 1991, naming himself as trustee, the bonds would be registered, using appropriate abbreviations, as follows: "Jason Brown Trustee Under Declaration of Trust Dated June 6, 1991."

b. When the trustee and the grantor are not the same person, bonds are registered "*Trustee's name*," under agreement with "*Grantor's name*," dated "*date of trust instrument.*" For example, if Jason Brown created a trust on June 6, 1991, naming Betty Brown as the trustee, the bonds would be registered, using appropriate abbreviations, as follows: "Betty Brown Trustee Under Agreement with Jason Brown Dated June 6, 1991."

Variations may be made depending on the particular circumstances of the case; for example, there may be co-trustees or the trust instrument may be an indenture of trust rather than a declaration of trust. Additional examples of authorized registrations are available from the BPD.

An individual should be designated by the name he or she is ordinarily known by or uses in business, including at least one full given name. It is important to note that the complete name of each trustee and grantor must be shown. For example, bonds should not be registered "John & Mary Brown Co-Trustees…"; the surname must be shown for each trustee and grantor even if they both have the same surname.

When more than one trustee is acting, what connective should be used in the registration of bonds?

When co-trustees are to be named in the registration of bonds, the connective "AND" is normally used to link the names of the co-trustees. All of the trustees are then required to jointly execute any subsequent request for payment or reissue of the bonds. However, if the trust instrument permits each trustee to act independently and without the consent of the other trustee, the connective "OR" may be used in the registration of bonds. When the connective "OR" is shown in the registration, any one trustee may execute a subsequent request for payment or reissue without the consent of the other trustee(s). Unless otherwise specifically requested, the connective "AND" is used in the registration of bonds.

Whose Taxpayer Identification Number should be shown in a trust registration on bonds?

The registration of bonds for a trust must include the social security account number or employer identification number which the grantor ordinarily uses to identify the trust. Depending upon the specific circumstances, this may be the grantor's social security account number or an employer identification number assigned to the trust by the Internal Revenue Service.

What is the difference between an Irrevocable Trust and a Revocable Trust, and which one has to be included in the bond registration?

An Irrevocable Trust is one which the grantor may not rescind or cancel, while a Revocable Trust is one which the grantor has the option of rescinding or canceling. The governing regulations do not require that either term be included in the registration of bonds.

How can existing bonds be reissued to a trust?

In order to reissue bonds into a trust form of registration, a PD F 1851 must be signed by all persons named in the current registration of the bonds, in the presence of an authorized certifying officer. If Series EE bonds or Series HH bonds are involved, the consent and signature of the beneficiary is not required. If one of the persons named on the bonds is deceased and he or she would have been required to join in completing the PD F 1851 if he or she were still living, then the PD F 1851 must be supported by a certified copy of his or her death certificate.

Special attention should be given to completing item 3 on the PD F 1851 as it concerns tax matters. If block (a) is checked, the reissue will not be taxable. However, if block (b) is checked, the transaction will be considered taxable for the owner or principal co-owner. In that event, the interest earned on any Series E bonds, Series EE bonds and Savings Notes from the date of issue until the date of receipt of the request for reissue, as well as any deferred interest on Series H bonds and Series HH bonds, will be reported to the Internal Revenue Service under the owner or principal co-owner's social security account number.

Are there any additional requirements for reissue of Series H and Series HH bonds to a trust?

Yes. When Series H/HH are reissued to a trust, the new owner must certify that the taxpayer identification number furnished is correct and that he or she is not subject to backup withholding. Certification is accomplished by completing an IRS Form W-9 or a similar certification statement on the PD F 1851 (reissue application). If a social security account number is furnished to identify the trust, the Form W-9 must be completed and signed by the person to whom the social security account number belongs. If an employer identification number is furnished to identify the trust, one of the trustees must complete and sign the Form W-9. The certification statement is incorporated in the most recent versions of the PD F 1851; therefore, if the person whose certification is required has joined in signing the PD F 1851 and provided the appropriate taxpayer identification number on that form, a separate Form W-9 will not be required.

The furnishing of direct deposit information is a condition of reissue of Series HH bonds bearing issue dates of October 1989 and thereafter. An SF 1199A must be completed for bonds dated October 1989 and thereafter which are submitted for reissue. One of the trustees must complete an SF 1199A providing the appropriate information for direct deposit of the semi-annual interest payments.

Both of the above-mentioned forms are available at financial institutions in the United States.

Where should requests for reissue be sent?

The bonds, PD F 1851, IRS Forms W-9 and SF 1199A (if appropriate), and any required evidence should be submitted to the nearest FRB. Most local banks can assist in this process.

What evidence is required to redeem bonds belonging to a trust and where can they be redeemed?

When bonds are registered in the name of a trust, they are payable to the trustees upon their request. Nothing other than a properly certified request for payment is required. Local banks are authorized to redeem bonds registered in the names of the trustee(s) of a personal trust.

Estate Planning Options—Run the Numbers

Remember rule number one of estate planning: There is an estate plan regardless of what the client thinks. Either they have devised a plan that reflects their personal desires and wishes, or the state and federal taxing agencies have devised one for them. Obviously if they plan now they have control and options for minimizing estate taxes. That way, most of the assets that they worked a lifetime to accumulate will be passed on to the heirs or charities of their choice.

Estate planning and all its intricacies are beyond the scope of this book. However, the unique tax characteristics of savings bonds need to be examined and incorporated into the "bigger picture." The remainder of this section will give you some items to consider during this process, including how income taxes and estate taxes interact with estate tax calculations.

The following example illustrates some of these considerations. The purpose is to show how different choices can change the amount of assets that end up in the hands of the heirs of a 75-year-old taxpayer. Here are the facts of the case, followed by possible courses of action (both before and after Mr. Taxpayer's death), and their outcomes.

Facts

1. Mr. Taxpayer's assets include a personal residence valued at $250,000; certificates of deposit totaling $150,000, invested at 6%; and Series EE savings bonds totaling $800,000, of which $400,000 is accumulated interest.

2. Mr. Taxpayer receives annual Social Security benefits of $10,000.

3. Taxable interest each year is $9,000 ($150,000 x 6% interest rate).

4. 1998 federal tax rates, personal exemptions, and standard deductions are used in tax calculations.

5. All proceeds from cashing any savings bonds, less applicable income taxes, are invested to earn 6% taxable interest.

6. All bonds are cashed on the last day of the year for figuring future year taxable interest income from proceeds.

7. A combined state and local income tax rate of 4% is used to calculate taxes.

8. Mr. Taxpayer dies on the last day of the fifth year of tax calculations.

9. No state inheritance tax or final expenses have been taken into account.

Options

1. Wait until the taxpayer's death and elect to have all of the $400,000 of accumulated savings bond interest taxed on the *taxpayer's final return* and then calculate the estate tax.

2. Systematically redeem $200,000 of bonds each year for four years before the taxpayer dies, generating $100,000 of taxable bond interest each year, and then calculate the estate tax.

3. Redeem all the bonds in the estate and have the *estate pay tax* on the $400,000 of accumulated interest in the estate and then figure the estate tax.

4. Wait and distribute the bonds to the beneficiaries (outside the estate) and have the *beneficiaries report the interest* when they cash the bonds.

The result of each option is shown below.

Table 16.1

Savings Bond Estate Planning Options

	Option 1	Option 2	Option 3	Option 4
Asset value left in estate before estate taxes:				
Personal residence	$250,000	$250,000	$250,000	$250,000
Other investments	150,000	150,000	150,000	150,000
Investments from bonds cashed	655,935	661,000	800,000	0
Savings bonds	0	0	0	800,000
Total estate value	$1,055,935	$1,061,000	$1,200,000	$1,200,000
Less federal income tax in estate	0	0	(157,215)	0
Estimated federal estate tax after $229,800 credit for year 2002	(138,933)	(141,010)	(198,000)	(198,000)
Net assets to distribute to heirs	$917,002	$919,990	$844,785	$1,002,000
Less estimated income tax for heirs when bonds are cashed (28% federal)	0	0	0	(112,000)
Plus personal tax saved when deducting federal estate tax paid on accumulated savings bond interest included in estate (28% federal)	0	0	0	**+44,800***
Projected net value to heirs after taking into account tax effect	$917,002	$919,990	$844,785	$934,800*

*If heirs are in the 36% federal tax bracket, however, the projected amount left for them would be about $13,000 less than $934,800. If the heirs are in the 39.6% bracket, the amount would be about $18,500 less. This assumes that the heirs itemize deductions and can use the federal estate tax-paid deduction (and that their other income does not limit their itemized deductions).

Use of the Qualified Disclaimer

In some estate planning situations, it may be beneficial for an heir to disclaim the assets. This is especially true when the beneficiary already has substantial assets and has a taxable estate without adding assets from a parent's or relative's estate. Careful consideration should be made before this decision is finalized because it is irrevocable and certain conditions must be met. This is another area where it is important that a competent estate tax advisor be consulted.

Internal Revenue Code Section 2418 defines a qualified disclaimer for federal estate tax purposes as an irrevocable and unqualified refusal by a person to accept an interest in a property if the following four conditions are met:

1. The refusal or disclaimer is in writing,

2. The written disclaimer is received by the transferor of the interest, his legal representative, or holder of the legal title to the property to which the interest relates not later than the date which is nine months after the later of...

   a. The day on which the transfer creating the interest in such person is made, or
   b. The day on which such person attains the age of 21,

3. The person has not accepted the interest or any of its benefits, and

4. As a result of such refusal, the interest passes without any direction on the part of the person making the disclaimer and passes either to the spouse of the decedent or to a person other than the person making disclaimer.

Example: A single person with assets of $1,000,000 receives a call from an attorney stating a distant relative has left her $200,000 in savings bonds. Before receiving the bonds, this single taxpayer has a projected federal estate tax of approximately $153,000. After the $200,000 in bonds have been received and included in her estate, her new projected federal estate tax is $235,000, an increase of $82,000. In this case, the net effect of the transfer of the $200,000, after the estate taxes, is $118,000 ($847,000 vs. $965,000). Since over 40% of the inheritance could potentially be taxed within her estate, this is a situation where a disclaimer might be considered. It is very important that all facts be thoroughly examined before the final decision to disclaim is made, because disclaiming is irrevocable.

One of the key facts when considering whether to use the disclaimer is, "Who will receive the assets if I disclaim them?" This can be answered by the decedent's will or living trust. The will treats the person disclaiming the property as if that person had died before the actual decedent (i.e., whose will or trust is being administered). The will or trust would then determine who would receive the assets on that basis. It is important to know how assets will be transferred even though the disclaiming person has no control over it, because that information will likely have an impact on the decision to disclaim.

Has any of the accrued interest been previously reported? There are several scenarios where the interest on savings bonds may have been previously reported without the current owner's knowledge. The specific history of each bond must be researched in an effort to avoid double taxation. If some or all of the interest has been previously reported, this amount can be deducted from the total amount of the 1099-INT when reporting the interest on the owner's tax return. Typical cases are provided in the following:

1. The owner of the savings bonds reported the interest income annually.

2. The interest was reported on the last tax return of the decedent, the bonds were subsequently reissued.

3. The bonds were reissued removing the first named co-owner. At the time of reissue, the original owner had to report the interest earned up to the point of the transfer of ownership.

Although time consuming, it can pay great dividends to research the history of each bond to determine if some or all the interest has been previously reported.

Savings Bond Abnormalities

Although mentioned at various intervals throughout the text, savings bond abnormalities (i.e., how bonds behave differently than other assets) are summarized here for your benefit:

- Savings bonds do not receive a stepped-up basis.

- If a first-named living owner of a bond wants to transfer or gift bonds (meaning removal of their name from the bond), it will normally create a taxable event (some exceptions may apply if they claim, under penalty of perjury, that they are not the principal owner—consult to the BPD for more information).

- Several different scenarios can result in double taxation (see page 185).

- If savings bonds remain unclaimed (after the death of a bond owner), the government gets to keep the money. At present they are under no obligation to attempt to contact bond owners or heirs.

Quick Tips on Trusts and Estate Planning

- Examine how your client's bonds are currently titled. The registration of the bond determines who is entitled to the bond.
- Do not assume all of a client's bonds are titled the same way: each bond needs to be examined.
- When determining how to incorporate the savings bonds into the estate planning process, the following are important: tax bracket of bond owner, anticipated tax bracket of heirs, size of the estate, tax treatment of other assets within the estate, and titling of the bonds.

The information in this chapter is based on current tax laws. Because tax laws are constantly changing, the information in these pages may become obsolete. It is not our intent to offer legal or tax advice. The author strongly suggests that anyone with a specific savings bond tax issue or legal issue consult a competent and experienced professional for advice.

Chapter 17

THE NEW I BOND

- ▶ *What Is an I Bond?*
- ▶ *How Does It Work?*
- ▶ *How Will It Perform?*
- ▶ *How Does the I Bond Compare to the EE Bond?*
- ▶ *Analyzing the I Bond's Potential*
- ▶ *Hey, Where's the Protection?*
- ▶ *I Bond Sales Predictions*
- ▶ *Purchasing the I Bond*
- ▶ *Quick Tips on the I Bond*

Who says big government never changes? For the first time in eighteen years they have launched a new product—the I bond. Much of the attention at the initial press conference was devoted to whose pictures will be on the bonds. And although this is a nice feature, I'd rather have a $100 dollar bill than a $1 dollar bill, regardless of whose picture is on it. Thus, this chapter goes into more detail about what type of investment the I bond is.

What Is an I Bond?

An I bond is a new savings bond issued by the Treasury designed to offer protection from inflation. By linking the return of the bond to an inflation index the bond is always guaranteed to earn a fixed rate above the inflation rate. It is sort of a hybrid between the Treasury Inflation Indexed Bond and the EE bond. As you will see later in this chapter, the I bond contains elements of both.

This bond represents yet another way for the government to borrow money to finance the debt. Since the debt stands at over $5.5 trillion one can understand the need for some creative new financing options. The trick for the Treasury is to offer a product that is attractive enough to gain investor's confidence and money, while keeping the cost of financing the debt as low as possible. If the entire debt were financed at 5%, the interest expense alone would top $275 billion a year. A 1% savings in the cost of borrowing represents a savings of over $55 billion a year in interest expense.

The I bonds were made available September 1, 1998. They can be purchased at banks where EE bonds are currently sold. Clients will also be able to purchase them through payroll deduction (although not immediately, it will depend on how quickly a company can be "set up" to handle the purchases).

The Window Dressing

Each I bond features an outstanding American—someone who has made significant contributions to our society. While this information may appear to be unnecessary detail, it will serve to keep you "in the know" should a client identify his or her bond by the name of a person, e.g., "How long will my Martin Luther King bond earn interest?"

The following is a list of the honorees and the denomination of the bond on which their likeness appears, as quoted from a press release the government used to introduce the new bonds:

- *$50 I bond: Helen Keller, a noted author and advocate for individuals with disabilities. Ms. Keller was also responsible for Braille becoming the standard for printed communication with the blind.*

- *$75 I bond: Dr. Hector Garcia, a leading advocate for Mexican-American veterans rights, an activist in the Latino civil rights movement, and the founder of the American GI forum.*

- *$100 I bond: Dr. Martin Luther King, Jr., one of the nation's most prominent civil rights leaders. Dr. King was also a minister and Nobel Peace Prize recipient.*

- *$200 I bond: Chief Joseph-Nez Perce Chief, one of the greatest Native American leaders.*

- *$500 I bond: General George Marshall, U.S. Army Chief of Staff during World War II, Secretary of State and Defense, author of the Marshall plan, and Nobel Peace Prize recipient.*

- *$1,000 I bond: Albert Einstein, a physicist and creator of the theory of relativity. Einstein was also a Nobel Prize recipient for physics.*

- *$5,000 I bond: Marian Anderson, a world-renowned vocalist and the first African-American to sing with the Metropolitan Opera.*

- *$10,000 I bond: Spark Matsunaga, a former U.S. Senator and Congressman and World War II hero.*

How Does It Work?

The I bond is an accrual bond. At redemption, the bond owner will receive the purchase price plus the gain in interest that has been added to the value of the bond. Here are the details:

Purchase price: All I bonds will be purchased at face value. A $100 I bond will be purchased for $100. This eliminates the confusion about when a bond will reach face value. In other words, you purchase at face value and interest is added to the bond to increase the value of the bond.

Minimum and Maximum Purchase: A bond owner can purchase up to $30,000 per person per year. This is double the limit available on EE bonds. Bond owners can purchase the limit of both EE bonds and I bonds in the same year. And, by adding co-owners, they can increase the amount purchased each year. (See "Purchasing" later in this chapter for registration options.) The minimum purchase is $50.

Denominations: The I bond is available in the following denominations: $50, $75, $100, $200, $500, $1,000, $5,000, and $10,000.

Where to buy: I bonds can be purchased at any financial institution (bank, savings & loan, credit union) that sells EE bonds. Not all financial institutions participate in the bond program. They can also be purchased directly through a FRB (see Chapter 18 for the closest one). The purchase application can be downloaded from the government web site at www.publicdebt.treas.gov.

Where to redeem: An I bond must be held for six months before cashing it. It can be cashed at any financial institution that handles savings bonds. If the person redeeming is not a customer of that institution, the institution can limit the redemption to $1,000 per person per day. These bonds can also be cashed at many FRBs. (See Chapter 18 for the FRB closest to you and call for instructions before proceeding with the transaction.)

Penalties: If an I bond is cashed before it turns five years old, three months of earnings are forfeited. This means if the bond is redeemed at four-years, six months old, four-years and three-months worth of interest is received.

Tax Issues: Interest earned on I bonds is treated as interest income and is reported in the year the bond is redeemed or reaches final maturity (thirty years), whichever comes first. A bond owner can elect to report interest annually (see Chapter 14 for the same conditions that apply to series E and EE bonds). Interest is subject to federal tax, but exempt from state and local taxes.

Maturity: The I bond will earn interest for thirty years. Since it is purchased at face value, bond owners don't need to be concerned about how long will it take to reach face value. The I bond does not have an original and an extended maturity period (like the older E and EE bonds).

Interest Rates: There are two components to the I bond interest rate: the fixed rate and the semi-annual inflation rate.

The fixed rate is assigned at purchase and remains with the bond for its life. The first fixed rate for bonds issued September and October 1998 is 3.4%. For bonds issued November 1998 through April 1999 the government lowered the fixed rate to 3.3%. Although a new fixed rate can be announced each May and November (for new issues of I bonds), don't look for much change. Future fixed rates, that will govern future purchases of the I bond, will probably vary slightly—less than 20 basis points up or down—if at all.

The semi-annual inflation rate is, as the name suggests, the portion of the bond's earnings that are tied to the inflation rate. The CPI-U (consumer price index-urban consumers) is the measuring stick used to determine this rate. The rate is published every May and November and is based on a time period that starts two months back from the publishing date and then measures the preceding six months for change in the CPI-U.

For instance: The initial fixed rate is 3.4% (for bonds purchased September and October 1998). The initial semi-annual inflation rate was based on measuring the CPI-U from October 1997 to March 1998. The CPI-U increased 62 basis points. When annualized with the fixed rate of 3.4% that provided a rate of 4.66% which was used to determine the earnings for the first six-month period. A $1,000 I bond purchased in September or October 1998, would be worth about $1,023.30 after six months. However, if the bond is cashed before five years have passed, three months of interest are forfeited, so the redemption table will show this bond valued at only $1,011.65 after the first six months.

When the increases occur: The I bond will increase in value monthly and interest is compounded semi-annually (at six-month intervals from the issue date). At every semi-annual period the values and rates are "locked" in. This means that the government cannot use a retroactive feature or any other gimmick to "take away" previous rates or earnings, as was possible under the old EE bond rules.

How Will It Perform?
A Historical View of Inflation: What If?

The CPI-U has increased at an annual average of 3.425% over the last sixteen years; 3.4% over the last ten years; 2.58% over the last five years; 2.5% over the last three years; and only 1.7% over the last twelve months. The only time there was no inflation in the last sixteen years was a six-month period in 1982/83.

The inflation rate at the time the I bond was introduced is one of the lowest rates we have seen since 1982/3. The first CPI-U number that was used is based on an annual rate of about 1.26%. Had the I bond been available in the mid-1980s it would have averaged an annual return of about 6.8% (based on the initial fixed rate of 3.4% and an average increase in the CPI-U of 3.4%).

How Does the I Bond Compare to the EE Bond?

Now that two savings bonds are available for purchase at the same time, "Which one is better (if any) for the client? How do they compare?"

Similarities

As mentioned earlier in the chapter, the new I bond is a hybrid of the EE bond and the Treasury Inflation Indexed Notes/Bonds. Here are the features shared by both the EE and I bonds:

- They earn interest for thirty years.

- They are interest accrual bonds. That is, the interest is added to the value of the bond and does not have to be reported as income until the bond is cashed or reaches final maturity, whichever comes first.

- They increase in value monthly, and the interest is compounded semi-annually.

- If not held five years, three months of interest is forfeited.

- You must hold them at least six months before cashing.

- The rates that affect the bond are published each May and November.

- They can be purchased at a bank or through payroll deduction.

- They can be used "tax free" for education if all the conditions are met. (See Chapter 11 for a list of the conditions.)

Differences

- Interest on EE bonds is based on 90% of five-year Treasury yields and the rate is reset every six months. Interest on I bonds has two parts: a fixed rate assigned at purchase that remains for the life of the bond and an inflation indexed rate that is adjusted every six months based on changes in the CPI-U.

- The purchase price for EE bonds is one-half the face value; purchasers pay $50 for a $100 face value. Purchase price for I bonds is face value; purchasers pay $100 for a $100 bond.

- The purchase limitation on EE bonds is $15,000 purchase price, per person, per year. The I bond limitation is $30,000 purchase price, per person, per year.

- EE bonds can be exchanged for HH bonds. The I bond cannot be exchanged for HH bonds.

Analyzing the I Bond's Potential

While the I bond is new, how would it perform if we examined it in a historical context? The following analysis covers data back to 1982—the year that the bond program introduced the market rate program. For the purposes of our discussion, we will assume that we could buy both the EE bond and the I bond under their current rules throughout the last sixteen years. Which one would have been the better deal?

Here is what was discovered: The grid shows a comparison of the bonds over a five-, ten-, and sixteen-year period. And because the fixed rate component of the I bond is critical to its performance, the grid reflects three assumed fixed rates—3%, 3.25%, and 3.5%. The first rate actually published for the I bond is 3.4%.

The initial fixed rate of 3.4% is assigned for the life of the I bond for those issued September and October 1998. The fixed rate was lowered to 3.3% on November 1, 1998. Thus, 3.3% will be the fixed rate for any I bond purchased November 1998 through April 1999.

Table 17.1

Average Annual Earnings
Rate Comparison of an I-bond and EE bond

	I Bond, 3.0% fixed rate	I Bond, 3.25% fixed rate	I Bond, 3.5% fixed rate	EE Bond, 90% of 5-Yr. Treasury
Last 5 years	5.23%	5.48%	5.74%	5.52%
Last 10 years	6.10%	6.35%	6.60%	6.18%
Last 16 years	6.21%	6.47%	6.74%	7.20%

© 1998 by The Savings Bond Informer, Inc. All Rights Reserved.

Here is the difference represented in basis points.

Table 17.2

Average Annual Basis Point Comparison
+/- Comparison of I Bonds and EE Bonds (May 1997 Rules)
Positive Number is EE Greater Than I; Negative Number is I Greater Than EE

	I Bond, 3.0% fixed rate	I Bond, 3.25% fixed rate	I Bond, 3.5% fixed rate	EE Bond, 90% of 5-Yr. Treasury
Last 5 years	29	4	-22	5.52%
Last 10 years	8	-17	-42	6.18%
Last 16 years	99	73	46	7.20%

© 1998 by The Savings Bond Informer, Inc. All Rights Reserved.

When measuring the performance of each bond over the last sixteen years, the EE bond would have done better in comparison to the I bond's assumed rates. In fact, it would have taken a fixed rate of 4% for the I bond to equal the performance of the EE bond. However, when looking at the last five or ten years, it would have taken a fixed rate of only 3.25% to equal the performance of the EE bond.

If we compare the last five- and ten-year periods of the five-year Treasury yields to the CPI, we see that the bonds would have performed about the same if the I bond's fixed rate had been 3.25% (basis point differential of 4 and –17). Consequently, anything less than 3.25% and the consumer would have been better off purchasing the EE bond. Anything at 3.25% or over, and the I bond would have been more attractive.

At the moment the I bond was first offered, it would have taken a fixed rate of about 3.75% (plus the inflation adjustment) to equal the EE bond rate of 5.06%. However, lower Treasury yields at the time of writing will likely pull the EE bond rate down 10 to 40 basis points for the next six-month period. Also, slightly higher inflation (about 1.7% annualized) will push the I bond earnings higher (10 to 50 basis points higher) for the next six-month period. Thus the initial fixed rate of 3.4% (and the new fixed rate of 3.3%, published November 1, 1998) on the I bond looks very competitive with the EE bond both for the short- and long-term.

Summary of Comparison: The key to determining which bond is the best buy is the fixed rate on the I bond. The fixed rate of 3.3% (at the time of writing) makes the I bond a pretty good bet under conditions where inflation is a moderate 2% to 4% and interest rates are low. Historically, during periods where interest rates are high (9% to 12% on five-year Treasury yields), the EE bond would have performed better.

Hey, Where's the Protection?

Although the I bond is dubbed as protection against inflation—meaning that the purchasing power is not eroded by inflation—it does not take into account another arm of government that may wipe out the very protection that bond owners thought they had.

In some cases, the tax paid on I bond income will eliminate the inflation protection. This is true if the percentage of the owner's earnings that is funded by the fixed rate component of the I bond is less than his or her tax rate.

Consider this scenario: Suppose a bond owner in a 36% tax bracket purchases an I bond. Assume the I bond has a fixed rate of 3% and we are experiencing an inflation rate of 6%. The fixed rate represents 33% of the total earnings. (To illustrate this for a one-year period, assume there is no three-month penalty when cashing prior to five years.)

At the end of the year, the investor has earned 9% on a $1,000 I bond. She cashes the bond and receives $1,090. The interest earned ($90) is subject to federal tax at her rate of 36%. The tax bill comes to $32.40. That means the net return after taxes was $57.60. With an inflation rate of 6%, she needed $60 just to keep pace with inflation. In some cases investors will not get the protection they thought they might be getting.

Although this example would be a considerable change from the economy at the time of writing, we know that it is historically possible. **Remember:** If the tax rate is greater than the percentage of the return covered by the fixed rate, the client will be in jeopardy of losing the expected "inflation protection."

I Bond Sales Predictions

Since the news broke that the I bond would go on sale, bond owners and investors have been asking, "Should I buy the I?" Ultimately we will see what they have decided as we watch the sales figures over the next twelve to eighteen months. The author expects a slow start for three reasons:

1. Those that are interested in the I bond are still unfamiliar with this new product. They will want to learn more about it and watch its performance before they buy.

2. Inflation is at one of the lowest points it has been in the last fifteen years. The idea of protection from something that, at the time of writing, does not seem threatening will deter some would-be buyers.

3. The backbone of savings bond sales is the payroll deduction plan. Since many companies will not offer the I bond right away, it may not be possible for those who want to purchase through their companies, to do so. The new EasySaver program offers an alternative form for systematic purchase (see Chapter 7, page 82).

However, if inflation starts to rise, this is a product that will be positioned to capture dollars that will be exiting from investments that are negatively affected by inflation. Also, a turbulent stock market may cause investors to seek a safer haven for their money (like for instance July through September 1998).

Purchasing the I Bond

The following points will help you advise clients who decide the I bond is for them:

- It is purchased at face value.

- When deciding how to register the bonds, the client has three options:

  Single Ownership: Purchase in one name alone

  Co-Ownership: Two names are listed on the bond with the word "or" between the names. Either co-owner can cash without the other's consent. The first named co-owner is generally considered the principal owner of the bond.

Single Owner with Beneficiary: One owner is named on the bond and one beneficiary. The word "POD" will precede the beneficiary's name. ("POD" means "Pay on Death.") The bond does not have to be cashed upon the death of the owner (see Chapter 15 for more on retitling bonds). The beneficiary can only cash the bond with a valid death certificate for the first-named owner.

- Purchasers should be ready with the proper spelling of the name(s), social security number(s), and addresses of those they want named on the bonds.

- Buy late in the month. The bond actually begins to earn interest as of the first day of the month you purchase.

- If purchasing as a gift, ask for a gift certificate for the recipient. The bond will be mailed to the address indicated at time of purchase. The certificate lets the gift recipient know who bought the gift.

- If the bond is purchased through a bank, make sure the bank teller understands that you want to buy the I bond, not the EE bond.

- If the new bond is not received within four weeks, contact the organization where the bond was purchased.

- For clients who want to buy the limit ($30,000 per person per year) each year, remember that the limit is reset every January 1st. Example: They can purchase the 1998 limit in December 1998 and then purchase the 1999 limit in January 1999.

- Call 1-800-USBONDS for the interest rate on new purchases.

Quick Tips on the I Bond

- The new I bond was first issued September 1, 1998, and is a Treasury product designed to offer protection from inflation.
- The interest rate has two parts: a fixed rate that remains with the bond for life, and an inflation adjusted rate that will change every six months.
- If we are in a period of high inflation, a purchaser in a high tax bracket may not get the inflation protection expected.
- The I bond is purchased at face value. It will always be worth at least face value.
- Interest is deferred until the bond is cashed or until the bond reaches final maturity, whichever is first.
- Interest earned is subject to federal tax, but exempt from state and local taxes.

Part IV

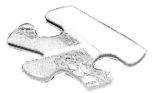

Resources

_____ Chapter 18

WHERE TO GET HELP

▶ *Organizations that Perform Savings Bond Services*
▶ *Common Savings Bond Activities: Who Do You Call?*
▶ *Forms, Publications, Tables, and How to Get Them*

This chapter is intended to guide you to the most established and reliable sources of savings bond information. The resources listed range from information tables for the do-it-yourselfer to full-service companies that will analyze bond holdings for you and your client. The first section lists the organizations, what they do, and how to contact them. The next section lists savings bonds activities and assigns the appropriate resource(s) to each. Finally, a listing of savings bond publications is given, with ordering information.

Organizations that Perform
Savings Bond Services

Government

The Bureau of the Public Debt (BPD)

There are two major offices within the BPD: the U.S. Savings Bond Marketing Office and the U.S. Savings Bond Operations Office.

U.S. Savings Bond Marketing Office

> Department of the Treasury
> Bureau of the Public Debt
> U.S. Savings Bond Marketing Office
> Washington, DC 20226
> www.savingsbonds.gov

The purpose of this office is to promote the sale and retention of U.S. Savings Bonds. Formerly known as "The Savings Bond Division," this office handles government responsibilities for the annual savings bond drive campaign activities. It also handles many of the press releases and media contacts for changes in the bond program.

U.S. Savings Bond Operations Office

> Bureau of the Public Debt
> U.S. Savings Bond Operations Office
> P.O. Box 1328
> Parkersburg, WV 26106-1328
> (304) 480-6112
> www.savingsbonds.gov

At the operations center, hundreds of activities critical to the bond program are maintained and performed. The Bureau has several "bond consultants" staffing phones each day from 8:00 a.m. to 4:30 p.m., Eastern Standard Time, Monday through Friday. The bond consultants are well-versed in a variety of savings bond issues and can answer questions or, at least, point you in the right direction. They do not have an 800 number. The phone number listed will put you into their automated answering system.

This is one government agency that the author has used extensively. They are taxed with thousands of calls each month, so it can be difficult to get through. Be persistent, though—the staff is knowledgeable and helpful.

The Savings Bond Wizard

The Savings Bond Wizard is a software program developed and distributed by the Treasury Department. The features of the program include redemption values and accrued interest. You input the issue date, series, denomination, and serial number.

Since bonds have been a do-it-yourself investment for fifty-seven years, a program that values bonds without using the government redemption table is viewed by many as a quantum leap forward. And from what the government did offer, it is. The danger is that many people think that the value of a bond is all they need to know.

The Wizard provides a quick way to determine the bond's value; it helps you keep an inventory of bond information; and the updates are offered at no charge. However, don't be mislead into thinking that it provides all you need to know about a savings bond investment. Note that the program does not provide a complete analysis, which should include interest rates, increase dates, dates bonds enter into extended maturities, date bonds stop earning interest, and a rating of projected future performance.

If you decide to use the Wizard, use it in conjunction with the information in Chapter 2 to build a complete analysis of your clients bond holdings. If you prefer to have a complete analysis done for your client, along with a rating of their bonds, see the last page of this book.

To obtain the program either buy it on 3.5" disk from the government for $17 or download it for free from www.publicdebt.treas.gov.

Federal Reserve Banks (FRB)

> As fiscal agents of the United States, Federal Reserve Banks and Branches (FRB) perform a number of activities in support of the Savings Bond program, including issuing, redeeming, and reissuing Savings Bonds and Notes. In recent years, both the Bureau of the Public Debt and Federal Reserve Offices have recognized that there would be benefits associated with consolidating certain Saving Bond activities....
>
> —Department of Treasury, BPD, Part 353, 3-80, 6th Amendment (3-4-94)

To help point you to the correct FRB, here is the list of consolidated sites as explained in the above publication:

Federal Reserve Bank of New York
Buffalo Branch
Attn: Savings Bond Examinations
P.O. Box 961
Buffalo, NY 14240-0961
(716) 849-5165

This office serves the reserve districts of New York and Boston. The geographic region served includes the following states or portions of states and/or territories: CT, MA, ME, NH, NJ (northern half), NY (city & state), RI, VT, Puerto Rico, and Virgin Islands.

Federal Reserve Bank of Kansas City
P.O. Box 419440
Kansas City, MO 64141-6440
(816) 881-2919
This number will also service Spanish-speaking customers.

This office serves the reserve districts of Dallas, San Francisco, Kansas City, and St. Louis. The geographic region served includes the following states or portions of states and/or territories: AK, AR, AZ, CA, CO, HI, ID, IL (southern half), IN (southern half), KS, KY (western half), LA (northern half), MO, MS, NE, NM, NV, OK, OR, TN (western half), TX, WA, WY, UT, and GU (Guam).

Federal Reserve Bank of Minneapolis
P.O. Box 214
Minneapolis, MN 55480
(612) 204-7000

This office serves the reserve districts of Minneapolis and Chicago. The geographic region served includes the following states or portions of states: IA, IL (northern half), IN (northern half), MI, MN, MT, ND, SD, and WI.

Federal Reserve Bank
Pittsburgh Branch
P.O. Box 299
Pittsburgh, PA 15230-0299
(412) 261-7900

This office serves the reserve districts of Cleveland and Philadelphia. The geographic region served includes the following states or portions of states: DE, KY (eastern half), NJ (southern half), OH, PA, and WV (northern panhandle).

Federal Reserve Bank of Richmond
P.O. Box 85053
Richmond, VA 23285
(804) 697-8370

This office serves the reserve districts of Richmond and Atlanta. The geographic region served includes the following states or portions of states: AL, DC, FL, GA, LA (southern half), MD, MS (southern half), NC, SC, TN (eastern half), VA, and WV (except northern panhandle).

Non-Government

Commercial Banks

A thorough description of the bank's relationship to the bond program is discussed in Chapter 3. Here is a summary of the highlights:

- ✓ U.S. Savings Bonds are not a bank product.

- ✓ Surveys indicate that they are not a reliable source of information for questions that deal with analyzing bonds, such as interest rates and timing issues.

- ✓ Many banks assist bond owners with processing paperwork when seeking to reissue or exchange savings bonds, although fees can be as high as $5 per bond on a reissue transaction.

When obtaining savings bond information from a bank, make sure you get it in writing.

The Savings Bond Informer, Inc.

The Savings Bond Informer, Inc.
P.O. Box 9249
Detroit, MI 48209
(800) 927-1901 for a free packet and description of services
www.bondinformer.com

This fee-based company was founded by the author in 1990 to service bond owners and financial professionals whose clients own U.S. Savings Bonds.

Products and Services:

- The book for investors—*Savings Bonds: When to Hold, When to Fold and Everything In-Between*

- The book for professionals—*U.S. Savings Bonds: The Definitive Guide for Financial Professionals*

- Savings Bond Statements—Customized analyses of bond holdings, including exclusive rating system, interest rates, increase dates, values, and maturity dates

- Paperwork completion for savings bond reissue and exchange transactions

- Consultations and analysis

- Seminars for bond owners and financial professionals

The primary service of this organization is to create bond statements. An example can be found on page 18. An order form and price list can be found on the last page of this book.

Important note: Consultations without ordering a bond statement are available for a fee of $35 per fifteen-minute segment (minimum billing $35). Credit card payment is required at the time of call.

National Bond & Trust, Co. (NBT)

National Bond & Trust, Co.
P.O. Box 846
Crown Point, IN 46307
(800) 426-9314 (**For business inquiries only**)
www.nbtco.com

NBT supplies a full range of support services to companies that would like to start a payroll deduction program and those that would like to consider service alternatives for the program they already have. They essentially do what the government does in terms of conducting a bond drive. However, as a private company, they add additional elements of service and product to the mix.

In many companies, accounting, payroll, or human resources staff handles savings bond activities. Having an outside firm handle the administrative aspects of the program reduces a company's cost of having a bond program.

NBT also offers a unique insurance component to participants of the bond program. This component is not mandatory for the bond owner

Other Financial Professionals

This next category is very difficult to characterize. There are hundreds of specialty areas within each profession, as you well know. Although a financial professional may be highly trained, often that training has not included a study of U.S. Savings Bonds. This section is neither an endorsement nor an indictment of any particular group of financial professionals but an attempt to give you some bond-related background for each.

Accountants: Accountants may be very helpful in evaluating tax issues related to bond holdings. Before you engage the services of an accountant, find out if he or she has had previous experience with bond-related work and establish a fee before proceeding.

Accountant, Professional Counsel: Brent Dawes is a CPA who specializes in tax questions, research, and counsel on savings bond issues. He is also a contributor to this book (see Chapter 14). His fee is $35 per fifteen minutes, minimum fee $35 (charged to Visa or Mastercard at the time of call). This may be helpful to other financial professionals or bond owners who have a particular situation that calls for tax advice. The firm is American Express Tax and Business Services, Inc; their number is (800) 851-2324. Tell them that you are calling for tax counsel regarding U.S. Savings Bonds.

Attorneys: Many attorneys handle savings bond transactions, most commonly for estate settlement or trust purposes. Many law offices use the services of The Savings Bond Informer, Inc. to value bonds, others calculate the data themselves. Fees vary depending on the complexity of the case and the pricing structure of the individual office.

Financial Planners: It is the author's assessment that a good financial planner will take the time to understand a client's financial situation and evaluate his or her status before they offer counsel. Related to savings bonds, a planner should be able to provide written details about a savings bond investment. The written analysis will allow the client to compare savings bond holdings to other options and will contribute to an accurate net worth statement.

Common Savings Bond Activities: Who Do You Call?

The following is a list of common bond activities. Listed after each activity are the organizations or institutions to contact regarding that particular activity. The address and phone number for many of the organizations can be found in the preceding pages of this chapter.

Buying Bonds

Financial Institutions: Most commercial banks still sell U.S. Savings Bonds, but call before you go. In our phone survey of banks, we discovered several banks that no longer sell bonds. (Some savings & loans and credit unions also sell U.S. Savings Bonds.) Commercial banks will take an application and money and forward it to a regional FRB site for processing.

Federal Reserve Banks: An application to purchase U.S. Savings Bonds can be mailed to any FRB. The check should be payable to "The Federal Reserve Bank." Include your telephone number so they can reach you if there are any questions.

Payroll Deduction: To buy bonds through payroll deduction, your company must have a Payroll Savings Plan in place. Printing and mailing the bonds is handled at a regional FRB, another qualified issuing agent, or through another party such as National Bond & Trust. (Typically, no fees are charged to deal with the organizations; however, the level and type of service they offer may differ.)

Redeeming Bonds and Exchanging Bonds

Financial Institutions: Most commercial banks will redeem and exchange U.S. Savings Bonds, but, again, have the client call first. In our phone survey of banks, we discovered several that no longer provide these services. Some savings & loans and credit unions redeem U.S. Savings Bonds. Commercial banks have a specific set of guidelines to follow when redeeming bonds. Cases that they are unable to process will be forwarded to the FRB or the BPD. H and HH bonds are forwarded to the FRB. A client redeeming less than $1,000 in E or EE bonds, with proper identification, should receive the money the same day.

Federal Reserve Banks: FRBs will act as a redemption site for bond owners, though the request may be forwarded to another FRB for processing. Expect to wait three to five business days for payment. Call for specific instructions from the FRB you intend to use.

Determining the Value of Your Bonds

Author's note: If the client has fifty bonds or more, none of the free services listed below will read the redemption values over the phone or in person. But they will mail a redemption table. Why? Consider it from a bank's perspective. It's Friday afternoon, hundreds of customers are cashing payroll checks, and your client's needs will consume at least one hour of a teller's time—for which the bank will not make any money. Savvy banks will direct bond owners to the customer service area so that their financial representative can pitch the bank's own products. Remember that bank information on savings bond interest rates and timing issues is often inaccurate (see Chapter 3).

Commercial Banks (no fee): The level of service here may vary, depending on the customer's status. Most banks will provide values for a reasonable number of bonds without any qualms. Larger numbers of bonds may not be serviced for the reasons noted above.

Federal Reserve Bank (no fee): FRBs will mail a redemption table and may price a couple of bonds over the phone.

Bureau of the Public Debt (no fee): BPD will mail a redemption table to you. The best free information is the Savings Bond Wizard, a program available on the government web site that can be used to provide the value of bonds at no cost.

The Savings Bond Informer, Inc. (fee). TSBI will produce a statement of savings bond holdings which includes values as well as interest rates, timing issues, explanation of maturity dates, accrued interest, and a rating for each bond. You supply the month/year of purchase (issue date), face value, and series. Refer to the last page of this book for prices.

Tables for Analyzing Bonds On Your Own

There are several current government tables you will need to analyze the details of savings bonds. There is no charge for these tables.

- ✓ Table of Redemption Values for Series E and EE bonds and SN
- ✓ Guaranteed Minimum Rates Table
- ✓ Interest Accrual Dates
- ✓ Earnings Report
- ✓ United States Savings Bonds/Notes Earnings Report

The **FRB** will mail most of the items; the **BPD** will mail any or all of the items. Contact:

Bureau of the Public Debt
P.O. Box 1328
Parkersburg, WV 26106-1328
(304) 480-6112
or download the information at www.savingsbonds.gov

Reissuing Bonds

Federal Reserve Bank: FRB regional sites accept all reissue transactions. Customer service representatives will answer questions related to reissue transactions. Some cases are forwarded to the BPD.

Commercial Banks: Banks may have the forms needed to complete reissue transactions. Some will help complete the forms, but there may be a fee involved, possibly as much as $5 a bond.

Bureau of the Public Debt: (304) 480-6112. Bond consultants staff phones from 8:00 a.m. to 4:30 p.m., EST. All reissue forms may be ordered from the BPD. Many forms can be downloaded from the web site at www.savingsbonds.gov.

Legal Questions

Bureau of the Public Debt: See address listing.

Attorneys: You may also want to consult with an attorney for estate, probate, custody issues, and other legal concerns.

Educational Feature of Bonds

Ask for both the "Questions and Answers" publication on the educational feature of EE bonds and the brochure that outlines the guidelines. These are available from:

- ✓ Bureau of the Public Debt
  P.O. Box 1328
  Parkersburg, WV 26106-1328
- ✓ Federal Reserve Bank Regional Sites
- ✓ Some commercial banks

Lost, Stolen, or Destroyed Bonds

Ask for form PD F 1048, available from:

- ✓ Bureau of the Public Debt (download from www.savingsbonds.gov)
- ✓ Federal Reserve Bank Regional Sites
- ✓ Some commercial banks

Forms, Publications, Tables, and How To Get Them

All of the following forms and regulations are available from the BPD, Savings Bond Operations Office. FRBs will also have most, if not all, of the forms. Many banks stock the forms used most often. Table 18.1 and the following lists are from "The Book on U.S. Savings Bonds" and the brochure, "U.S. Savings Bonds, Buyers Guide 1993-94."

Table 18.1

Treasury Circulars

Subject	CFR Part	Treasury Circular
Offering of Series E Bonds	316	No. 653
Offering of Series EE Bonds	351	No. 1-80
Offering of Savings Notes	342	No. 3-67
Offering of Series H Bonds	332	No. 905
Offering of Series HH Bonds	352	No. 2-80
Regulations Governing Series E and H Bonds	315	No. 530
Regulations Governing Series EE and HH Bonds	353	No. 3-80
Regulations Governing Exchange Transactions	352	No. 2-80

Adapted from "The Book on U.S. Savings Bonds," p.1.

The following is a list of PD forms pertinent to U.S. Savings Bonds and Notes. The government often revises forms to accommodate changes that have occurred in the bond program. When ordering a form, explain why you need it. That way, if there have been any changes you will get the most recent and appropriate form. If you use the government's web site here is the exact page you need:

www.savingsbonds.gov/sav/savforms.htm

PD F 1048
Application for Relief on Account of Loss, Theft, or Destruction of United States Savings and Retirement Securities

PD F 1455
Request by Fiduciary for Reissue of United States Savings Bonds/Notes

PD F 1522
Special Form of Request for Payment of United States Savings Bonds/Notes and Retirement Securities Where Use of a Detached Request is Authorized

PD F 1849

Disclaimer of Consent With Respect to United States Savings Bonds/Notes

PD F 1851

Request for Reissue of United States Savings Bond/Notes in Name of Trustee of Personal Trust Estate

PD F 1938

Request for Reissue of United States Savings Bond/Notes During the Lives of Both Co-owners

PD F 1980

Description of United States Savings Bonds Series H/HH

PD F 1993

Request for Purchase of United States Savings Bonds With Proceeds of Payment of Matured Savings Bonds

PD F 2216

Application by Preferred Creditor for Disposition Without Administration Where Deceased Owner's Estate Includes United States Registered Securities and/or Related Checks in Amount not Exceeding $500

PD F 2458

Certificate of Entitlement—United States Savings and Retirement Securities and Checks After Administration of Decedent's Estate

PD F 2488-1

Certificate by Legal Representative(s) of Decedent's Estate, During Administration, of Authority to Act and of Distribution Where Estate Holds No More Than $1,000 (Face Amount) United States Savings Bonds/Notes, Excluding Checks Representing Interest

PD F 2513

Application by Voluntary Guardian of Incompetent Owner of United States Savings Bonds

PD F 2966

Special Bond of Indemnity to the United States of America

PD F 3062

Claim for Relief on Account of Inscribed United States Savings Bonds Lost, Stolen or Destroyed Prior to Receipt by Owner, Co-owner, or Beneficiary

PD F 3253

Exchange Subscription for United States Savings Bonds or Series HH

PD F 3360

Request for Reissue of United States Savings Bond/Notes in the Name of a Person or Persons Other Than the Owner (Including Legal Guardian, Custodian for a Minor Under a Statute, etc.)

PD F 4000

Request by Owner for Reissue of United States Savings Bonds/Notes to Add Beneficiary or Co-owner, Eliminate Beneficiary or Decedent, Show Change of Name, and/or Correct Error in Registration

PD F 4881

Application for Payment of United States Savings Bonds of Series EE or HH and/or Related Checks in an Amount Not Exceeding $1,000 by the Survivor of a Deceased Owner Whose Estate is Not Being Administered

PD F 5263

Order for Series EE U.S. Savings Bonds (RDS)

PD F 5336

Application for Disposition of United States Savings Bonds/Notes and/or Related Checks Owned by Decedent Whose Estate is Being Settled Without Administration

---

This resource section should provide you with an organization to contact for virtually any question that was not addressed in this book. Since change is ongoing within the bond program, you may want to contact the publisher for revised copies of this book in future years.

Appendix A: Savings Bond Series at a Glance: Your Official "Cheat Sheet"

Series	Purchase Price	Face Value	Issue Date	Tax Features	Original Maturity	Final Maturity	When Cashable	Who Can Cash	When Exchangeable
I	Face value (A bond with a face value of $100 is purchased for $100)	$50, $75, $100, $200, $500, $1,000, $5,000 $10,000	9/98 to present	Subject to federal tax, exempt from state & local tax. Reporting of interest usually deferred until the bond is cashed or reaches final maturity.	N/A	30 yrs. from issue date	Anytime after first 6 mos. 3-month interest penalty for bonds not held 5 years	Bond Owner or Co-Owner. Pay on Death listee can cash with a valid death certificate.	N/A
EE	One-half face value (A bond with a face value of $100 is purchased for $50)	$50, $75, $100, $200, $500, $1,000, $5,000 $10,000	1/80 to present	Same as above	8 to 18 yrs. depending on date of issue. Interest rate determines length of original maturity period.	30 yrs. from issue date	Anytime after first 6 mos. For bonds issued after April 1997, a 3-month interest penalty if not held 5 years	Same as above	6 months from issue date and up to 1 yr. past final maturity.
E	75% of face value (A bond with a face value of $100 was purchased for $75)	$25, $50, $75, $100, $200, $500, $1,000, $5,000, $10,000	1941 to 6/80	Same as above	5 yrs. to 9 yrs., 8 mos. (Interest rate determines length.)	40 yrs. if issued prior to 12/65; 30 years if issued after 11/65	Anytime	Same as above	Any bond currently earning interest and up to 1 yr. past final maturity.
SN FS	81% of face value (A bond with a face value of $100 was purchased for $81)	Same as E bond	5/67 to 10/70	Same as above	4 yrs., 6 mos.	30 yrs. from issue date	Same as above	Same as above	Same as above
H	Face value (A bond with a face value of $500 was purchased for $500)	$500 $1,000 $5,000 $10,000	1952 to 12/79	Semi-annual interest payments must be reported annually. Interest deferred from series E, EE, or SN is reported upon redemption or final maturity of bonds, whichever comes first.	10 yrs.	30 yrs. from issue date	Anytime after first 6 mos.	Same as above	Can be reinvested into HH bonds upon final maturity, however deferred interest on H bonds must be reported at time of reinvestment.
HH	Same as H bond	Same as H bond	1/80 to present	Same as H bond	Same as H bond	20 yrs. from issue date	Same as H bond	Same as above	N/A

245

FORM PD 3600
DEPT. OF THE TREASURY
BUR. OF THE PUBLIC DEBT
[REV. SEP 1998]

TABLES OF REDEMPTION VALUES

$50 SERIES EE BONDS $25 SERIES E BONDS $25 SAVINGS NOTES
FOR REDEMPTION MONTHS SEPTEMBER 1998 THROUGH FEBRUARY 1999

TABLES OF REDEMPTION VALUES FOR $50 SERIES EE SAVINGS BONDS

ISSUE YEARS	SEPTEMBER 1998		OCTOBER 1998		NOVEMBER 1998		DECEMBER 1998		JANUARY 1999		FEBRUARY 1999		ISSUE YEARS
	ISSUE MONTHS	$50	ISSUE MONTHS	$50	ISSUE MONTHS	$50	ISSUE MONTHS	$50	ISSUE MONTHS	$50	ISSUE MONTHS	$50	
1999	*	*	*	*	*	*	*	*	Jan.	*	Jan.-Feb.	*	**1999**
1998	Apr.-Sep.	*	May-Oct.	*	June-Nov.	*	July-Dec.	*	Aug.-Dec.	*	Sep.-Dec.	*	**1998**
	Mar.	25.34	Apr.	25.34	May	25.32	June	25.32	July	25.32	Aug.	25.32	
	Feb.	25.46	Mar.	25.46	Apr.	25.46	May	25.42	June	25.42	July	25.42	
	Jan.	25.58	Feb.	25.58	Mar.	25.58	Apr.	25.58	May	25.52	June	25.52	
			Jan.	25.70	Feb.	25.70	Mar.	25.70	Apr.	25.70	May	25.64	
					Jan.	25.80	Feb.	25.80	Mar.	25.80	Apr.	25.80	
							Jan.	25.92	Feb.	25.92	Mar.	25.92	
									Jan.	26.02	Feb.	26.02	
											Jan.	26.14	
1997	Dec.	25.70	Dec.	25.80	Dec.	25.92	Dec.	26.02	Dec.	26.14	Dec.	26.24	**1997**
	Nov.	25.80	Nov.	25.92	Nov.	26.02	Nov.	26.14	Nov.	26.24	Nov.	26.36	
	Oct.	25.96	Oct.	26.08	Oct.	26.20	Oct.	26.32	Oct.	26.44	Oct.	26.56	
	Sep.	26.08	Sep.	26.20	Sep.	26.32	Sep.	26.44	Sep.	26.56	Sep.	26.66	
	Aug.	26.20	Aug.	26.32	Aug.	26.44	Aug.	26.56	Aug.	26.66	Aug.	26.78	
	July	26.32	July	26.44	July	26.56	July	26.66	July	26.78	July	26.88	
	June	26.44	June	26.56	June	26.66	June	26.78	June	26.88	June	27.00	
	May	26.56	May	26.66	Jan.-May	26.78	May	26.88	May	27.00	May	27.10	
	Apr.	26.18	Jan.-Apr.	26.78			Jan.-Apr.	26.78	Feb.-Apr.	26.78	Mar.-Apr.	26.78	
	Jan.-Mar.	26.78							Jan.	27.38	Jan.-Feb.	27.38	
1996	Nov.-Dec.	26.78	Nov.-Dec.	26.78	Dec.	26.78	Nov.-Dec.	27.38	Nov.-Dec.	27.38	Nov.-Dec.	27.38	**1996**
	Oct.	26.72	May-Oct.	27.32	Nov.	27.38	July-Oct.	27.32	Aug.-Oct.	27.32	Sep.-Oct.	27.32	
	May-Sep.	27.32	Jan.-Apr.	28.00	June-Oct.	27.32	May-June	27.94	May-July	27.94	May-Aug.	27.94	
	Apr.	27.38			May	27.94	Jan.-Apr.	28.00	Feb.-Apr.	28.00	Mar.-Apr.	28.00	
	Jan.-Mar.	28.00			Jan.-Apr.	28.00			Jan.	28.62	Jan.-Feb.	28.62	
1995	Nov.-Dec.	28.00	Nov.-Dec.	28.00	Dec.	28.00	Nov.-Dec.	28.62	Nov.-Dec.	28.62	Nov.-Dec.	28.62	**1995**
	Oct.	28.10	May-Oct.	28.74	Nov.	28.62	July-Oct.	28.74	Aug.-Oct.	28.74	Sep.-Oct.	28.74	
	May-Sep.	28.74	Apr.	28.72	June-Oct.	28.74	May-June	29.38	May-July	29.38	May-Aug.	29.38	
	Apr.	28.64	Mar.	28.82	May	29.38	Apr.	28.92	Apr.	29.02	Apr.	29.10	
	Mar.	28.72	Feb.	28.92	Apr.	28.82	Mar.	29.02	Mar.	29.10	Mar.	29.20	
	Feb.	28.82	Jan.	29.02	Mar.	28.92	Feb.	29.10	Feb.	29.20	Feb.	29.30	
	Jan.	28.92			Feb.	29.02	Jan.	29.20	Jan.	29.30	Jan.	29.40	
					Jan.	29.10							
1994	Dec.	29.02	Dec.	29.10	Dec.	29.20	Dec.	29.30	Dec.	29.40	Dec.	29.50	**1994**
	Nov.	29.10	Nov.	29.20	Nov.	29.30	Nov.	29.40	Nov.	29.50	Nov.	29.60	
	Oct.	29.20	Oct.	29.30	Oct.	29.40	Oct.	29.50	Oct.	29.60	Oct.	29.70	
	Sep.	29.30	Sep.	29.40	Sep.	29.50	Sep.	29.60	Sep.	29.70	Sep.	29.78	
	Aug.	29.40	Aug.	29.50	Aug.	29.60	Aug.	29.70	Aug.	29.78	Aug.	29.88	
	July	29.50	July	29.60	July	29.70	July	29.78	July	29.88	July	29.98	
	June	29.60	June	29.70	June	29.78	June	29.88	June	29.98	June	30.08	
	May	29.70	May	29.78	May	29.88	May	29.98	May	30.08	May	30.18	
	Apr.	29.78	Apr.	29.88	Apr.	29.98	Apr.	30.08	Apr.	30.18	Apr.	30.28	
	Mar.	29.88	Mar.	29.98	Mar.	30.08	Mar.	30.18	Mar.	30.28	Mar.	30.38	
	Feb.	29.98	Feb.	30.08	Feb.	30.18	Feb.	30.28	Feb.	30.38	Jan.-Feb.	32.34	
	Jan.	30.08	Jan.	30.18	Jan.	30.28	Jan.	30.38	Jan.	32.34			

* NOT ELIGIBLE FOR PAYMENT.

TABLES OF REDEMPTION VALUES FOR $50 SERIES EE SAVINGS BONDS

ISSUE YEARS	SEPTEMBER 1998 ISSUE MONTHS	$50	OCTOBER 1998 ISSUE MONTHS	$50	NOVEMBER 1998 ISSUE MONTHS	$50	DECEMBER 1998 ISSUE MONTHS	$50	JANUARY 1999 ISSUE MONTHS	$50	FEBRUARY 1999 ISSUE MONTHS	$50	ISSUE YEARS
1993	Dec.	30.18	Dec.	30.28	Dec.	30.38	July-Dec.	32.34	Aug.-Dec.	32.34	Sep.-Dec.	32.34	**1993**
	Nov.	30.28	Nov.	30.38	June-Nov.	32.34	May-June	33.12	May-July	33.12	May-Aug.	33.12	
	Oct.	30.38	May-Oct.	32.34	May	33.12	Mar.-Apr.	33.16	Mar.-Apr.	33.16	Mar.-Apr.	33.16	
	May-Sep.	32.34	Mar.-Apr.	33.16	Mar.-Apr.	33.16	Jan.-Feb.	34.62	Feb.	34.62	Jan.-Feb.	35.66	
	Apr.	32.30	Jan.-Feb.	34.62	Jan.-Feb.	34.62			Jan.	35.66			
	Mar.	33.16											
	Jan.-Feb.	34.62											
1992	Oct.-Dec.	34.62	Nov.-Dec.	34.62	Dec.	34.62	July-Dec.	35.66	Aug.-Dec.	35.66	Sep.-Dec.	35.66	**1992**
	Apr.-Sep.	35.66	May-Oct.	35.66	June-Nov.	35.66	Jan.-June	36.72	Feb.-July	36.72	Mar.-Aug.	36.72	
	Jan.-Mar.	36.72	Jan.-Apr.	36.72	Jan.-May	36.72			Jan.	37.82	Jan.-Feb.	37.82	
1991	Oct.-Dec.	36.72	Nov.-Dec.	36.72	Dec.	36.72	July-Dec.	37.82	Aug.-Dec.	37.82	Sep.-Dec.	37.82	**1991**
	Apr.-Sep.	37.82	May-Oct.	37.82	June-Nov.	37.82	Jan.-June	38.96	Feb.-July	38.96	Mar.-Aug.	38.96	
	Jan.-Mar.	38.96	Jan.-Apr.	38.96	Jan.-May	38.96			Jan.	40.12	Jan.-Feb.	40.12	
1990	Oct.-Dec.	38.96	Nov.-Dec.	38.96	Dec.	38.96	July-Dec.	40.12	Aug.-Dec.	40.12	Sep.-Dec.	40.12	**1990**
	Apr.-Sep.	40.12	May-Oct.	40.12	June-Nov.	40.12	Jan.-June	41.34	Feb.-July	41.34	Mar.-Aug.	41.34	
	Jan.-Mar.	41.34	Jan.-Apr.	41.34	Jan.-May	41.34			Jan.	42.58	Jan.-Feb.	42.58	
1989	Oct.-Dec.	41.34	Nov.-Dec.	41.34	Dec.	41.34	July-Dec.	42.58	Aug.-Dec.	42.58	Sep.-Dec.	42.58	**1989**
	Apr.-Sep.	42.58	May-Oct.	42.58	June-Nov.	42.58	Jan.-June	43.84	Feb.-July	43.84	Mar.-Aug.	43.84	
	Jan.-Mar.	43.84	Jan.-Apr.	43.84	Jan.-May	43.84			Jan.	45.16	Jan.-Feb.	45.16	
1988	Oct.-Dec.	43.84	Nov.-Dec.	43.84	Dec.	43.84	July-Dec.	45.16	Aug.-Dec.	45.16	Sep.-Dec.	45.16	**1988**
	Apr.-Sep.	45.16	May-Oct.	45.16	June-Nov.	45.16	Jan.-June	46.52	Feb.-July	46.52	Mar.-Aug.	46.52	
	Jan.-Mar.	46.52	Jan.-Apr.	46.52	Jan.-May	46.52			Jan.	47.92	Jan.-Feb.	47.92	
1987	Oct.-Dec.	46.52	Nov.-Dec.	46.52	Dec.	46.52	July-Dec.	47.92	Aug.-Dec.	47.92	Sep.-Dec.	47.92	**1987**
	Apr.-Sep.	47.92	May-Oct.	47.92	June-Nov.	47.92	Jan.-June	49.34	Feb.-July	49.34	Mar.-Aug.	49.34	
	Jan.-Mar.	49.34	Jan.-Apr.	49.34	Jan.-May	49.34			Jan.	50.82	Jan.-Feb.	50.82	
1986	Nov.-Dec.	49.34	Nov.-Dec.	49.34	Dec.	49.34	Nov.-Dec.	50.82	Nov.-Dec.	50.82	Nov.-Dec.	50.82	**1986**
	Oct.	55.42	May-Oct.	56.54	Nov.	50.82	July-Oct.	56.54	Aug.-Oct.	56.54	Sep.-Oct.	56.54	
	Apr.-Sep.	56.54	Jan.-Apr.	57.66	June-Oct.	56.54	Jan.-June	57.66	Feb.-July	57.66	Mar.-Aug.	57.66	
	Jan.-Mar.	57.66			Jan.-May	57.66			Jan.	58.82	Jan.-Feb.	58.82	
1985	Oct.-Dec.	57.66	Nov.-Dec.	57.66	Dec.	57.66	July-Dec.	58.82	Aug.-Dec.	58.82	Sep.-Dec.	58.82	**1985**
	Apr.-Sep.	58.82	May-Oct.	58.82	June-Nov.	58.82	Jan.-June	60.00	Feb.-July	60.00	Mar.-Aug.	60.00	
	Jan.-Mar.	60.00	Jan.-Apr.	60.00	Jan.-May	60.00			Jan.	61.20	Jan.-Feb.	61.20	
1984	Nov.-Dec.	60.00	Nov.-Dec.	60.00	Dec.	60.00	Nov.-Dec.	61.20	Nov.-Dec.	61.20	Nov.-Dec.	61.20	**1984**
	Oct.	60.16	May-Oct.	61.72	Nov.	61.20	July-Oct.	61.72	Aug.-Oct.	61.72	Sep.-Oct.	61.72	
	May-Sep.	61.72	Jan.-Apr.	64.66	June-Oct.	61.72	May-June	63.22	May-July	63.22	May-Aug.	63.22	
	Apr.	63.00			May	63.22	Jan.-Apr.	64.66	Feb.-Apr.	64.66	Mar.-Apr.	64.66	
	Jan.-Mar.	64.66			Jan.-Apr.	64.66			Jan.	66.22	Jan.-Feb.	66.22	
1983	Nov.-Dec.	64.66	Nov.-Dec.	64.66	Dec.	64.66	Nov.-Dec.	66.22	Nov.-Dec.	66.22	Nov.-Dec.	66.22	**1983**
	Oct.	65.74	May-Oct.	67.48	Nov.	66.22	July-Oct.	67.48	Aug.-Oct.	67.48	Sep.-Oct.	67.48	
	May-Sep.	67.48	Mar.-Apr.	71.24	June-Oct.	67.48	May-June	69.02	May-July	69.02	May-Aug.	69.02	
	Apr.	69.38	Jan.-Feb.	72.30	May	69.02	Mar.-Apr.	71.24	Mar.-Apr.	71.24	Mar.-Apr.	71.24	
	Mar.	71.24			Mar.-Apr.	71.24	Jan.-Feb.	72.30	Feb.	72.30	Jan.-Feb.	74.46	
	Jan.-Feb.	72.30			Jan.-Feb.	72.30			Jan.	74.46			
1982	Nov.-Dec.	72.30	Nov.-Dec.	72.30	Dec.	72.30	Nov.-Dec.	74.46	Nov.-Dec.	74.46	Nov.-Dec.	74.46	**1982**
	Oct.	78.78	May-Oct.	81.14	Nov.	74.46	July-Oct.	81.14	Aug.-Oct.	81.14	Sep.-Oct.	81.14	
	Apr.-Sep.	81.14	Jan.-Apr.	83.58	June-Oct.	81.14	Jan.-June	83.58	Feb.-July	83.58	Mar.-Aug.	83.58	
	Jan.-Mar.	83.58			Jan.-May	83.58			Jan.	86.08	Jan.-Feb.	86.08	
1981	Oct.-Dec.	83.58	Nov.-Dec.	83.58	Dec.	83.58	July-Dec.	86.08	Aug.-Dec.	86.08	Sep.-Dec.	86.08	**1981**
	May-Sep.	86.08	May-Oct.	86.08	June-Nov.	86.08	May-June	88.66	May-July	88.66	May-Aug.	88.66	
	Apr.	88.18	Jan.-Apr.	90.82	May	88.66	Jan.-Apr.	90.82	Feb.-Apr.	90.82	Mar.-Apr.	90.82	
	Jan.-Mar.	90.82			Jan.-Apr.	90.82			Jan.	93.54	Jan.-Feb.	93.54	
1980	Nov.-Dec.	90.82	Nov.-Dec.	90.82	Dec.	90.82	Nov.-Dec.	93.54	Nov.-Dec.	93.54	Nov.-Dec.	93.54	**1980**
	Oct.	95.28	May-Oct.	98.14	Nov.	93.54	July-Oct.	98.14	Aug.-Oct.	98.14	Sep.-Oct.	98.14	
	May-Sep.	98.14	Jan.-Apr.	100.10	June-Oct.	98.14	May-June	101.10	May-July	101.10	May-Aug.	101.10	
	Apr.	97.18			May	101.10	Jan.-Apr.	100.10	Feb.-Apr.	100.10	Mar.-Apr.	100.10	
	Jan.-Mar.	100.10			Jan.-Apr.	100.10			Jan.	103.10	Jan.-Feb.	103.10	

TABLES OF REDEMPTION VALUES FOR $25 SERIES E SAVINGS BONDS

ISSUE YEARS	SEPTEMBER 1998 ISSUE MONTHS	$25	OCTOBER 1998 ISSUE MONTHS	$25	NOVEMBER 1998 ISSUE MONTHS	$25	DECEMBER 1998 ISSUE MONTHS	$25	JANUARY 1999 ISSUE MONTHS	$25	FEBRUARY 1999 ISSUE MONTHS	$25	ISSUE YEARS
1980	May-June	69.47	May-June	69.47	June	69.47	May-June	70.86	May-June	70.86	May-June	70.86	**1980**
	Apr.	68.77	Jan.-Apr.	70.15	May	70.86	Jan.-Apr.	70.15	Feb.-Apr.	70.15	Mar.-Apr.	70.15	
	Jan.-Mar.	70.15			Jan.-Apr.	70.15			Jan.	71.55	Jan.-Feb.	71.55	
1979	Nov.-Dec.	70.15	Nov.-Dec.	70.15	Dec.	70.15	Nov.-Dec.	71.55	Nov.-Dec.	71.55	Nov.-Dec.	71.55	**1979**
	Oct.	69.50	June-Oct.	70.89	Nov.	71.55	July-Oct.	70.89	Aug.-Oct.	70.89	Sep.-Oct.	70.89	
	June-Sep.	70.89	May	70.72	June-Oct.	70.89	June	72.30	June-July	72.30	June-Aug.	72.30	
	May	70.72	Jan.-Apr.	71.44	May	72.14	May	72.14	May	72.14	May	72.14	
	Apr.	70.04			Jan.-Apr.	71.44	Jan.-Apr.	71.44	Feb.-Apr.	71.44	Mar.-Apr.	71.44	
	Jan.-Mar.	71.44							Jan.	72.87	Jan.-Feb.	72.87	
1978	Dec.	71.43	Dec.	71.43	Dec.	71.43	Dec.	72.86	Dec.	72.86	Dec.	72.86	**1978**
	Nov.	71.24	Nov.	71.24	Nov.	72.66	Nov.	72.66	Nov.	72.66	Nov.	72.66	
	Oct.	70.57	July-Oct.	71.98	July-Oct.	71.98	July-Oct.	71.98	Aug.-Oct.	71.98	Sep.-Oct.	71.98	
	July-Sep.	71.98	June	71.97	June	71.97	June	73.41	July	73.42	July-Aug.	73.42	
	June	71.97	May	71.79	May	73.22	May	73.22	June	73.41	June	73.41	
	May	71.79	Mar.-Apr.	75.50	Mar.-Apr.	75.50	Mar.-Apr.	75.50	May	73.22	May	73.22	
	Apr.	73.52	Jan.-Feb.	80.76	Jan.-Feb.	80.76	Jan.-Feb.	80.76	Mar.-Apr.	75.50	Mar.-Apr.	75.50	
	Mar.	75.50							Feb.	80.76	Jan.-Feb.	83.18	
	Jan.-Feb.	80.76							Jan.	83.18			
1977	Dec.	80.76	Dec.	80.76	Dec.	80.76	Dec.	83.18	Dec.	83.18	Dec.	83.18	**1977**
	Nov.	80.53	Nov.	80.53	Nov.	82.95	Nov.	82.95	Nov.	82.95	Nov.	82.95	
	Oct.	87.82	July-Oct.	90.45	July-Oct.	90.45	July-Oct.	90.45	Aug.-Oct.	90.45	Sep.-Oct.	90.45	
	July-Sep.	90.45	June	90.46	June	90.46	June	93.18	July	93.16	July-Aug.	93.16	
	June	90.46	May	90.28	May	92.99	May	92.99	June	93.18	June	93.18	
	May	90.28	Jan.-Apr.	92.08	Jan.-Apr.	92.08	Jan.-Apr.	92.08	May	92.99	May	92.99	
	Apr.	89.40							Feb.-Apr.	92.08	Mar.-Apr.	92.08	
	Jan.-Mar.	92.08							Jan.	94.84	Jan.-Feb.	94.84	
1976	Dec.	92.08	Dec.	92.08	Dec.	92.08	Dec.	94.84	Dec.	94.84	Dec.	94.84	**1976**
	Nov.	91.81	Nov.	91.81	Nov.	94.57	Nov.	94.57	Nov.	94.57	Nov.	94.57	
	Oct.	90.93	July-Oct.	93.66	July-Oct.	93.66	July-Oct.	93.66	Aug.-Oct.	93.66	Sep.-Oct.	93.66	
	July-Sep.	93.66	June	93.67	June	93.67	June	96.48	July	96.47	July-Aug.	96.47	
	June	93.67	May	93.46	May	96.27	May	96.27	June	96.48	June	96.48	
	May	93.46	Jan.-Apr.	95.36	Jan.-Apr.	95.36	Jan.-Apr.	95.36	May	96.27	May	96.27	
	Apr.	92.59							Feb.-Apr.	95.36	Mar.-Apr.	95.36	
	Jan.-Mar.	95.36							Jan.	98.22	Jan.-Feb.	98.22	
1975	Dec.	95.35	Dec.	95.35	Dec.	95.35	Dec.	98.21	Dec.	98.21	Dec.	98.21	**1975**
	Nov.	95.14	Nov.	95.14	Nov.	98.00	Nov.	98.00	Nov.	98.00	Nov.	98.00	
	Oct.	94.22	June-Oct.	97.05	June-Oct.	97.05	July-Oct.	97.05	Aug.-Oct.	97.05	Sep.-Oct.	97.05	
	June-Sep.	97.05	May	96.82	May	99.73	June	99.96	June-July	99.96	June-Aug.	99.96	
	May	96.82	Jan.-Apr.	98.78	Jan.-Apr.	98.78	May	99.73	May	99.73	May	99.73	
	Apr.	95.90					Jan.-Apr.	98.78	Feb.-Apr.	98.78	Mar.-Apr.	98.78	
	Jan.-Mar.	98.78							Jan.	101.74	Jan.-Feb.	101.74	
1974	Dec.	98.79	Dec.	98.79	Dec.	98.79	Dec.	101.75	Dec.	101.75	Dec.	101.75	**1974**
	Nov.	98.55	Nov.	98.55	Nov.	101.50	Nov.	101.50	Nov.	101.50	Nov.	101.50	
	Oct.	97.61	June-Oct.	100.54	June-Oct.	100.54	July-Oct.	100.54	Aug.-Oct.	100.54	Sep.-Oct.	100.54	
	June-Sep.	100.54	May	100.30	May	103.31	June	103.56	July	103.55	July-Aug.	103.55	
	May	100.30	Jan.-Apr.	102.33	Jan.-Apr.	102.33	May	103.31	June	103.56	June	103.56	
	Apr.	99.35					Jan.-Apr.	102.33	May	103.31	May	103.31	
	Jan.-Mar.	102.33							Feb.-Apr.	102.33	Mar.-Apr.	102.33	
									Jan.	105.40	Jan.-Feb.	105.40	
1973	Dec.	102.33	Dec.	102.33	Dec.	102.33	Dec.	105.40	Dec.	105.40	Dec.	105.40	**1973**
	Sep.-Nov.	105.30	Sep.-Nov.	105.30	Sep.-Nov.	105.30	Sep.-Nov.	105.30	Oct.-Nov.	105.30	Nov.	105.30	
	Aug.	105.29	Aug.	105.29	Aug.	105.29	Aug.	108.45	Sep.	108.46	Sep.-Oct.	108.46	
	July	105.06	July	105.06	July	108.22	July	108.22	Aug.	108.45	Aug.	108.45	
	June	104.05	June	107.17	June	107.17	June	107.17	July	108.22	July	108.22	
	Feb.-May	106.92	Feb.-May	106.92	Feb.-May	106.92	Mar.-May	106.92	June	107.17	June	107.17	
	Jan.	106.65	Jan.	106.65	Jan.	109.85	Feb.	110.13	Apr.-May	106.92	May	106.92	
							Jan.	109.85	Feb.-Mar.	110.13	Feb.-Apr.	110.13	
									Jan.	109.85	Jan.	109.85	

TABLES OF REDEMPTION VALUES FOR $25 SERIES E SAVINGS BONDS

ISSUE YEARS	SEPTEMBER 1998		OCTOBER 1998		NOVEMBER 1998		DECEMBER 1998		JANUARY 1999		FEBRUARY 1999		ISSUE YEARS
	ISSUE MONTHS	$25	ISSUE MONTHS	$25	ISSUE MONTHS	$25	ISSUE MONTHS	$25	ISSUE MONTHS	$25	ISSUE MONTHS	$25	
1972	Dec.	105.64	Dec.	108.81	Dec.	108.81	Dec.	108.81	Dec.	108.81	Dec.	108.81	**1972**
	Aug.-Nov.	108.57	Aug.-Nov.	108.57	Aug.-Nov.	108.57	Sep.-Nov.	108.57	Oct.-Nov.	108.57	Nov.	108.57	
	July	108.33	July	108.33	July	110.50	Aug.	110.74	Aug.-Sep.	110.74	Aug.-Oct.	110.74	
	June	107.29	June	109.44	June	109.44	July	110.50	July	110.50	July	110.50	
	Mar.-May	109.13	Mar.-May	109.13	Mar.-May	109.13	June	109.44	June	109.44	June	109.44	
	Feb.	109.12	Feb.	109.12	Feb.	109.12	Mar.-May	109.13	Apr.-May	109.13	May	109.13	
	Jan.	108.86	Jan.	108.86	Jan.	111.04	Feb.	111.30	Mar.	111.31	Mar.-Apr.	111.31	
							Jan.	111.04	Feb.	111.30	Feb.	111.30	
									Jan.	111.04	Jan.	111.04	
1971	Dec.	107.82	Dec.	109.98	Dec.	109.98	Dec.	109.98	Dec.	109.98	Dec.	109.98	**1971**
	Aug.-Nov.	109.70	Aug.-Nov.	109.70	Aug.-Nov.	109.70	Sep.-Nov.	109.70	Oct.-Nov.	109.70	Nov.	109.70	
	July	109.50	July	109.50	July	111.69	Aug.	111.89	Aug.-Sep.	111.89	Aug.-Oct.	111.89	
	June	108.84	June	111.77	June	111.77	July	111.69	July	111.69	July	111.69	
	Feb.-May	111.45	Feb.-May	111.45	Feb.-May	111.45	June	111.77	June	111.77	June	111.77	
	Jan.	111.20	Jan.	111.20	Jan.	113.78	Mar.-May	111.45	Apr.-May	111.45	May	111.45	
							Feb.	114.04	Feb.-Mar.	114.04	Feb.-Apr.	114.04	
							Jan.	113.78	Jan.	113.78	Jan.	113.78	
1970	Dec.	125.98	Dec.	128.50	Dec.	128.50	Dec.	128.50	Dec.	128.50	Dec.	128.50	**1970**
	Aug.-Nov.	128.20	Aug.-Nov.	128.20	Aug.-Nov.	128.20	Sep.-Nov.	128.20	Oct.-Nov.	128.20	Nov.	128.20	
	July	127.90	July	127.90	July	130.46	Aug.	130.77	Aug.-Sep.	130.77	Aug.-Oct.	130.77	
	June	126.66	June	129.19	June	129.19	July	130.46	July	130.46	July	130.46	
	Mar.-May	128.58	Mar.-May	128.58	Mar.-May	128.58	June	129.19	June	129.19	June	129.19	
	Feb.	128.57	Feb.	128.57	Feb.	128.57	Mar.-May	128.58	Apr.-May	128.58	May	128.58	
	Jan.	128.25	Jan.	128.25	Jan.	130.82	Feb.	131.14	Mar.	131.15	Mar.-Apr.	131.15	
							Jan.	130.82	Feb.	131.14	Feb.	131.14	
									Jan.	130.82	Jan.	130.82	
1969	Dec.	127.05	Dec.	129.59	Dec.	129.59	Dec.	129.59	Dec.	129.59	Dec.	129.59	**1969**
	Sep.-Nov.	128.92	Sep.-Nov.	128.92	Sep.-Nov.	128.92	Sep.-Nov.	128.92	Oct.-Nov.	128.92	Nov.	128.92	
	Aug.	128.91	Aug.	128.91	Aug.	128.91	Aug.	131.49	Sep.	131.50	Sep.-Oct.	131.50	
	July	128.63	July	128.63	July	131.20	July	131.20	Aug.	131.49	Aug.	131.49	
	June	127.39	June	129.94	June	129.94	June	129.94	July	131.20	July	131.20	
	May	133.21	May	133.21	May	135.88	May	135.88	June	129.94	June	129.94	
	Apr.	131.94	Jan.-Apr.	134.58	Jan.-Apr.	134.58	Jan.-Apr.	134.58	May	135.88	May	135.88	
	Jan.-Mar.	134.58							Feb.-Apr.	134.58	Mar.-Apr.	134.58	
									Jan.*	137.27	Jan.-Feb.*	137.27	
1968	Dec.	134.59	Dec.	134.59	Dec.	134.59	Dec.*	137.28	Dec.	137.28	Dec.	137.28	**1968**
	Nov.	132.79	Nov.	132.79	Nov.*	135.44	Nov.	135.44	Nov.	135.44	Nov.	135.44	
	Oct.	131.51	July-Oct.*	134.14	July-Oct.	134.14	July-Oct.	134.14	July-Oct.	134.14	July-Oct.	134.14	
	July-Sep.*	134.14	June	134.16	June	134.16	June	134.16	June	134.16	June	134.16	
	June	134.16	May	132.57	May	132.57	May	132.57	May	132.57	May	132.57	
	May	132.57	Jan.-Apr.	131.28	Jan.-Apr.	131.28	Jan.-Apr.	131.28	Jan.-Apr.	131.28	Jan.-Apr.	131.28	
	Jan.-Apr.	131.28											
1967	Dec.	131.28	Dec.	131.28	Dec.	131.28	Dec.	131.28	Dec.	131.28	Dec.	131.28	**1967**
	Nov.	129.70	Nov.	129.70	Nov.	129.70	Nov.	129.70	Nov.	129.70	Nov.	129.70	
	July-Oct.	128.45	July-Oct.	128.45	July-Oct.	128.45	July-Oct.	128.45	July-Oct.	128.45	July-Oct.	128.45	
	June	128.46	June	128.46	June	128.46	June	128.46	June	128.46	June	128.46	
	May	127.06	May	127.06	May	127.06	May	127.06	May	127.06	May	127.06	
	Jan.-Apr.	125.86	Jan.-Apr.	125.86	Jan.-Apr.	125.86	Jan.-Apr.	125.86	Jan.-Apr.	125.86	Jan.-Apr.	125.86	
1966	Dec.	125.85	Dec.	125.85	Dec.	125.85	Dec.	125.85	Dec.	125.85	Dec.	125.85	**1966**
	Nov.	124.46	Nov.	124.46	Nov.	124.46	Nov.	124.46	Nov.	124.46	Nov.	124.46	
	July-Oct.	123.27	July-Oct.	123.27	July-Oct.	123.27	July-Oct.	123.27	July-Oct.	123.27	July-Oct.	123.27	
	June	123.28	June	123.28	June	123.28	June	123.28	June	123.28	June	123.28	
	May	122.02	May	122.02	May	122.02	May	122.02	May	122.02	May	122.02	
	Mar.-Apr.	121.94	Mar.-Apr.	121.94	Mar.-Apr.	121.94	Mar.-Apr.	121.94	Mar.-Apr.	121.94	Mar.-Apr.	121.94	
	Jan.-Feb.	128.13	Jan.-Feb.	128.13	Jan.-Feb.	128.13	Jan.-Feb.	128.13	Jan.-Feb.	128.13	Jan.-Feb.	128.13	

* BONDS ISSUED BETWEEN DECEMBER 1965 AND THIS DATE HAVE REACHED FINAL MATURITY AND WILL EARN NO ADDITIONAL INTEREST.

TABLES OF REDEMPTION VALUES FOR $25 SERIES E SAVINGS BONDS

ISSUE YEARS	SEPTEMBER 1998 ISSUE MONTHS	$25	OCTOBER 1998 ISSUE MONTHS	$25	NOVEMBER 1998 ISSUE MONTHS	$25	DECEMBER 1998 ISSUE MONTHS	$25	JANUARY 1999 ISSUE MONTHS	$25	FEBRUARY 1999 ISSUE MONTHS	$25	ISSUE YEARS
1965	Dec.	128.12	Dec.	128.12	Dec.	128.12	Dec.	128.12	Dec.	128.12	Dec.	128.12	**1965**
	Sep.-Nov.	138.43	Sep.-Nov.	138.43	Sep.-Nov.	138.43	Oct.-Nov.	138.43	Nov.	138.43	Sep.-Nov.	141.65	
	Aug.	137.72	Aug.	137.72	Aug.	140.92	Sep.	141.65	Sep.-Oct.	141.65	Aug.	140.92	
	July	138.47	June-July	142.19	June-July	142.19	Aug.	140.92	Aug.	140.92	June-July	142.19	
	June	142.19	Apr.-May	151.27	Apr.-May	151.27	June-July	142.19	June-July	142.19	Apr.-May	155.81	
	Apr.-May	151.27	Mar.	151.28	Mar.	151.28	Apr.-May	151.27	May	151.27	Mar.	155.82	
	Mar.	151.28	Feb.	150.55	Feb.	155.07	Mar.	155.82	Apr.	155.81	Feb.	155.07	
	Feb.	150.55	Jan.	169.05	Jan.	169.05	Feb.	155.07	Mar.	155.82	Jan.	169.05	
	Jan.	164.13					Jan.	169.05	Feb.	155.07			
									Jan.	169.05			
1964	Dec.	169.05	Dec.	169.05	Dec.	169.05	Dec.	169.05	Dec.	169.05	Dec.	169.05	**1964**
	Sep.-Nov.	167.97	Sep.-Nov.	167.97	Sep.-Nov.	167.97	Oct.-Nov.	167.97	Nov.	167.97	Sep.-Nov.	173.01	
	Aug.	167.18	Aug.	167.18	Aug.	172.20	Sep.	173.01	Sep.-Oct.	173.01	Aug.	172.20	
	July	165.57	June-July	170.54	June-July	170.54	Aug.	172.20	Aug.	172.20	June-July	170.54	
	June	170.54	Apr.-May	169.41	Apr.-May	169.41	June-July	170.54	June-July	170.54	Apr.-May	174.49	
	Apr.-May	169.41	Mar.	169.42	Mar.	169.42	Apr.-May	169.41	May	169.41	Mar.	174.51	
	Mar.	169.42	Feb.	168.62	Feb.	173.68	Mar.	174.51	Apr.	174.49	Feb.	173.68	
	Feb.	168.62	Jan.	172.03	Jan.	172.03	Feb.	173.68	Mar.	174.51	Jan.	172.03	
	Jan.	167.02					Jan.	172.03	Feb.	173.68			
									Jan.	172.03			
1963	Dec.	172.03	Dec.	172.03	Dec.	172.03	Dec.	172.03	Dec.	172.03	Dec.	172.03	**1963**
	Sep.-Nov.	170.97	Sep.-Nov.	170.97	Sep.-Nov.	170.97	Oct.-Nov.	170.97	Nov.	170.97	Sep.-Nov.	176.10	
	Aug.	170.15	Aug.	170.15	Aug.	175.26	Sep.	176.10	Sep.-Oct.	176.10	Aug.	175.26	
	July	168.50	June-July	173.56	June-July	173.56	Aug.	175.26	Aug.	175.26	June-July	173.56	
	June	173.56	Apr.-May	172.25	Apr.-May	172.25	June-July	173.56	June-July	173.56	Apr.-May	177.42	
	Apr.-May	172.25	Mar.	172.27	Mar.	172.27	Apr.-May	172.25	May	172.25	Mar.	177.44	
	Mar.	172.27	Feb.	171.47	Feb.	176.61	Mar.	177.44	Apr.	177.42	Feb.	176.61	
	Feb.	171.47	Jan.	174.91	Jan.	174.91	Feb.	176.61	Mar.	177.44	Jan.	174.91	
	Jan.	169.82					Jan.	174.91	Feb.	176.61			
									Jan.	174.91			
1962	Dec.	174.91	Dec.	174.91	Dec.	174.91	Dec.	174.91	Dec.	174.91	Dec.	174.91	**1962**
	Oct.-Nov.	174.20	Oct.-Nov.	174.20	Oct.-Nov.	174.20	Oct.-Nov.	174.20	Nov.	174.20	Sep.-Nov.	179.42	
	Sep.	174.19	Sep.	174.19	Sep.	174.19	Sep.	179.42	Sep.-Oct.	179.42	Aug.	178.15	
	Aug.	172.96	Aug.	172.96	Aug.	178.15	Aug.	178.15	Aug.	178.15	June-July	176.46	
	July	171.32	June-July	176.46	June-July	176.46	June-July	176.46	June-July	176.46	Apr.-May	181.28	
	June	176.46	Apr.-May	176.00	Apr.-May	176.00	Apr.-May	176.00	May	176.00	Mar.	181.30	
	Apr.-May	176.00	Mar.	176.02	Mar.	176.02	Mar.	181.30	Apr.	181.28	Feb.	179.99	
	Mar.	176.02	Feb.	174.75	Feb.	179.99	Feb.	179.99	Mar.	181.30	Jan.	178.26	
	Feb.	174.75	Jan.	178.26	Jan.	178.26	Jan.	178.26	Feb.	179.99			
	Jan.	173.07							Jan.	178.26			
1961	Dec.	178.26	Dec.	178.26	Dec.	178.26	Dec.	178.26	Dec.	178.26	Dec.	178.26	**1961**
	Oct.-Nov.	177.75	Oct.-Nov.	177.75	Oct.-Nov.	177.75	Oct.-Nov.	177.75	Nov.	177.75	Oct.-Nov.	183.08	
	Sep.	177.76	Sep.	177.76	Sep.	177.76	Sep.	183.09	Oct.	183.08	Sep.	183.09	
	Aug.	175.79	Aug.	175.79	Aug.	181.07	Aug.	181.07	Sep.	183.09	Aug.	181.07	
	July	174.13	June-July	179.35	June-July	179.35	June-July	179.35	Aug.	181.07	June-July	179.35	
	June	179.35	Apr.-May	178.82	Apr.-May	178.82	Apr.-May	178.82	June-July	179.35	Apr.-May	184.19	
	Apr.-May	178.82	Mar.	178.83	Mar.	178.83	Mar.	184.20	May	178.82	Mar.	184.20	
	Mar.	178.83	Feb.	176.79	Feb.	182.10	Feb.	182.10	Apr.	184.19	Feb.	182.10	
	Feb.	176.79	Jan.	180.37	Jan.	180.37	Jan.	180.37	Mar.	184.20	Jan.	180.37	
	Jan.	175.11							Feb.	182.10			
									Jan.	180.37			

TABLES OF REDEMPTION VALUES FOR $25 SERIES E SAVINGS BONDS

ISSUE YEARS	SEPTEMBER 1998 ISSUE MONTHS	$25	OCTOBER 1998 ISSUE MONTHS	$25	NOVEMBER 1998 ISSUE MONTHS	$25	DECEMBER 1998 ISSUE MONTHS	$25	JANUARY 1999 ISSUE MONTHS	$25	FEBRUARY 1999 ISSUE MONTHS	$25	ISSUE YEARS
1960	Dec.	180.37	Dec.	180.37	Dec.	180.37	Dec.	180.37	Dec.	180.37	Dec.	180.37	**1960**
	Oct.-Nov.	180.01	Oct.-Nov.	180.01	Oct.-Nov.	180.01	Oct.-Nov.	180.01	Nov.	180.01	Oct.-Nov.	183.61	
	Sep.	180.00	Sep.	180.00	Sep.	180.00	Sep.	183.60	Oct.	183.61	Sep.	183.60	
	Aug.	177.94	Aug.	177.94	Aug.	181.50	Aug.	181.50	Sep.	183.60	Aug.	181.50	
	July	176.26	June-July	179.79	June-July	179.79	June-July	179.79	Aug.	181.50	June-July	179.79	
	June	179.79	Mar.-May	179.48	Mar.-May	179.48	Apr.-May	179.48	June-July	179.79	Mar.-May	183.07	
	Mar.-May	179.48	Feb.	177.44	Feb.	180.99	Mar.	183.07	May	179.48	Feb.	180.99	
	Feb.	177.44	Jan.	179.26	Jan.	179.26	Feb.	180.99	Mar.-Apr.	183.07	Jan.	179.26	
	Jan.	175.75					Jan.	179.26	Feb.	180.99			
									Jan.	179.26			
1959	Dec.	179.26	Dec.	179.26	Dec.	179.26	Dec.	179.26	Dec.	179.26	Dec.	179.26	**1959**
	Oct.-Nov.	178.86	Oct.-Nov.	178.86	Oct.-Nov.	178.86	Oct.-Nov.	178.86	Nov.	178.86	Oct.-Nov.	182.43	
	Sep.	178.84	Sep.	178.84	Sep.	178.84	Sep.	182.42	Oct.	182.43	Sep.	182.42	
	Aug.	176.86	Aug.	176.86	Aug.	180.39	Aug.	180.39	Sep.	182.42	Aug.	180.39	
	July	175.84	June-July	180.57	June-July	180.57	June-July	180.57	Aug.	180.39	June-July	180.57	
	June	180.57	Jan.-May	187.16	Jan.-May	187.16	Feb.-May	187.16	June-July	180.57	Apr.-May	187.16	
	May	183.49					Jan.	190.90	Mar.-May	187.16	Mar.	190.90	
	Jan.-Apr.	187.16							Feb.	190.90	Jan.-Feb.**	191.53	
									Jan.**	191.53			
1958	Dec.	185.02	Dec.	185.02	Dec.	188.72	Dec.**	189.34	Dec.	189.34	Dec.	189.34	**1958**
	Nov.	182.45	Nov.	186.10	Aug.-Nov.**	186.71	Aug.-Nov.	186.71	Aug.-Nov.	186.71	Aug.-Nov.	186.71	
	Oct.	186.10	Aug.-Oct.**	186.71	July	186.72	July	186.72	July	186.72	July	186.72	
	Aug.-Sep.**	186.71	July	186.72	June	184.53	June	184.53	June	184.53	June	184.53	
	July	186.72	June	184.53	Jan.-May	183.12	Jan.-May	183.12	Jan.-May	183.12	Jan.-May	183.12	
	June	184.53	Jan.-May	183.12									
	Jan.-May	183.12											
1957	Dec.	180.97	Dec.	180.97	Dec.	180.97	Dec.	180.97	Dec.	180.97	Dec.	180.97	**1957**
	Aug.-Nov.	205.07	Aug.-Nov.	205.07	Aug.-Nov.	205.07	Aug.-Nov.	205.07	Aug.-Nov.	205.07	Aug.-Nov.	205.07	
	July	205.08	July	205.08	July	205.08	July	205.08	July	205.08	July	205.08	
	June	202.72	June	202.72	June	202.72	June	202.72	June	202.72	June	202.72	
	Feb.-May	199.90	Feb.-May	199.90	Feb.-May	199.90	Feb.-May	199.90	Feb.-May	199.90	Feb.-May	199.90	
	Jan.	199.56	Jan.	199.56	Jan.	199.56	Jan.	199.56	Jan.	199.56	Jan.	199.56	

** BONDS WITH THIS AND PRIOR ISSUE DATES HAVE REACHED FINAL MATURITY AND WILL EARN NO ADDITIONAL INTEREST.

TABLES OF REDEMPTION VALUES FOR MATURED $25 SERIES E BONDS

ISSUE YEARS	ISSUE MONTHS	$25		ISSUE YEARS	ISSUE MONTHS	$25		ISSUE YEARS	ISSUE MONTHS	$25
	SEP 98 - FEB 99				SEP 98 - FEB 99				SEP 98 - FEB 99	
1956	Dec.	199.56		**1952**	Dec.	178.14		**1946**	Dec.	123.38
	Nov.	198.47			Nov.	177.66			Nov.	121.42
	Oct.	198.48			Oct.	177.69			June-Oct.	120.25
	Sep.	196.19			Sep.	175.46			May	118.41
	June-Aug.	194.29			June-Aug.	173.78			Jan.-Apr.	117.28
	Apr.-May	193.83			May	173.38		**1945**	Dec.	117.28
	Mar.	188.59			Jan.-Apr.	170.66			Nov.	114.43
	Jan.-Feb.	186.79		**1951**	Dec.	170.65			June-Oct.	113.33
1955	Dec.	186.79			Nov.	168.23			May	111.54
	Oct.-Nov.	186.29			July-Oct.	166.60			Jan.-Apr.	110.47
	Sep.	183.82			June	166.61		**1944**	Dec.	110.47
	June-Aug.	182.05			May	164.16			Nov.	108.75
	Apr.-May	181.57			Jan.-Apr.	162.60			June-Oct.	107.70
	Mar.	179.26		**1950**	Dec.	154.26			May	106.11
	Jan.-Feb.	177.53			Nov.	151.99			Jan.-Apr.	105.09
1954	Dec.	177.53			June-Oct.	150.53		**1943**	Dec.	105.09
	Nov.	177.17			May	148.48			Nov.	103.48
	Oct.	177.16			Jan.-Apr.	147.06			June-Oct.	102.48
	Sep.	174.81		**1949**	Dec.	147.06			May	100.91
	June-Aug.	173.12			Nov.	145.23			Jan.-Apr.	99.95
	Apr.-May	172.69			June-Oct.	143.83		**1942**	Dec.	99.95
	Mar.	170.51			May	138.02			Nov.	98.40
	Jan.-Feb.	168.86			Jan.-Apr.	136.69			June-Oct.	97.45
1953	Dec.	168.86		**1948**	Dec.	136.69			May	96.00
	Nov.	168.44			Nov.	134.51			Jan.-Apr.	94.35
	Oct.	168.43			June-Oct.	133.23		**1941**	Dec.	94.35
	Sep.	166.33			May	131.09			Nov.	92.86
	June-Aug.	165.81			Jan.-Apr.	131.41			June-Oct.	91.96
	Apr.-May	165.41		**1947**	Dec.	131.41			May	90.59
	Mar.	163.38			Nov.	129.34				
	Jan.-Feb.	178.14			June-Oct.	126.57				
					May	124.57				
					Jan.-Apr.	123.38				

ALL BONDS ON THIS PAGE HAVE CEASED TO EARN INTEREST; THEY CANNOT BE EXCHANGED FOR SERIES HH BONDS.

TABLES OF REDEMPTION VALUES FOR $25 SAVINGS NOTES

ISSUE YEARS	SEPTEMBER 1998 ISSUE MONTHS	$25	OCTOBER 1998 ISSUE MONTHS	$25	NOVEMBER 1998 ISSUE MONTHS	$25	DECEMBER 1998 ISSUE MONTHS	$25	JANUARY 1999 ISSUE MONTHS	$25	FEBRUARY 1999 ISSUE MONTHS	$25	ISSUE YEARS
1970	Oct.	125.62	June-Oct.	128.14	June-Oct.	128.14	July-Oct.	128.14	Aug.-Oct.	128.14	Sep.-Oct.	128.14	**1970**
	June-Sep.	128.14	May	127.53	May	130.08	June	130.70	June-July	130.70	June-Aug.	130.70	
	May	127.53	Jan.-Apr.	128.82	Jan.-Apr.	128.82	May	130.08	May	130.08	May	130.08	
	Apr.	126.30					Jan.-Apr.	128.82	Feb.-Apr.	128.82	Mar.-Apr.	128.82	
	Jan.-Mar.	128.82							Jan.	131.40	Jan.-Feb.	131.40	
1969	Dec.	128.81	Dec.	128.81	Dec.	128.81	Dec.	131.39	Dec.	131.39	Dec.	131.39	**1969**
	Nov.	128.23	Nov.	128.23	Nov.	130.79	Nov.	130.79	Nov.	130.79	Nov.	130.79	
	Oct.	127.00	June-Oct.	129.54	June-Oct.	129.54	July-Oct.	129.54	Aug.-Oct.	129.54	Sep.-Oct.	129.54	
	June-Sep.	129.54	May	128.89	May	131.47	June	132.13	June-July	132.13	June-Aug.	132.13	
	May	128.89	Jan.-Apr.	132.62	Jan.-Apr.	132.62	May	131.47	May	131.47	May	131.47	
	Apr.	129.15					Jan.-Apr.	132.62	Feb.-Apr.	132.62	Mar.-Apr.	132.62	
	Jan.-Mar.	132.62							Jan.*	135.70	Jan.-Feb.*	135.70	
1968	Dec.	132.62	Dec.	132.62	Dec.	132.62	Dec.*	135.70	Dec.	135.70	Dec.	135.70	**1968**
	Nov.	131.91	Nov.	131.91	Nov.*	134.97	Nov.	134.97	Nov.	134.97	Nov.	134.97	
	Oct.	132.62	Sep.-Oct.*	136.18	Sep.-Oct.	136.18	Sep.-Oct.	136.18	Sep.-Oct.	136.18	Sep.-Oct.	136.18	
	Sep.*	136.18	June-Aug.	145.68	June-Aug.	145.68	June-Aug.	145.68	June-Aug.	145.68	June-Aug.	145.68	
	June-Aug.	145.68	May	143.37	May	143.37	May	143.37	May	143.37	May	143.37	
	May	143.37	Jan.-Apr.	156.29	Jan.-Apr.	156.29	Jan.-Apr.	156.29	Jan.-Apr.	156.29	Jan.-Apr.	156.29	
	Jan.-Apr.	156.29											
1967	Dec.	156.28	Dec.	156.28	Dec.	156.28	Dec.	156.28	Dec.	156.28	Dec.	156.28	**1967**
	Nov.	155.52	Nov.	155.52	Nov.	155.52	Nov.	155.52	Nov.	155.52	Nov.	155.52	
	July-Oct.	154.05	July-Oct.	154.05	July-Oct.	154.05	July-Oct.	154.05	July-Oct.	154.05	July-Oct.	154.05	
	June	154.04	June	154.04	June	154.04	June	154.04	June	154.04	June	154.04	
	May	153.33	May	153.33	May	153.33	May	153.33	May	153.33	May	153.33	

* SAVINGS NOTES WITH THIS AND PRIOR ISSUE DATES HAVE REACHED FINAL MATURITY AND WILL EARN NO ADDITIONAL INTEREST.

INSTRUCTIONS

VALUE: Locate the redemption month at the top of the appropriate table; follow the column down to the year and month of issue. During February 1999, a $50 Series EE bond issue dated December 1997 has a value of $26.24, a $25 Series E bond issue dated June 1980 has a value of $70.86 and a $25 Savings Note issue dated October 1970 has a value of $128.14. The values of higher denomination securities are multiples of the amounts shown in the tables. For a $75 Series EE bond, multiply the value in the table by 1.5; for a $50 Series E bond or Savings Note, multiply the value in the table by 2.
INTEREST EARNED: To determine the interest earned to date, subtract the issue price from the value at redemption. The issue price of a Series EE bond is 50% of the amount shown on the face of the security, a Series E bond 75% and a Savings Note 81%. For the issue and redemption dates and denominations shown above, the Series EE bond earned $1.24, the Series E bond earned $52.11 and the Savings Note earned $107.89.

FINAL MATURITIES FOR SERIES E/EE BONDS AND SAVINGS NOTES
SAVINGS BONDS AND NOTES WILL CONTINUE TO EARN INTEREST ACCORDING TO THE FOLLOWING SCHEDULE

Series	Date of Issue	Date of Maturity	Term of Bond
Series E*	May 1941-Nov 1965	May 1981-Nov 2005	40 Years
Series E*	Dec 1965-Jun 1980	Dec 1995-Jun 2010	30 Years
Series EE	Jan 1980 and after	Jan 2010 and after	30 Years
Savings Notes	May 1967-Oct 1970	May 1997-Oct 2000	30 Years

* All Series E bonds do not increase in value on the same basis. Maturity and yield have been revised several times; thus, older bonds may have less redemption value than more current bonds.

* SERIES A-D Bonds. All bonds of Series A, B, C, and D have matured and the redemption value of each bond of these series is the face amount printed on the bond.

NOTE:
Savings Bonds and Notes are eligible for exchange to Series HH Bonds for one year from the month in which they reach final maturity. For example, a Series E Savings Bond issued in September 1958 or September 1968 is eligible for exchange through September 1999.

*U.S. Government Printing Office: 1998 - 432-320/97910

Glossary

Accrual method (or basis) of income reporting: Income is reported when earned or when the taxpayer has an unrestricted right to the income. The timing of the actual receipt of the income does not matter under this reporting method.

Amended returns: An income tax return filed after the original tax return has been filed to correct or change items filed on the original return. Amended returns can be filed within three years of filing the original return to claim refunds.

Automatic default: The result that will take place if no specific steps are taken to choose another alternative.

Average market-based rate: The rate produced by totaling all the individual market-based rates published during the life of a bond and then dividing that total by the number of rates. *See* Market rates. The individual market rates used for this average are always based on 85% of the five-year Treasury yields.

Basis Points: A small measurement used to describe the change in a bond's yield and/or interest rate. For example: An interest rate that changes from 5.25% to 5.15% would represent a drop of 10 basis points or $1/10^{th}$ of one percent. One basis point equals $1/100^{th}$ of one percent. One hundred basis points equal one percent.

Beneficiary: The person designated as a POD (Pay on Death) on a savings bond. This person is entitled to the bond only upon the death of the first-named party on the bond.

Bureau of the Public Debt (BPD): Government office that acts under the direction of the Department of Treasury. It has two main functions pertaining to the bond program: The U.S. Savings Bond Marketing Office promotes the sale and retention of bonds; the

U.S. Savings Bond Operations Office oversees all operational issues related to the bond program.

Cash method (or basis) of income reporting: Income is reported only when it is actually received, not when it was earned.

CPI-U: The CPI-U represents the Consumers Price Index for Urban Consumers. This measures the cost of a "basket" of goods. A change in the CPI-U used to measure inflation would take the cost of the basket of goods at two different time periods and then compute that change into an annualized percentage. For instance: Suppose that the basket of goods cost $160 on January 1st and $162 dollars on July 1st. This represents a change of $2. The change ($2) divided by the cost of the first time period measured ($160) equals 1.25%. Since this is a six-month period, we multiply the percentage change by two to get an annual representation (1.25% times two equals 2.5%). Thus we would say that inflation was growing at a 2.5% annual rate over the first six months.

Current income bonds: Bonds that produce an interest payment to the bond owner. H and HH bonds are examples of current income securities because they pay an interest payment to the bond owner every six months.

Date of purchase: *See* Issue date

Decedent: The person named on a bond who is now deceased.

Deferral: Postponing the reporting of interest income in a legal manner until a later time.

Denomination: *See* Face value

Disposition: To transfer or part with by gift or sale.

Extended maturity: The term(s) of life-bearing interest granted to a bond after the bond reaches original maturity. It is normally ten years, except for the final extension, which may be less than ten years.

Exchange for HH bonds: The process of exchanging Series E or EE bonds, Savings Notes, or eligible H bonds for Series HH bonds.

Face value: The dollar amount printed on the front of the bond.

Federal Reserve Bank (FRB): "As fiscal agents of the United States, Federal Reserve Banks and Branches (FRB) perform a number of activities in support of the Savings

Bond program, including issuing, redeeming, and reissuing Savings Bonds and Notes." (Department of Treasury, BPD, Part 353, 3-80, 6th Amendment, 3-4-94.)

Final maturity: The date on which a bond stops earning interest.

Fixed rate: A rate that does not fluctuate for a designated period of time.

FRB: *See* Federal Reserve Bank

Freedom Share: *See* Savings Notes

GATT: General Agreement on Trades and Tariffs. Legislation passed by the United States Congress in December 1994.

Guaranteed interest rate: A fixed rate of interest that applies to a bond in an original maturity period or an extended maturity period. This rate is not tied to any specific market condition and is set at the discretion of the Department of Treasury.

HH direct deposit: For all new issues of HH bonds, the interest must be directly deposited to an account of the bond holder's choosing. This means that a check is not issued; the money is sent to the designated account on the day the interest is to be paid to the investor.

Interest accrual security: A bond in which the interest is added to the value of the bond; thus, the bond increases in value over time.

Interest income: The difference between the purchase price and the redemption value of Series E and EE bonds and SNs is interest income. For H and HH bonds, the amount received every six months via check (for older bonds) or direct deposit is considered interest income in the year in which it is received.

Issue date: The specific date assigned to a bond. This appears in the top right-hand corner of each bond. It will always include a month and year. This date determines the set of interest rates, values, and timing issues that will apply to a given bond.

Market rate: Three market rates are published every May and November.

- For Series E, EE, and Savings Notes purchased prior to May 1995, the market rate is based on 85% of the five-year Treasury yields for the six months immediately preceding the month of publication. This rate will apply to bonds purchased May 1995 to April 1997 *after* they are five years old.

- For Series EE bonds purchased May 1995 to April 1997, the market rate is based on 85% of the six-month Treasury bill yields for three months immediately preceding the month of publication. This rate will only affect these bonds for a given six-month period. Once the bond is five years old, it will receive the market rate described above.

- For Series EE bonds purchased May 1997 and after, the market rate is based on 90% of the five-year Treasury yields for the six months immediately preceding the month of publication.

Maturity periods: Bonds have an original maturity period, extended maturity period, and a final maturity period. Because each bond is unique, the maturity periods differ for each bond.

New guaranteed rate: The guaranteed rate most recently assigned to purchases of Series EE bonds from March 1, 1993 to April 30, 1995, and to Series HH bonds obtained after February 28, 1993. As of March 1, 1993, the guaranteed rate is 4%. This rate does not affect Series EE bonds purchased after April 30, 1995.

Nominee: A co-owner of a bond who redeems the bond, but is not legally liable for the tax on the interest received because the principal owner is living and the principal owner's funds were used to purchase the bond.

Original maturity: The time period that it will take a bond to reach face value at the guaranteed interest rate in effect at the time of purchase, or a set period of seventeen years for Series EE bonds purchased after April 30, 1995.

Payroll Savings Plan: A program that many companies offer that allows employees the option to have a regular amount deducted from each paycheck to apply to the purchase of U.S. Savings Bonds. Also known as payroll deduction and systematic purchase.

PD Forms: Forms issued by the BPD for the purpose of collecting the appropriate information to authorize specific bond transactions. See Chapter 18 for a listing.

Purchase application: The form a person completes to purchase a Series EE savings bond.

Rating: *See* The Savings Bond Informer Rating System℠

Redemption: The act of presenting bonds for payment.

Redemption value: The value of a bond at a given point in time.

Regional distribution site: A FRB that has been chosen as one of five sites to service bond transactions.

Registered security: A bond that is inscribed with the name or names of persons entitled to the bond.

Registration: The form of inscription upon a bond.

Reissue: The act of changing a registration upon a bond. This can only be done by a FRB or the BPD. A bond owner can never make marks on a bond to change the registration of that bond.

Residuary beneficiaries: The person(s) entitled to assets of an estate after all expenses have been paid by the estate and all assets that were designated to specific individuals have been distributed.

Savings Notes (SN): A bond also known as the "Freedom Share," it was issued during the Vietnam War era, from May 1967 to October 1970. It is similar to Series E and EE bonds in that it is an interest accrual bond. The major difference is that this bond was purchased for 81% of face value. These bonds will earn interest for thirty years.

Schedule B: Internal Revenue Service tax form to list itemized deductions.

Selective redemption: The process of specifically choosing one bond over another to redeem, based on the bond owner's evaluation of interest rates, timing issues, and maturity dates.

Series E: Commonly referred to as the old "War Bonds" because they were issued to help finance World War II. The first bonds in this series were issued in May 1941 and the last in June 1980. The purchase price was 75% of face value and these bonds are all worth more than their face value. Bonds issued before December 1965 earn interest for forty years. Bonds issued in December 1965 and after earn interest for thirty years.

Series EE: Issued since January 1980 to the present. An interest accrual bond, the value of the bond grows over time. It is always purchased for one-half of face value. The time period to original maturity varies from eight to eighteen years, depending on the date of purchase. This series will earn interest for thirty years from date of purchase.

Series H: A current income bond with an interest-producing life of thirty years. It was issued from June 1952 through December 1979.

Series HH: A current income bond that can be obtained only by exchanging Series E and EE bonds and Savings Notes, or through the reinvestment of eligible H bonds. This bond produces an interest payment to the bond owner every six months. It has been available since January 1980.

Series identification: This is the specific series that is printed on the face of the bond, indicating the type of bond. The most common bonds will be one of the following series: Series E, EE, H, HH, I or Savings Notes (also known as Freedom Shares).

SN: *See* Savings Notes

Stepped-up basis: When qualifying assets are inherited, the value of the asset at the original owner's death becomes the basis for determining the gain or loss when the new owner sells the asset. This is called "the basis" from the original cost of the asset to the fair market value in the decedent's estate. U.S. Savings Bonds do not qualify for "stepped-up basis" treatment.

Systematic Purchase: *See* Payroll Savings Plan

1099-INT: The form a bond owner will receive from the redeeming institution when a bond transaction results in reporting interest income. A copy of the information on this form is also supplied to the Internal Revenue Service.

The Savings Bond Informer Rating System℠: This is a system that is a part of the savings bond statement developed by the author. It provides a two- and five-year rating based on the bond's future performance. Ratings are made based on rules and rates in effect at the time of rating. This provides an opportunity to identify the best and worst performing bonds in a portfolio.

Timing issues: Bonds are affected by time periods. Bonds purchased prior to March 1, 1993, will increase in value semi-annually. Timing a redemption or exchange to coincide with the increase pattern will result in the bond owner receiving a greater return on the bond investment. Another timing concern is the date that a bond enters an extended maturity period and is assigned a different guaranteed interest rate. Timing also is a factor when a bond reaches final maturity: The bond owner has only one year past final maturity to exchange bonds for Series HH bonds.

U.S. Savings Bonds report or statement: A detailed analysis of U.S. Saving Bonds. This can be created by using government tables (and following the instructions in Chapter 7 of the book "Savings Bonds: When to Hold, When to Fold and Everything In-Between") or ordered for a fee from The Savings Bond Informer, Inc. (see last page of this book).

Bibliography

Bamford, Janet. "The Class of 2013." *Sesame Street Parents* (September 1994): 52-55.

Nadler, Paul S. "Uncle Sam Out of Line." *Banker's Monthly* 109 (November 1992): 8.

Research Institute of America. *The Complete Internal Revenue Code.* New York: Research Institute of America, 1997.

"Save-Bond." *Associated Press* (24 August 1994): 2209PDT.

"Series EE Savings Bond pays interest at differing rates over life of bond." *The Providence Journal-Bulletin* (8 October 1996): sec. 6, p.1.

U.S. Department of the Treasury, Bureau of the Public Debt. *31 CFR Part 351*, "Public Debt Series No. 1-80; Final Rule." (March 1995).

U.S. Department of the Treasury, Bureau of the Public Debt. *Federal Register*, vol. 59, pt. 3, "Offering and Governing Regulations for United States Savings Bond; Final Rule." No. 43 (4 March 1994).

U.S. Department of the Treasury, Bureau of the Public Debt. *Federal Register*, vol. 59, "Offering of United States Savings Bonds Series HH." No. 43 (4 March 1994).

U.S. Department of the Treasury, Bureau of the Public Debt. *Federal Register*, vol. 58, pt. 4, "Offering of United States Savings Bonds and United States Savings Notes; Final Rule." No. 221 (18 November 1993).

U.S. Department of the Treasury, Bureau of the Public Debt. *Federal Register*, vol. 55, "Regulations Governing United States Savings Bonds, Series EE and HH." No. 4 (5 January 1990).

U.S. Department of the Treasury, Bureau of the Public Debt, U.S. Savings Bond Division. "A History of the United States Savings Bond Program." Washington, D.C.: Government Printing Office (1991).

U.S. Department of the Treasury, Bureau of the Public Debt, U.S. Savings Bond Division. "Buyer's Guide: 1993-1994." No. SBD-2085. Washington, D.C.: Government Printing Office (1993).

U.S. Department of the Treasury, Bureau of the Public Debt, U.S. Savings Bond Division. "The Savings Bond Question & Answer Book." Washington, D.C.: Government Printing Office (1994).

U.S. Department of the Treasury, Bureau of the Public Debt, U.S. Savings Bond Division. "U.S. Savings Bonds: Now Tax-Free for Education." No. SBD-2017.

U.S. Department of the Treasury, Bureau of the Public Debt, Savings Bond Marketing Division. "The Book on U.S. Savings Bonds." No. SBD-2080. Washington, D.C.: Government Printing Office (1994).

U.S. Department of the Treasury, Bureau of the Public Debt, Savings Bond Marketing Division. "Legal Aspects of United States Savings Bonds" No. SBD-2113. Washington, D.C.: Government Printing Office.

U.S. Department of the Treasury, Internal Revenue Service. "Investment Income and Expenses: For use in preparing 1993 Returns." Pubn. No. 550. Washington, D.C.: Government Printing Office (1994).

U.S. Department of the Treasury, Internal Revenue Service. "Your Federal Income Tax: For use in preparing 1993 Returns." Pubn. No. 17. Washington, D.C.: Government Printing Office (1994).

Index

U.S. Savings Bond Record Keeping Sheet
(Savings Bond List)

This form was designed to serve as a helpful document for you and your clients. It can also be used to order a customized savings bond statement from The Savings Bond Informer, Inc. (TSBI). Record the issue date (month/year of purchase), face value (denomination) and series (E, EE, H, HH, I, SN, FS) for each bond to be analyzed.

Name(s) to appear on Bond Statement:

To receive an analysis for each bond, attach this list to the TSBI order form and mail, with your payment, to the address below. **Note**: You do *not* have to use this form to order a statement if a list including <u>issue date</u>, <u>face value</u>, and <u>series</u> already exists or if you would prefer to photocopy each bond.

The Savings Bond Informer, Inc.   **OR**   Fax your order:
P.O. Box 9249   (313) 843-1912
Detroit, MI 48209   VISA, MasterCard, AMEX, DISCOVER

*If you have any questions regarding how to order a bond statement or need additional order forms, call **(800) 927-1901**. The cost for a savings bond statement is determined by the total number of bonds included in the statement.*

Quantity	Issue date (Month/Yr.)	Face value	Series (E,EE,H,HH,I, FS, or SN)	Quantity	Issue date (Month/Yr.)	Face value	Series (E,EE,H,HH,I, FS, or SN)

The cost of a statement is determined by the total number of bonds included.   30

Savings Bond Statement Order Form

1. Obtain a list of your client's U.S. Savings Bonds. (The form entitled, "U.S. Savings Bonds List," can be used by you or your client.) The list can be written, typed, or an actual photocopy of the bonds. If your clients already have a list—just photocopy theirs. **Make sure to include the following:** date of purchase (month/year in top right hand corner of most bonds), series (E, EE, H, HH, I, SN, FS), and face value ($25, 50, 75, 100, 200, 500, 1000, 5000, or 10,000).

2. **Name to appear on Bond Statement:** _____

   Name of Financial Professional: _____

   Company: _____ **Phone:** _____ **Fax:** _____

   "Mail to:" Name: _____

   "Mail to:" Address: _____

   City: _____ **State:** _____ **Zip:** _____ **E-Mail Address:** _____

3. The cost of a statement is determined by the number of bonds included. ***Enter the total number of bonds, to be listed on the bond statement:*** [_____]

NUMBER OF BONDS	TOTAL COST	ENTER COST
1 to 10 bonds	$15.00	
11 to 25 bonds	$24.00	
26 to 50 bonds	$34.00	
51 to 100 bonds	$49.00	
101 to 200 bonds	$59.00	
201 to 300 bonds	$69.00	
301 to 400 bonds	$79.00	
401 to 500 bonds	$89.00	
Over 500 bonds	Call for Quote	
The Book -*U.S. Savings Bonds: The Definitive Guide for Financial Professionals*	$29.95 plus $3 shipping	
The Book - *Savings Bonds: When to Hold, When to Fold and Everything In-Between* Consumer Version	$19.95 plus $3 shipping	
	Total Cost of Order:	

4. Please indicate payment information below. If you would like a standing credit account, fill in your card information below and mark the box labeled "Keep Card on File." All future orders, unless otherwise indicated, will automatically be charged to your account, saving you time and paper work. If your card is already on file with us, mark the box labeled "Charge Credit Card on File." If you need a paid receipt for this order, mark the box labeled "Send Paid Receipt." I would like to pay for this order by: check _____   credit card _____

Name on Card: _____ Card Number: _____ Exp. Date: _____

Keep Card on File: [ ]   Charge Credit Card on File: [ ]   Send Paid Receipt: [ ]

5. Mail, fax or phone your client's list and payment information to:

   The Savings Bond Informer, Inc.   **Fax: *(313) 843-1912***   **Phone orders for 25 bonds or less: *(800) 927-1901***
   PO Box 9249 Detroit, MI 48209
   Orders processed within two business days of receipt. Choose one method of delivery.

   Mail Two Copies: [ ]   Fax and Mail: [ ]   Fax only: [ ]

6. If you have questions/comments or need additional information packets for other associates in your office or brochures for clients, please inform us in the space provided below.